FREE TIME

Benjamin Kline Hunnicutt

FREE TIME

The Forgotten American Dream

TEMPLE UNIVERSITY PRESS
PHILADELPHIA

To the memory of my mother, Cassie Horton Hunnicutt

TEMPLE UNIVERSITY PRESS
Philadelphia, Pennsylvania 19122
www.temple.edu/tempress

Library of Congress Cataloging-in-Publication Data

Hunnicutt, Benjamin Kline.
    Free time : the forgotten American Dream / Benjamin Kline
Hunnicutt.
        p. cm.
    Includes bibliographical references.
    ISBN 978-1-4399-0714-6 (cloth : alk. paper) —
ISBN 978-1-4399-0715-3 (pbk. : alk. paper) —
ISBN 978-1-4399-0716-0 (e-book)   1. Hours of labor—United
States.   2. Leisure—United States.   I. Title.
    HD5124.H858 2013
    331.25′760973—dc23
                                                    2012025886

♾ The paper used in this publication meets the requirements of the
American National Standard for Information Sciences—Permanence
of Paper for Printed Library Materials, ANSI Z39.48-1992

Printed in the United States of America

2 4 6 8 9 7 5 3 1

CONTENTS

PREFACE

For nearly thirty-six years I have been struggling to solve what I am convinced is one of the great mysteries of our time. Like all good stories, this one can be sketched out quickly and simply. Beginning in the early nineteenth century and continuing for over a hundred years, working hours in America were gradually reduced—cut in half according to most accounts—and this is true for most modern industrial nations. Few other economic or social movements lasted as long or involved as many people. Few developments excited the imaginations of so many or encouraged such hope for the future. Counted as one of the great blessings of technology, the process lasted so long that observers during the first decades of the twentieth century agreed that it was bound to continue.

No one predicted that it was going to end. On the contrary, prominent figures such as John Maynard Keynes, Julian Huxley, and Dorothy Canfield Fisher regularly predicted that, well before the twentieth century ended, a Golden Age of Leisure would arrive, when no one would have to work more than two hours a day. Humans seemed to be on the verge of meeting the ancient economic challenge. Able to ensure everyone the necessities of life at last, technology would soon present humanity with what Keynes, the best-known economist of the century, called its "greatest challenge":

> Thus for the first time since his creation Man will be faced with his real, his permanent problem—how to use his freedom from pressing economic cares, how to occupy the leisure, which science and compound interest have won for him, to live wisely and agreeably and well.[1]

However, the shorter-hour process stopped after the Great Depression. Since then we have had little or no decrease in our work. Abandoning hope for the abundant life Keynes so confidently predicted for us (his grandchildren), we moderns for some reason no longer expect work to ever become a subordinate part of life. We no longer look forward to gradually getting enough material goods and services so that we are able to turn our main attention to the business of living free. Unlike previous generations, we no longer worry about leisure's challenge.

What happened?

I began trying to unravel this mystery while I attended the University of North Carolina back in the 1970s. I still remember the day I stumbled on this curiosity down in the dark stacks of Wilson Library, poring over John Owen's article in the *Monthly Labor Review*.[2] His conclusion that Americans have had no increase in leisure since the Great Depression left me incredulous and sent me scurrying from journals to dissertations to academic tomes only to discover that a substantial body of scholarship backed up this respected economist's remarkable conclusion: work hours had remained stable for over forty years.[3]

For a while during the late 1970s and early 1980s, I began to suspect that the shorter-hours process might begin again. I admit that the predictions of such notables as Eric Sevareid and Henry Luce that leisure would soon become the nation's primary problem concerned me. From my purely selfish point of view such a prospect was disturbing—a forty-year pause in the work-reduction process would not be much of a historical mystery. I need not have worried. Far from resolving itself, the mystery deepened. Even as I watched, the historical work-reduction process began to reverse. The trend lines that had prompted Keynes and so many others to predict a ten-hour week began to run in the opposite direction. More and more people began entering the labor force. Most of us began working longer and longer from year to year, and observers began to predict that the future would bring still more work, not less.

Instead of Keynes's leisure "problem," we began to face a time famine. The statistics were harder and harder to ignore. While I suspected that a sea change had occurred, the publication of Juliet Schor's book *The Overworked American* in 1991 excited me nearly as much as Owen's original research.[4] Confirming my suspicions, Schor concluded that the average American was working about a month more a year in 1991 than in the mid-1970s; she later updated her figures to show that the trend has accelerated since the early 1990s. Now we average *five* weeks more (199 hours) than in 1973.[5]

Since the mid-1970s, we have been working longer and longer each year, about half a percentage point more from year to year—the exact reverse of what happened during the nineteenth and early twentieth centuries.[6] Moreover, because more women have entered the work force, more of us are working as a percentage of the total population. However, housework has neither magically disappeared nor been completely absorbed by the marketplace. Men have shouldered little of the extra burden. As Arlie Hochschild and Anne Machung pointed out, women routinely face a "second shift" when they get home from their paid job.[7]

Now it is commonplace for both spouses to work full time and for both to shortchange parts of their lives not connected to their paid jobs. Television talk-show hosts and their guests regularly comment on the strange fact that today it takes two parents working full time to support a family, whereas previous generations were able to survive, perhaps even thrive during the 1950s and 1960s, on one salary.

Groups in addition to women are hard pressed. The salaried middle classes, for example, have seen their yearly working hours increase by 660 hours—20 percent more than twenty-five years ago. *U.S. News and World Report* concluded in 2003 that nearly 40 percent of this group worked more than fifty hours a week.[8] Within a few years most of us will likely be working sixty hours a week if things continue the way they have since the 1980s.[9]

The pride that our nation once took in being the world leader in freeing its citizens from constant, urgent need is now but a dim memory, preserved in odd places such as bumper stickers that remind us that our labor unions represent "the people that gave us the weekend." The most recent studies from the Bureau of Labor Statistics show that workers in the United States work longer hours than those of other modern industrial nations, with the exception of South Korea.[10]

One small, hopeful trend seemed to develop in the 1980s—earlier retirements. Some overly optimistic economists, eager to show America leading the world in all categories of wealth, declared that there had been historical "shift" in "leisure preferences" from shorter work weeks and years to more leisure (two or three more years) during retirement.[11]

Now it appears that even such modest predictions of a few extra years of retirement were premature. The slight retirement trend of the 1980s and 1990s has also reversed. Over the last decade or so Americans have extended their work life, retiring later and later, opting for phased retirement, or reentering the work force after they retire. Many are now trading in careers and stable jobs for McJobs when they get old. The *New York Times* reported a "steep turnaround" in workforce participation rates of males fifty-five to sixty-four years old, concluding that "retirement [is] turning into a brief rest stop."[12] Among men sixty-five and older, labor force participation rates rose from a low of 15.8 percent in 1996 to 21.5 percent in 2008.[13] The *Monthly Labor Review* reported in 2008 that "over the past dozen or so years, older men—especially those 65 years or older—have increased their labor force participation and full-time employment, thereby reversing long-run declines; increases for older women also have occurred and have been proportionately greater."[14] The Bureau of Labor Statistics predicts that these new trends will gather speed as more baby boomers reach retirement age.[15]

Just as in a popular novel, then, the plot of the historical mystery *The Death of Shorter Working Hours* thickened in my lifetime.

What happened, indeed?

Now my questions are, Why did the century-long shorter-hours movement end and then go in reverse? Why do the confident predictions that we would be working less than ten hours a *week* by now, made by respected, thoughtful men and women throughout the first half of the twentieth century, appear not only wrong but a bit harebrained by those of us working ten hours a *day*? Why have complaints about overwork and the frantic pace of life replaced the old debates about how best to use our coming abundant leisure? What happened to the widespread expectation that we would soon solve the economic problem and, finding it increasingly easy to make a living, get on with the much more important business of living? What happened to the seemingly irresistible movement to steadily reduce hours of labor—a movement that was once centrally important to this nation and considered by many Americans to be the essence of progress and highest expression of liberty?

For some yet unexplained reasons, the anticipation of "abundance"—the enduring and widespread belief that it was possible to get enough and move on to better things as the economy advanced—has been replaced by desperate hopes that the economy will expand forever, the standard of living will perpetually improve, and new work will be created ad infinitum through the everlasting invention of new "necessities." Unlike John Stuart Mill and Keynes, few economists still believe that the satisfaction of basic economic needs will ever be possible. Indeed, the mere weakening of consumer demand is universally heralded as the harbinger of hard times. Many now dismiss talk about "abundance" and hopes for more free time as unrealistic, utopian, or perfectionist.

I have spent untold effort, overworking myself trying to solve these mysteries, exploring social, economic, and historical developments in what one reviewer called "excruciating detail."[16] I have come at last to the simple conclusion that one of the most important reasons for the end of shorter hours, the recent decline of leisure, and the substitution of the rhetoric of perpetual need for the traditional language of "abundance" is something like a nationwide amnesia.

We have forgotten what used to be the other, better half of the American dream. In our rushing about for more, we have lost sight of the better part of freedom—of what Walt Whitman, with so many others throughout American history, called Higher Progress.[17]

Early in the 1930s, James Truslow Adams complained that "money making and material improvements . . . mere extensions of the material basis of existence," were beginning to be valued as "good in themselves [exhibiting] the aspects of moral virtues." Belief that a growing economy was the one and only definition of progress was beginning to obscure the traditional "American dream" (a term usually attributed to him), which had always before been about "quality and spiritual values": "The American dream that has lured tens of millions of all nations to our shores in the past century has not been a dream of merely material plenty, although that has doubtless counted heavily. It has been much more than that." He feared that "in our struggle to 'make a living'" we

were forgetting "to *live*." Thus, he wrote *The Epic of America* to call his generation back to what he knew as America's "priceless heritage"—a vision of progress as real as "gold or corn crops," of progress as "a genuine individual search
and striving for the abiding values of life," of progress as the growth of opportunities for the "*common man* to rise to full stature" in the free realms of "communal spiritual and intellectual life."[18]

Over the last two or three decades, Adams's "American dream" has been
virtually forgotten, his fears largely realized. The American dream has been
reduced to economic growth and confined by government budgets. What I do
in this book is take up Adams's standard and cause. Following his lead I attempt to re-present that traditional American dream and, challenging those
who imagine the dream has become unrealistic or utopian, reestablish it on
the solid economic ground it occupied for over a century—what for decades
the labor movement called the "progressive shortening of the hours of labor."[19]

INTRODUCTION

Higher Progress—the Forgotten American Dream

> The order of things should be somewhat reversed; the seventh
> should be man's day of toil, wherein to earn his living by
> the sweat of his brow; and the other six his Sabbath of the
> affections and the soul,—in which to range this widespread
> garden, and drink in the soft influences and sublime revelations
> of Nature.
> —Henry David Thoreau, "Commencement Essay," 1837

> Thoreau spoke as a conservative and a traditionalist. For the
> first American dream, before the others shoved it rudely aside,
> had been one not of work but of leisure.
> —Daniel Rodgers, *The Work Ethic in Industrial America*

At one time economic progress and technological advances were understood to have a definite goal: abundance. After adequate economic
progress was made so that everyone was able to afford the necessities
of life, a condition Monsignor John Ryan (the "Right Reverend New Dealer")[1]
described as a life of "reasonable and frugal comfort," our nation would be able
to make real progress, exploring liberty that transcended material concerns
and the marketplace.[2]

Scarcity has not always seemed to be eternal—it was not always understood
as the everlasting human condition or the foundation of our nation's economy.
For the most part, perpetual scarcity is a twentieth-century invention. Before
then, most Americans assumed that it would be possible for reasonable people
to eventually satisfy their needs as the economy and technology improved and
the nation advanced. Traditionally, too much wealth, too much materialism,
was understood to impede human progress, leading to greed and envy (twin
sins that fed on each other), luxury, indolence, and the slavery of selfishness.

As we began to solve what John Maynard Keynes called the "economic
problem," our time would become more valuable to us than new goods and services we had never needed before.[3] Then we would welcome the opportunity to
live more of our lives outside the marketplace. No longer preoccupied with economic concerns, we could begin to develop our potential to live together peace-
fully and agreeably, spending more of our time and energy forming healthy

families, neighborhoods, and cities; increasing our knowledge and appreciation of nature, history, and other peoples; freely investigating and delighting in the mysteries of the human spirit; exploring our beliefs and values together; finding common ground for agreement and conviviality; living virtuous lives; practicing our faiths; expanding our awareness of God; and wondering in Creation—a more complete catalog of the free activities envisioned over the course of our nation's history is one of the burdens of this book.

Walt Whitman called such a project "higher progress."[4] Claiming a vantage point as democracy's poet that opened to him "Democratic Vistas," he imagined scenes from an American future in which all would be free to celebrate and sing. Monsignor John Ryan envisioned Higher Progress as increasing opportunities beyond necessary work to "know the best that is to be known, and to love the best that is to be loved."[5] Struggling to save the Jewish Sabbath in America, Abba Hillel Silver wrote that the Sabbath was "much more than mere relaxation from labor. It is a sign and symbol of man's higher destiny." He believed the Sabbath provided a model for Higher Progress (free Saturdays were simply one step forward) because it represented the importance of time for tradition, family, spiritual exercise, and the development of our higher potentials and humane interests.[6]

Higher Progress and Republican Virtue

The Declaration of Independence's list of unalienable rights, "life, liberty, and the pursuit of happiness," originally identified Higher Progress. When he wrote the phrase "pursuit of happiness," Thomas Jefferson was concerned with questions about America's destiny. What is the highest that we can achieve? What would make us truly happy? Where do we go and what do we do when we have done all our chores, performed our duties, and met our responsibilities? What kinds of human activities or states of being lay beyond social responsibilities and material necessity and are worthwhile in and for themselves?

The same enlightened reason that led to scientific knowledge, the mastery of nature, and rational solutions to economic and political problems led inevitably to the challenges of Higher Progress. It was all a matter of a reasonable approach to life, of a rational chain of means and ends. Scientific knowledge and technology had practical purposes: the mastery of nature to satisfy human needs. The rational organization of society and the state had reasonable ends: peace, security, justice, and the rule of law. Liberal education and a democratic, civil order promoted virtue and good manners—informal living *skills* that included consideration, tolerance, openness, and attentiveness to others.[7]

But such economic, political, and civic ends, vital though they may be, were seldom seen as final or absolute. They were most often understood as means to other, more important ends that were more complete in themselves. They led to the pursuit of happiness—to open-ended freedom and liberty expanding into ever-higher realms of human experience and potential. The customary practice of virtue ended in good character that Jefferson and others around him recognized in Aristotle's *Eudaimonia* and that still others, more religiously minded, saw as selfless charity ("disinterested benevolence") that was prerequisite for the establishment of God's earthly kingdom.[8]

Higher Progress as the pursuit of happiness was once understood by many in this nation to be something of an arena—a cultural opening in which humans practiced the skills of living together. Government's main responsibility was to make sure that citizens were as safe and unencumbered as possible. Government had absolutely no business supporting one brand of felicity over another.

Similarly, the economy was also understood to be the servant of Higher Progress. Its ultimate purpose was to free humans from scarcity; its goal, abundance. Creating a stable democracy, taming the frontier, establishing successful farms, and building industry all had a purpose, an end: the end of the day, the weekend, retirement, and posterity—and for many, God's kingdom on earth. Until the end of the nineteenth century, few expected that the economy might be the place where humans would realize our full potential—our full, *free* humanity was to be discovered outside the economy, beyond pecuniary concerns.

Gordon Wood concluded, "Indeed, there was hardly an educated person in all of 18th-century America who did not at one time or another try to describe people's moral sense and the natural forces of love and benevolence holding society together."[9] Instead of assuming the modern Durkheimian view that the economy's divisions of labor make society stable and peaceful, most people in the eighteenth and nineteenth centuries were moral sentimentalists, continuing to believe that the economy owed its existence to stable human associations outside commerce, that "traditional enemy of classical virtue." The regular practice of virtue in pursuit of happiness was the glue that held societies together.[10] Even commitment to hard work, an ethic so vigorously promoted by Protestantism and republicanism, was seldom valued as an end in itself. Religiously as well as rationally understood, devotion to work was virtuous because it was a means to other, higher cultural and spiritual ends. Work provided for the necessities of life—a reasonable and finite undertaking. Work also disciplined the human spirit, preparing selfish and unruly humans in a kind of work-school for the larger liberty that followed a busy and productive workday, workweek, and work life.

However, the ultimate reason for working hard six days a week was not to pile luxury on luxury, wealth on wealth. It was not to outdo others in a splendor of possessions. The purpose of work was not to create more work to do forevermore. More often, work was viewed as part of God's original curse that separated humans from the divine and from each other. It was not until the middle to latter part of the ninetieth century, when in the United States the Protestant work ethic lost its theological supports and rationalist underpinnings, mutating into what Max Weber called "the Spirit of Capitalism," that work became the modern cardinal virtue and its own reason for being, separate from the complex of republican virtues and Christian theology.[11] Before then, the virtue of work lay in its goals and purposes: building a good character ready for freedom, obtaining the (finite) necessaries of life in obedience to God's call or nature's dictates, practicing the moral disciplines of selflessness essential for living in communities, acquiring the wealth needed for charity, and then finding greater opportunities for fellowship, worship, and the free practice of civic virtues.

The reward for working hard six days a week was the Sabbath. The reward for a lifetime of hard work was an "Eternal Sabbath" when "man works no more," being too busy singing everlasting hymns of joy. Technology and the hard work of humans might even lead to the kingdom of God on earth—to the millennium of human happiness when, as Jonathan Edwards's disciple Samuel Hopkins confidently predicted, "it will not be necessary for each one, to labour more than two or three hours in a day."[12]

Together with Jefferson and Hopkins, other of the nation's founders were eager to recommend their vision of Higher Progress. John Adams, for example, had suggestions that he included in a now famous letter to his wife, Abigail. He concluded his letter with what has become a familiar passage:

> I must study Politicks and War that my sons may have liberty to study Mathematicks and Philosophy. My sons ought to study Mathematicks and Philosophy, Geography, natural History, Naval Architecture, navigation, Commerce and Agriculture, in order to give their Children a right to study Painting, Poetry, Musick, Architecture, Statuary, Tapestry and Porcelaine.[13]

Thus, Adams envisioned America's future as the progress of liberty: his generation concerned with providing a finer freedom to their children by establishing a stable democracy and a secure nation, the second generation employing its new political liberties in practical matters and economic endeavors to ensure the third generation new rights to the most refined of human activities. Ascending into these new freedoms, American democracy would then rise in a Renaissance surpassing anything Europe had yet produced.

In his history of the early years of the nation, John Adams's great-grandson Henry Adams, writing toward the close of the nineteenth century, reiterated the republican vision of Higher Progress:

> Leaders like Jefferson, [Albert] Gallatin, and [Joel] Barlow might without extravagance count upon a coming time when diffused ease and education should bring the masses into familiar contact with higher forms of human achievement, and their vast creative power, turned toward a nobler culture, might rise to the level of that democratic genius which found expression in the Parthenon ... might create for five hundred million people the America of thought and art which alone could satisfy their omnivorous ambition.[14]

Benjamin Franklin, agreeing that "the happiness of individuals is evidently the ultimate end of political society," offered his vision of Higher Progress:

> If every man and woman would work for four hours each day on something useful, that labor would produce sufficient to procure all the necessaries and comforts of life, want and misery would be banished out of the world, and the rest of the twenty-four hours might be leisure and happiness.[15]

Franklin added a new dimension to the dream: democratic abundance and leisure. Living freely and rationally, *all* Americans would eventually be able to provide their "necessaries." Scarcity would be abolished, necessity would become obsolete, and abundance would be ensured. Unlike the old European versions, the American cultural renaissance would then have a firm democratic and egalitarian base. Indeed, that would be its genius.

To be sure, for Jefferson and Adams, "humane and moral freedom" was available mainly to the aristocrat—if not by birth, then certainly by accomplishment. Higher Progress would open primarily to those educated in the liberal arts and wealthy enough to avoid full-time work on the farm or for wages. The mass of humanity still did not have the time, education, or character for Higher Progress. For the time being, most people would need to devote themselves to the business of making a living and founding a nation. Moreover, many of the Founders were devoted to an agrarian ideal, understanding that liberty's goal was the small freeholder farmer, largely self-reliant, close to fructifying nature, and practicing the Virgilian virtues of simplicity and duty in relation to family, religion, and community as he daily tilled the soil.

Nevertheless, most of America's wealthiest individuals understood that their privileged leisure represented an obligation to demonstrate Higher Progress to the rest of the nation. Wealth entailed a duty to lead others into an abundant existence beyond material concerns and beyond the marketplace, to a *democratic* culture in which everyone would have the "right to study Painting, Poetry, Musick, Architecture, Statuary, Tapestry and Porcelaine."

Gordon Wood observed that Jefferson was

> by no means unique in his concern for refining the sensibilities of himself and those of the American people. This was a moral and political imperative of all of the founders. To refine popular taste was in fact a moral and political imperative of all the enlightened of the eighteenth century.[16]

Refined tastes and manners would promote the republican virtues of tolerance, mutuality, and openness—the cornerstones of democracy.[17] These were not culturally relative values, because no democratic culture could exist without them—no set of shared beliefs and values (the very definition of democratic culture) could ever be put together. As the nineteenth century wore on and the nation's economy and power grew, more Americans began to share the vision of progress as the opening of freedom beyond the marketplace.

Higher Progress and Labor

Vigorously opposed by industry and the business world, the shorter-hours movement initiated by American workers challenged the new "Spirit of Capitalism" that was seeking to transform wealth and work into ends in themselves, divorced from Higher Progress. Following its inception during the first half of the nineteenth century, labor's shorter-hours movement sustained the republican and millennial visions of Higher Progress, of civic virtue and "disinterested benevolence," gradually transforming them from the dreams of republican patriots, agrarian aristocrats, religious leaders, romantic poets, and utopians into practical democratic possibilities for all, in a process that lasted well into the second half of the twentieth century.

Shorter working hours was the cause that awakened the labor movement in the United States, providing laborers with a modicum of working-class identity. Throughout labor's century-long shorter-hours campaign, workers were led by a vision of freedom and progress that drew heavily from existing republican expectations and millennial hopes—visions of a future in which work was reduced to a minimum and ordinary people, liberated from necessity, would spend the best part of their lives as only the wealthy had before, pursuing Higher Progress.

Such a vision was manifest at the beginning of the American labor movement in the struggle for the ten-hour day. In 1827, displaying what historians have called "the earliest evidence of [labor] unrest" in the United States and employing the Revolutionary rhetoric of the preceding generation, Philadelphia journeymen carpenters resolved that "all men have a just right, derived from their Creator, to have sufficient time each day for the cultivation of their mind and for self-improvement."[18] Giving voice to the carpenters' sentiment, William Heighton envisioned American progress as the reduction of working hours from "12 to 10, to 8, to 6, and so on," until "the development and progress of science have reduced human labor to its lowest terms."[19]

The history of labor from then until World War II unfolded, at least in part, as the "progressive shortening of the hours of labor."[20] George Meany once observed, "The progress toward a . . . shorter work week is a history of the labor movement itself."[21] Other issues were certainly important. But only higher wages competed with shorter hours for the attention and passion of organized workers.

Labor's shorter-hours campaign came to embody a distinctive working-class vision of Higher Progress, similar to, but distinguishable from, millennial, republican, and romantic hopes. The movement had clear rhetorical and ideological ties to the Declaration of Independence, republican virtue, and "the kingdom of God in America."[22] However, laborites added a sharp critique of the new forms of exploitation and oppression that were emerging with technological advances and with changes in work and the labor market. Whereas America's Revolutionary generation had struggled to overthrow the tyranny of England and claim their natural right to govern themselves, workers after the 1820s attempted to throw off their new industrial chains, demanding their fair share of the wealth they produced and their "just right, derived from their Creator," to sell as much or as little of their own time as they wanted—to be free of bosses and "wage-slavery" and have some time each day to call their own.[23] What laborites called their "Ten Hour System" developed as a distinct alternative to laissez-faire capitalism—to what for decades they called the "selfish system."[24]

Workers embraced the Higher Progress that Jefferson, Adams, Franklin, and the other Founders guaranteed as "the pursuit of happiness" and made it their own. Moreover, they turned the vision into their own reform cause, shorter working hours, that unified workers for over a hundred years. Supporting practical reforms such as the ten- and eight-hour day, workers reshaped the vision of Higher Progress, adding new dimensions and expressing a more democratic hope for the future. American workers translated the republican aristocrats' hope for refined culture and the theologian's speculation about the spiritual possibilities of increased leisure into the down-to-earth terms of their daily lives. For working men and women in Fall River, Lowell, and Boston, Massachusetts; New York; Philadelphia; and Cincinnati, Ohio, Higher Progress was a tangible reality: getting out from under the boss's thumb a little sooner each day, having a few additional minutes down at the saloon with friends, and finding a little extra time at home with the family.

Higher Progress might very well advance civilization, facilitate virtue, promote a cultural Renaissance, and even bring about the kingdom of God in the long run, as some of the Founders envisioned. But in the meantime relief from the tyranny of the job and the increase of daily freedom to live a little outside work were welcome improvements.

Still, the very practical benefits of shorter hours did not rule out a larger vision for laborites. Increasing leisure promised workers liberation from an economic system that was fundamentally exploitative (the "selfish system"), opening up new democratic forms of civic engagement and individual expression—what Heighton called the "cultivation of the mind and for self-improvement."[25]

Higher Progress Realized through Shorter Hours

The history of American workers' and the labor movement's struggle for "the progressive shortening of the hours of labor" is this book's central, recurring theme that binds its narrative together and grounds the story of Higher Progress in the reality of economic and political developments. Like the Mississippi River in Mark Twain's *Huckleberry Finn*, it organizes the book, providing a center from which depend visions of progress and dreams of freedom, such as Walt Whitman's *Democratic Vistas* and Frank Lloyd Wright's Broadacre City.

In the book's four labor chapters, workers and union leaders speak for themselves, describing their hopes for freedom's future and envisioning an alternative to laissez-faire capitalism. In the new freedom shorter hours represented, workers hoped to develop better ways of living together beyond competition, consumerism, and perpetual self-seeking, without having to change existing governmental forms or economic systems. Working within a constitutional democracy and a capitalist economic order, workers hoped simply to work less and less (buying back their time), thus gradually freeing themselves from the constraints that are inherent parts of those systems. Instead of changing political and economic orders, most hoped simply to move beyond them, using them, as Walt Whitman suggested, as stepping stones to a "larger liberty."[26] Labor's opponents came to recognize this desire to escape as the very essence of worker radicalism—a revolutionary possibility lurking within existing constitutional and free market forms.

The freedom of leisure was no abstract speculation for American workers. They began, as Jacques Rancière observed, to "live into" their new freedom, experimenting with various possibilities, revising and enlarging their vision of what their new leisure meant for them and might mean for future generations, and enjoying their lives in ways never before possible.[27]

Through the nineteenth century, poets, religious leaders, utopian writers, and visionaries shared labor's vision of liberation from the "selfish system," providing vital support for labor's practical efforts to reduce working hours. Such writers as Henry Ward Beecher, Charles Dudley Warner, Edward Everett, and John Spalding, the Catholic bishop of Peoria, continued to speculate about what freedom from work would mean and what could be done in the new leisure opening up for all people. Organizations, institutions, and professions began to make provisions for the coming leisure: enlarging the public sphere; building camps, parks, and playgrounds; and founding community centers, theaters, schools, libraries, forums, and lyceums. To serve the new mass leisure, a vigorous parks and recreation movement formed and began to build community and recreation centers, vacation resorts, and community sports complexes—free public places for free people. Luminaries such as Frederick Law Olmsted designed facilities such as New York's Central Park to serve and promote the nation's "sense of enlarged freedom."[28] Frank Lloyd Wright deliberately devoted his career to building for America's coming freedom.

The twentieth century saw such dreams appearing to come to fruition, such preparations justified. Early in the century observers recognized that working hours had been cut nearly in half. Higher Progress then came to the forefront of the nation's attention during the 1920s, where it remained for decades. During much of the twentieth century, abundance seemed to be just around the corner, disturbing some who fretted about "economic maturity," "overproduction," and ordinary people having too much time on their hands, delighting others who continued to look forward to progress and equality in the arenas of life beyond the marketplace.

Just as Whitman and so many others had expressed distinctive and diverse ideas about the promise of Higher Progress during the eighteenth and nineteenth centuries, new voices joined during the twentieth, swelling in a magnificent chorus, singing the praises and possibilities of Higher Progress. Bubbling up from the ranks of workers and their organizations, the chorus was taken up by social critics and middle-of-the-road politicians, visionaries and intellectuals, educators and professionals, scientists and naturalists, artists and poets, utopian writers and environmentalists, radicals and inventors, businessmen and industrialists, theologians and philosophers, librarians and cooks, architects and musicians, and craftsmen and amateur sports enthusiasts.

Educators such as Dorothy Canfield Fisher, president of the Adult Education Association in the 1920s, and later Robert Hutchins, legendary president of the University of Chicago, advised teachers and administrators to retool their schools to teach people "the worthy use of leisure" and provide the skills and public facilities that would soon be in demand. Led by Hutchins, American colleges began to rediscover the reason that liberal arts had been the heart of higher education for over two millennia: the practical need to teach free people the arts of freedom.

Conservative business people such the British soap-king Lord Leverhulme and America's celebrated cereal maker W. K. Kellogg took the initiative, instituting a six-hour workday in the 1920s and 1930s. Walter Gifford, from 1925 to 1948 president of AT&T, one of the largest corporations in the United States in the twentieth century, recognized that "industry . . . has gained a new and astonishing vision." The final, best achievement of business and the free market need not be perpetual economic growth, eternal job creation, and everlasting consumerism, but "a new type of civilization," in which "how to make a living becomes less important than how to live." Gifford predicted:

> Machinery will increasingly take the load off men's shoulders. . . . Every one of us will have more chance to do what he wills, which means greater opportunity, both materially and spiritually. . . . [Steadily decreasing work hours] will give us time to cultivate the art of living, give us a better opportunity for . . . the arts, enlarge the comforts and satisfaction of the mind and spirit, as material well-being feeds the comforts of the body.[29]

Labor leaders, having fought for the five-day workweek and the six-hour workday in the 1920s and 1930s, reaffirmed their commitment to "progressive shortening of the hours of labor" to rally their forces after World War II.[30]

Radicals and socialists such as Helen and Scott Nearing, Norman O. Brown, and Herbert Marcuse, praising idleness and play and forming communes, saw increasing leisure as a form of bloodless, democratic revolution. They saw progressively shorter hours as the practical way for Americans to free themselves from the tyranny of corporations and what had become a charade of a free market, to regain control over their own destinies. Such critics hoped that abundant leisure and public education would enable ordinary citizens to study and understand public issues and, recognizing their own best interest, reclaim the political power rightfully theirs. With increased leisure, they might begin to understand that perpetual work and everlasting scarcity were the creatures of capitalism and corporations rather than laws of nature. Thus, increasing free time might translate into the political power necessary to counterbalance the building tyranny of concentrated wealth.[31]

Naturalists and environmentalists were inspired by Higher Progress. Aldo Leopold suggested that there was a "law of diminishing returns in progress."[32] Industrial and economic expansion steadily encroached on nature, gradually destroying it and prospects for its renewal. Many, including Sigurd Olson, agreed.[33] The natural world offered opportunities that could never be manufactured: natural beauty, companionship, solitude, joy, and a sense of belonging. An economy that produced leisure instead of ever more consumption was the last best hope for a sustainable economy and for the preservation of the natural world. Parks, wilderness preserves, and national rivers and forests held open the possibility that humans could discover an alternative relationship with nature, one based on wonder and celebration rather than exploitation and development.

Sociologists such as David Riesman asked, "Abundance for what?" and for a while during the early 1950s believed that increasing leisure offered the opportunity to rebuild families and reenergize communities weakened by urbanization and industrial development. Poets such as Vachel Lindsay; playwrights and theater builders such as Percy MacKaye, Paul Green, and E. C. Mabie; painters such as Grant Wood and Thomas Hart Benton; architects such as Frank Lloyd Wright and Ernest Flagg; musicians such as Shin'ichi Suzuki and Andrés Segovia; chefs such as Julia Child; and craftsmen such as Gustav Stickley and Elbert Hubbard envisioned a world in which citizens wrote their own poetry, staged their own local dramas, performed pageants, played and sang their own music together as naturally as they spoke their mother tongue, cooked gourmet meals for each other, and helped design, build, and decorate their own homes in their free time.

Understanding our lives as the subjects of our own community-based literature, drama, fine arts, and quotidian discourse, we moderns had the potential to transfigure the commonplace, elevating everydayness with the do-it-yourself creations of democratic artist and artisan. Higher Progress's free, creative endeavors would join people in vigorous, free civic engagement, creating communities held together by virtue, tolerance, conviviality, and perhaps even affection.

The days of the Grand Master, the Diva, the Star, the once-in-a-lifetime Genius, and the Great American Novelist, and of the masses passively watching and consuming what paid cultural experts and professionals produced, were

passing, being replaced by an age of ordinary excellence and the everyday practice of what had previously been the preserve of the few. Famous painters, poets, chefs, actors, and musicians were becoming more notable for sharing their
skills—for making it possible for everyone to practice them—than for mere dis-
plays of their brilliance.

The days foreseen by John Adams were arriving when America's children
devoted more and more of their lives to "Painting, Poetry, Musick, Architecture, Statuary, Tapestry and Porcelaine," to what William Heighton envisioned
as the "cultivation of the mind and . . . self-improvement," and to what John
Ryan imagined as the opportunity to "know the best that is to be known, and to
love the best that is to be loved." The day of democratic community and culture
was dawning. Real progress was just beginning.

Most of this book is devoted to recalling a *sampling* of that chorus of voices,
re-presenting the diverse visions of how abundance and increasing freedom from work would soon open the original American dream to all. The
sampling will, of course, be selective and limited; a complete catalog of voices
supporting Higher Progress would be vast—and impossible to gather at this
point of historical scholarship. Readers may be concerned with what has been
left out. But no more so than I. Having had to cut the book nearly in half for the
final proof, I am keenly aware of things omitted, still on my computer's hard
drive awaiting publication.

For example, I have had to be selective in my choice of radical voices, including Juliet Stuart Poyntz, the Bread and Roses strikers, Sidney Lens, Norman O.
Brown, and Herbert Marcuse, while omitting others, notably Eugene Debs. I
made these choices in an attempt to shift the historical understanding of American radicalism from the traditional focus on the radical's desire to change governmental forms (to socialism or communism—typically more European than
American) to a focus on what I argue is more typical of American worker radicalism, contained by *progressively* shorter work hours. As Herbert Marcuse suggested, "Advanced industrial society is in permanent mobilization against" the
working-class threat to abandon capitalism an hour at a time—a threat that was
regularly repeated and acted on in America from the 1820s and into the 1970s.[34]

I also had to make choices about what parts of labor history to include,
concentrating on the AFL (American Federation of Labor) and on auto workers and steel unions in the CIO (Congress of Industrial Organizations) after
World War II. I also chose to focus attention on the International Ladies' Garment Workers' Union (the ILGWU, which is part of the book's core narrative)
instead of the CIO itself because its membership was mostly women and it was
one of the most important and largest industrial unions in existence, leading
the way to shorter hours. Moreover, since David R. Roediger and Philip Sheldon Foner do an excellent job covering the history of the CIO on the shorter-
hours issue in *Our Own Time*, I decided to rely on their account, offering my
own only when I had something new to say.[35]

Worker's voices are also somewhat muted. Concerns about the length of the book prompted me to remove a good deal of new material about the Kellogg's and Goodyear six-hour workers whom I have been interviewing since 1988.

Even though I have left important voices out of this account, I hope to have included a broad enough sample to make a beginning in re-presenting the forgotten American dream. The historical visions of Higher Progress were built on the foundation of workers' quest for shorter hours. Such visions became, in turn, essential supports for labor's century-long campaign. But when these visions were obscured by the rise of Full-Time, Full Employment, the shorter-hours movement collapsed.[36] Re-presenting Higher Progress in the following history, limited and selective though the result may be, is a necessary first step toward reawakening both the dream and the very real process that sustained it for well over a century.

The Kingdom of God in America

Progress as the Advance of Freedom

J.G.A. Pocock emphasized that personal independence, selfless duty to the state, and military valor were the primary virtues of pre-Revolutionary America's "Country Ideology"—an ideology that, "belonging to a tradition of classical republicanism and civic humanism" and "looking unmistakably back to antiquity and to Aristotle," exhibited a "civic and patriotic" rather than a "leisure or Arcadian . . . character."[1] However, Gordon Wood recognized the importance of the "leisured and Arcadian" aspects of civic humanism during the colonial and early national periods. He pointed out that "the classical devotion to leisure among the gentry" was not for the practice of disinterested politics alone but was also for "promoting social affection . . . the object of the civilizing process."[2]

Nevertheless, republican expectations about the promotion of civic humanism in leisure were limited, confined for the most part to an educated aristocracy still struggling with old Machiavellian notions about the importance of competition for distinction and recognition. Moreover, most of the Founders were pessimistic about the future, more often expecting decline into chaos than the dawn of new freedoms for all. For most secular leaders of Jefferson's generation, the average person would need to endure the discipline of work well into the future—leisure and Arcadia were not for the masses.

Higher Progress—the *democratic* advance of freedom beyond political liberty and economic struggles—was first described in the American colonies in sermons and religious tracts speculating about the coming of God's kingdom. Predating the Revolutionary-period debates about civic humanism, and long before the advent of the secular American dream, what H. Richard Niebuhr called the "symbolic form" of "the kingdom of God in America" appeared in the writings of Jonathan Edwards and other religious leaders of his day as forerunner.[3]

Niebuhr concluded that the discourse about the kingdom of God in America "seemed closely related to that 'American dream' which James Truslow Adams had used so effectively in interpreting American history." John Wilson observed that Niebuhr understood "Edwards' theme of God's redemption of the world" as both "the core of the Christian movement in America and the central meaning and significance of the [American] culture."[4]

Niebuhr's "kingdom of God in America" included what he saw as a set of interrelated, widely shared, and enduring beliefs: that by whatever cause, human or divine, earthly progress was not only possible but well under way; that modern scientific and material advances and the spread of human rights had profound moral, religious, and spiritual implications; and that such advances were obviously good things, in accord with reason as well as God's beneficent will. Such advances were good things primarily because they were beginning to free humans from the tyranny of the state, exploitation by the powerful, and the chains of material necessity, making it possible for more and more people to claim their full humanity.

For many churchmen and churchwomen a new and different kind of liberty, represented through the ages by the promises of the Sabbath and sired by science and the Enlightenment, seemed to be aborning: a new freedom in which the majority of humans, at last able to satisfy their material needs by God's grace and with their new machines, would escape the Adamic curse of constant toil to welcome the millennium. The "kingdom of God in America," then, developed in part as an ongoing discourse, what Niebuhr called a "guiding idea which unfolds itself,"[5] though which individuals struggled to imagine what the newly emerging realm of freedom might look like, what humans might be doing there, and what needed to be done in preparation.

Niebuhr explained the similarities between the kingdom of God in America and James Truslow Adams's American dream in terms of the church's influence on secular beliefs. He reasoned that the church's hopes for the advance of freedom expressed through the image of the kingdom led the way to the modern faith in progress and initiated exploration of what might be possible in the freer realms of human existence opening up in the modern age. Three of the best examples of those conducting such initial explorations are Jonathan Edwards, Samuel Hopkins, and William Ellery Channing.

Jonathan Edwards

Jonathan Edwards's *A History of the Work of Redemption* contained one of the first and finest postmillennial accounts of the kingdom of God to appear in America.[6] Edwards explored the theoretical ground, struggling with new questions of freedom and progress by using the symbolic form of the kingdom, providing insights and sounding themes that guided theologians and secular writers for over a century. A child of the Enlightenment, and breaking away from the traditional Puritan focus on life after death, Edwards observed that human life was improving remarkably. For reasons that humans could only speculate about, God had begun to move his spirit on the earth in America, awakening the souls of men and women at the very time that he was filling the land with material blessings.

Edwards's view of human progress certainly included diligent work for material necessities. But wealth and ordinary occupations (what Edwards called "necessary secular business") were decidedly means to the "main end." With growing wealth, "ease" might increase as the necessity to work decreased.[7] With increasing ease and as God granted humans their "contrivances and inventions," the redeemed would have ever "more time for more noble exercise" and for "spiritual employments." He foresaw:

> 'Tis probable that the world shall be more like Heaven in the millennium in this respect: that contemplation and spiritual employments, and those things that more directly concern the mind and religion, will be more the saint's ordinary business than now. There will be so many contrivances and inventions to facilitate and expedite their necessary secular business that they will have more time for more noble exercise, and . . . the whole earth may be as one community, one body in Christ.[8]

For one who is remembered today as a dour Puritan, preaching sermons filled with hellfire and damnation, he offered some remarkable advice:

> A man should be so much at liberty that he Can Pursue his main End without distraction. Labour to Get thoroughly Convinced that there is something else needs Caring for more than this world. . . . The Care of his soul will thrust out the Care of his body.[9]

Niebuhr concluded, "[Edwards and other 'New Light' revival leaders and evangelicals of his day] said 'love,' whereas the Puritans had said 'holiness.'" They "thought more in terms of man's nonprofessional relations to his fellow man than in those of the calling."[10]

God's grace lavished on America was beginning to provide enough and to spare of the goods of this world to satisfy all reasonable desires. However, "unruly passions" for ever more material goods, novel earthly gratifications, and the vainglory of display were creating discontent in the soul and divisions in the community, propagating the twin vices of greed and envy. Such irrational appetites had no place in a world of enlightened reason, let alone in God's kingdom. The only way out of such "a poor starved condition" was "to eat and be satisfied," in peace, "abundantly comforted" by enough of the "objective," "extrinsic" goods of life.[11]

Struggling with the question of how best to use the new freedoms reason and God were providing, Edwards found an example, a foretaste of the kingdom, revealed by the recent past. During the initial stages of the first Great

Awakening, he noted that every day came to resemble the Sabbath. Describing a set of behaviors that by today's standards may be seen as delusional, even scandalous, Edwards reported that the people were so filled by the Holy Spirit that ordinary business took second place throughout the week, giving way to "exercises" and "recreations" of the spirit. The revival begun in Edwards's church in Northampton in 1733 became so intense that it seemed to threaten the town's economy, prompting Edwards to fret about his congregation neglecting "worldly affairs":

> Yet there then was the reverse of what commonly is. Religion was with all sorts the great concern and the world was a thing only by the by. The only thing in their view was to get the kingdom . . . and eve'y day seemed, in many respects, like a sabbath-day.[12]

With the help of such tangible revelations, Edwards discerned a group of activities complete, worthwhile, meaningful, and delightful in and for themselves emerging in history: experiencing the peace of God; waiting and watching expectantly for him; delighting in true community and fellowship; doing acts of charity and penance; seeking to catch a glimpse of God in his work through history (Edward's favorite recreation); finding a heightened understanding and appreciation of the natural world; taking joy in the everydayness of life; finding the "comfort of our meat and drink"; praising, giving thanks, repenting and trembling before the Divine Majesty; reading the bible; praying; and singing and in all these things "experiencing His presence" more and more. Such activities might fill an individual's life entirely. Such recreations and spiritual exercises anticipated the coming of the earthly kingdom and could fill eternity. Edwards concluded his sermon on "Christian Liberty" with "[God] will give you liberty to recreate and delight yourself in the best, the purest and most exquisite pleasures, as much as you please, without restraint."[13]

Samuel Hopkins

Jonathan Edwards's close friend and disciple Samuel Hopkins presented an even stronger case for liberty's role in the postmillennial kingdom. The historian and scholar of religion Peter Jauhiainen observed that "it is in [Hopkins's] projection of the rapid increase in *nonreligious* knowledge that we see clearly the intersection of millennial and Enlightenment theories of progress."[14] As wealth grew with the progress of science and the useful arts, work, as well as charity, would become less burdensome and demanding. Since Adam's fall, humans had been condemned to earn a living by the sweat of their brows. However, it was as apparent to Hopkins as it was to Edwards that God was gradually lifting the original curse. As work served its intended purpose, chastising and correcting the soul's sinful tendencies, God was granting humans increasing liberty to progress in holiness and community, expanding opportunities for spiritual exercises. Humans were gradually regaining their original, free nature as God's own:

> In the days of the millennium there will be a fullness and plenty of all the necessaries and conveniences of life to render all much more easy and comfortable in their worldly circumstances and enjoyments . . . and with much less labor and toil, . . . it will not be then necessary for any men or women to spend all or the greatest part of their time in labor in order to procure a living, and enjoy all the comforts and desirable conveniences of life. It will not be necessary for each one to labor more than two or three hours in a day, . . . and the rest of their time they will be disposed to spend in reading and conversation, . . . to improve their minds and make progress in knowledge, especially in the knowledge of divinity, and in studying the Scriptures, and in private and social and public worship, and attending on public instruction, . . . [and] in business more entertaining and important.[15]

Indeed, for Hopkins the free-kingdom condition, complete and satisfying in itself, might become such a present fullness that all concerns about future punishments or rewards would be crowded out. For him the Christian life was not an austere struggle sustained by a dim hope for future deliverance. Rather, it involved an increasing focus on the intrinsic rewards of God's nearness here and now. Even suffering and deprivation were precious experiences in and for themselves so long as one was serving God. Hopkins envisioned such a radical giving up of self and future rewards that modern scholars have compared him to Zen Buddhists and medieval mystics.[16]

Whereas Edwards provided a list of free activities that signaled the kingdom's approach, Hopkins concentrated on what he believed was the one best virtue, "disinterested benevolence." Hopkins insisted that "disinterested benevolence," life's supreme and "beautiful good in itself," its *bonum formosum*, would more than compensate for the renunciation of selfish rewards and gratifications. Abandoning self and future reward, individuals could still experience a rational and present enjoyment in the happiness of others. A key precept shared by Edwards and Hopkins and underlying the "New Divinity" was that the individual soul was not loved separate from the rest of creation. Nevertheless, since the self is part of the whole, the individual's delight in the joys of others was perfectly reasonable. For Hopkins, "holiness" was primarily "disinterested benevolence toward man, including ourselves."[17]

As what many have called America's most important philosopher-theologian and as the "father of American postmillennialism,"[18] Jonathan Edwards influenced generations of churchmen and churchwomen who continued to wrestle with the novel questions of freedom, wealth, and ease that economic progress, scientific advance, and political reforms were presenting to the modern age. Both Edwards and Hopkins employed the symbolic form of the millennium partly as metaphor, mostly in expectation, as they struggled with freedom's new challenges, attempting to discover human actions and conditions beyond the marketplace and the courthouse worthwhile in and for themselves, setting a pattern for those who followed.

Their speculations about the coming of the kingdom focused in part on the ultimate purposes of human mastery of the natural world—on centrally important eschatological questions raised by the Enlightenment and technological progress: What is freedom for? What is worth doing in and for itself? While it was God who was acting in history, granting humans power to control their world and prepare for the coming of his kingdom, it remained the human responsibility to understand and respond. For Edwards and Hopkins freedom offered the possibility of turning to the recreations of the spirit—to such entertainments provided by community life, charity, and to the rational "delight in meat and drink."[19] These kingdom-like activities were God's best gifts: the fulfillment of human longing and the final end of working.

Beginning in the eighteenth century, "human agency" began to replace "God's providence" in discussions about the progress of freedom. However, the focus on how to use the new freedom continued even as men and women began to claim larger roles in determining their own destiny. Subsequently, the questions about the direction of progress and the uses of freedom have echoed down through the centuries in the secular world—Edwards's and Hopkins's inquiries into the *bonum formosum* deeply influenced the nineteenth and twentieth centuries' discourse about Higher Progress and the American dream.

William Ellery Channing

William Ellery Channing helped translate theological insights and speculations about the kingdom of God in America into practical action and social reforms. Because of his efforts to reach out to workers and because of his support of labor's ten-hour cause, he represents the transition from the kingdom of God in America to the secular American dream of Higher Progress. Moreover, his views concerning progressive revelation and disinterested benevolence as the unfolding of *inherent* human potential (rather than exclusively the gift of God's grace), together with his Universalist beliefs, led him to try to find new social and cultural opportunities for everyone, further democratizing Edwards's and Hopkins's millennial vision.[20]

As a Unitarian, convinced of the inherent worth and goodness of all people, he was committed to what he understood as human rights and to social reform in the areas of relief for the poor, peace, education, free speech, temperance, and the abolition of slavery. Historian David Robinson observed, "Social reformers of all stripes looked to him with hope to support their endeavors."[21] Channing believed that practical means must be found to educate everyone and that parks, libraries, and other public facilities to accommodate all in their new freedom needed to be built. Therefore, he was a leading advocate of public education, working with reformers such as Dorothea Dix, Elizabeth Peabody, and Horace Man, and became one of the first and most prominent supporters of labor's demands for the ten-hour day.

Channing and the Ten-Hour System

Today Channing is best known, and frequently castigated, for his lectures "On the Elevation of the Laboring Classes" and "Self-Culture."[22] In support of the workers in his city, Channing adopted phrases, such as "self-culture" and "elevation," that were distinctive parts of labor's rhetoric and demands for the ten-hour workday in Boston, New York, and other cities during the 1820s and 1830s.[23]

Speaking to a group of mechanic apprentices in 1841, Channing endorsed labor's primary goal of the ten-hour day. He agreed with laborites that industry's productive power would continue to increase and that as industry became "more efficient . . . the means of living will grow easier."[24] Thus, freedom from material necessity and from labor were bound to increase. The "human mind" would continue to "create a new world around it, corresponding to itself . . . securing time and means for improvement to the multitude": "With the increase of machinery, and with other aids which intelligence and philanthropy will multiply, *we may expect more and more time will be redeemed* from manual labor for intellectual and social occupations."[25]

He invited his audience to speculate with him about the importance of the new free time and how it might be used. In the process, he blended his views about the kingdom of God with working-class rhetoric and with labor's explicit demands for shorter work hours and public education. Channing reasoned that spiritual and economic development advanced together, the one supporting the other. The advance of knowledge and spiritual growth sustained economic progress by making work more efficient and humans more trusting and better able to cooperate. In turn, economic progress made it possible to "redeem the time," so that more people could devote more of their attention to family and community life, cultural pursuits, spiritual activities, and the arts of living freely together, stimulating even further economic development and spiritual growth.[26]

Whereas he was concerned that the increase in leisure should accomplish the ends of the Deity, he also stressed the importance of cultivating those virtues that would make community and conviviality possible. For Channing, as for Hopkins, republican virtue was encapsulated by the single Christian virtue "disinterested benevolence," which, coupled with labor-saving machinery, would provide increasing living "room" for humans to flourish. From the start of his career he had argued:

> One great end of the Deity . . . [is] that he may give *room* to the benevolent exertions of his children. . . . [H]appiness flows from . . . benevolent reciprocation. . . . [T]he good heart, therefore, will . . . rejoice in the happiness

which it has produced. . . . Let [the soul] behold a kingdom of endless and increasing glory . . . and let it be invited to press forward to this kingdom, and its benevolence will give it vigor to pursue the prize.[27]

Channing also employed the Sabbath as a symbolic form to write and speak about freedom and progress toward a higher life. The traditional Sabbath had humanized society for thousands of years, freeing people for one day in seven. Visions of the eternal Sabbath might thus guide the future.[28] "[The Sabbath] may be clothed with a new interest and a new sanctity. It may give a new impulse to the nation's soul."[29]

Threats of Idleness and the Work-School

However, the threat remained that people, rich and poor, would refuse or misuse their new freedom. The innate capacity for selfless benevolence and for cultural, spiritual, and convivial progress might not be cultivated and would be left to atrophy. Whereas no original sinfulness confounded human strivings, free people were certainly free to deny their destiny. Forgetting those immutable truths that make community and true progress possible, the nation might abandon its new freedoms and regress to tyranny, ignorance, selfishness, and economic chaos.

Idleness was one of the greatest pitfalls. The view held by the "fashionable" few that "idleness is a privilege and work a disgrace, is among the deadliest errors." Channing hammered the point home in his lecture "On the Elevation of the Laboring Classes," attacking the notion that release from labor was the occasion for idleness: "No toil is so burdensome as the rest of him who has nothing to task and quicken his powers."[30]

To preserve the new liberties made possible by the ten-hour day, workers (as well as the idle rich) needed to understand the importance of free *activity*. The "higher life" required vigorous effort, not passive indulgence.[31] Like the body, the mind and spirit would never strengthen and grow without resistance and exercise. Channing wrote of lust, greed, and sloth together, reasoning that each paralyzed souls and "hardened ourselves against the claims of humanity."[32] Thus, he mounted a spirited defense of active and socially engaged leisure.

Rather than appealing to scriptural or church authority, however, he more often used what he understood to be reasonable arguments. Supporting the ten-hour day, he sought common ground with workers, "room" to recommend and defend his beliefs about what should be done with the newly freed time. Channing argued that the best teacher to instruct all, rich and poor, in the importance of vigorous leisure activities was work. In arguments similar to Hopkins's explanation of God's purpose in imposing the Adamic work-curse, Channing proposed that work was nature's original teacher and guide.

In his essay on slavery, Channing compared free labor in accord with the "laws of nature" with its unnatural, perverted form, slavery.[33] He agreed with some of slavery's apologists that there were similarities. Both slave and free person "act from necessity." Whereas the slave had a human master, the free person's master was "hunger and thirst. . . . [T]he elements and seasons . . . [are] so many lashes driving us to our daily tasks." But to equate the two forms of working was monstrous. Unlike slavery, the "necessity laid on us by natural wants" served a larger purpose: "to awaken all our faculties, to give full play to body and mind, and thus to give us a new consciousness of the powers derived to us."[34] Moreover, through the discipline of labor the worker would eventually "gain mastery over himself" and "be able to diminish the toil of the hands, and to mix with it more intellectual and liberal occupations."[35] Slaves toiled unendingly, with no prospect of liberation, forever given new burdens by their human taskmasters who sought to "curb their wills, break their spirits, and shut them up forever in the same narrow and degrading work." Thus, slavery perverted nature. By contrast, nature "invites us to throw off her yoke, and to make her our servant. . . . To call forth the intellect is a principle purpose of the circumstances [of being forced by nature to work] in which we are placed."[36]

He explained further in his essay "On the Elevation of the Laboring Classes" that for free men and women labor "is a school in which [they] are placed to get energy of purpose and character." The idle rich were less likely than workers to make virtuous use of their leisure because many of them had been able to avoid the work-school. The struggle with necessity that defines natural, authentic work disciplined the body and soul, built skills, and strengthened the will, preparing both manual and mental workers for the freedom that resulted from the "diminishing" of labor.[37] Humans were blessed with the work-school

> to get energy of purpose and character,—a vastly more important endowment than all the learning of all other schools. They are placed, indeed, under hard masters, physical sufferings and wants, the power of fearful elements, and the vicissitudes of all human things; but these stern teachers do a work which no compassionate, indulgent friend could do for us; and true wisdom will bless Providence for their sharp ministry.[38]

Throughout his writings, Channing made a fundamental distinction between work as toil (mental as well as manual), driven by necessity in accord with the "laws of nature," and "intellectual and liberal *occupations*" that are chosen and done freely in accord with "another state of being," beyond necessity, pecuniary concerns, and the marketplace—in leisure.[39]

Channing's Leisure List

As did Edwards and Hopkins, Channing struggled with freedom's autotelic questions: What activities (*occupations*) are worthy of the kingdom/the Sabbath/heaven/Eden? What actions are worthwhile in and for themselves? He also began to outline specifics. Prominent on his list were everyday forms of conviviality. Ordinary conversation, stories, and political discourse were the very stuff of the kingdom and showed the way to human progress.

Channing agreed with Edwards that a new relationship with the natural world would also be possible as technology advanced: "Nature should be studied for its own sake, because so wonderful a work of God, because impressed with his perfection, because radiant with beauty, and grandeur, and wisdom, and beneficence."[40]

Intelligence, guiding labor and making it more efficient, leads to a higher end than the mere conflict with nature and competition in the marketplace. Instead of continually trying to control and dominate the natural world to meet their material needs, individuals could freely return to nature to understand, appreciate, enjoy, and recreate.

Moreover, "physical vigor is . . . valuable for its own sake." Together with the natural world, the human body merited careful attention and enjoyment on its own terms.[41] Channing pointed out that physical exercise opens the mind "to cheerful impressions . . . by removing those indescribable feelings of sinking, disquiet, depression." He observed, "Our whole nature must be cared for." The physical body would be very much at home in the kingdom. Thus, Channing recommended that physical education be given "greater attention" at home and in schools.[42]

He was particularly fond of dancing and suggested that dancing become "an every-day amusement, and may mix with our common intercourse. . . . The body as well as the mind feel the gladdening influence. No amusement seems more to have a foundation in our nature. . . . [G]race in motion . . . is one of the higher faculties of our nature." Along with disinterested benevolence, God had "implanted a strong desire for recreation after labor."[43] An example for all, Christ had developed his "human nature by active sports. . . . He, who has thus formed us, cannot have intended us for a dull, monotonous life, and cannot frown on pleasures which solace our fatigues and refresh our spirits."[44]

Channing was consistent in his view that activities of the mind and soul are superior to the physical struggles with the material world. He nevertheless caught a glimpse of a possible transformation of the body and the natural world. Freed from the prisons of material necessity into the new arenas of the kingdom, humans might redeem the body and experience it joyfully for its own sake. Others would later extend Channing's tentative suggestions about the freeing and transforming of the material world and the body. Writers such as Walt Whitman and Norman O. Brown would explore in detail how Higher Progress might free and then eroticize the complete body in play, as well as mind and spirit: the laborer as well as the theologian and poet.[45]

Channing concluded that "the increase of machinery" would provide increasingly more free time that, if patterned after the Sabbath, would allow humans to do things that were more and more their own reward: delighting in nature and their physical being, enlivening the human community, growing the soul, "developing the idea of God," and dancing the night away.

Channing's Critics

Perhaps Channing will never escape his reputation for class bias. However, he anticipated the accusations that would be leveled against him—that his efforts to "elevate" and "uplift" workers were products of his narrow bourgeois values and class agenda: "But some will say, 'Be it granted that the working classes may find some leisure; should they not be allowed to spend it in relaxation? Is it not cruel to summon them from toils of the hand to toils of the mind?'"[46]

In the face of such likely criticism, Channing remained unapologetic, retorting:

> Is the laborer then [to be] defrauded of pleasure by improvement? . . . Yes, let them have pleasure. Far be it from me to dry up the fountains, to blight the spots of verdure, where they refresh themselves after life's labors. But I maintain that self-culture multiplies and increases their pleasures, that it creates new capacities of enjoyment, that it saves their leisure from being what it too often is, dull and wearisome.[47]

Channing assailed those who would deny laborers access to the things of the mind, the joys of the spirit, and virtues of community, maintaining that the kingdom of God in America would be thoroughly democratic and egalitarian in the sense that all would have the time for "higher achievements."[48] Growth in the new, egalitarian "room" of leisure would gradually put the activities of mind and spirit within the reach of all:

> The doctrine is too shocking to need refutation, that the great majority of human beings, endowed as they are with rational and immortal powers, are placed on earth simply to toil for their own animal subsistence, and to minister to the luxury and elevation of the few. It is monstrous, it approaches impiety, to suppose that God has placed insuperable barriers to the expansion of the free, limitless soul.[49]

However, Channing had a conventional view of equality, as evidenced by his rejection of political attempts to redistribute wealth and his support of property rights: "That some should be richer than others is natural, and is necessary, and could only be prevented by gross violations of right. Leave men to the free use of their powers, and some will accumulate more than their neighbors."[50]

Channing struggled to reconcile liberty with equality, maintaining that his was the truly egalitarian, democratic way. He explained, "To be prosperous is not to be superior, and should form no barrier between men."[51] While he certainly included workers' wages in his understanding of "elevation," he valued the equality that was to be found beyond the marketplace. Wealth was no guarantee of superior virtue or happiness—more frequently wealth encouraged greed, envy, idleness, and selfishness, leading to isolation and despair.

True "elevation" and equality were to be found during leisure and would soon be available to all.

Better wages were important not because laborers would be able to mimic the idleness of the wealthy, wield power over and separate themselves from other people, or amass luxuries and wealth. Wages were important because once workers were paid enough to satisfy their material needs they could gradually claim a higher "mode of . . . future existence."[52]

Mounting a critique of his own, Channing made accusations against those in the privileged classes who held on to their position and status by perpetuating feudal-like forms of exploitation. Channing was suspicious of claims that a laborer would never have "time . . . [for] intellectual, social, and moral culture without starving his family, and impoverishing the community." Those who held such views were usually "people [who] are at ease; who think more of property than of any other human interest; who have little concern for the mass of their fellow creatures . . . and [who believe] that any social order should continue which secures to themselves personal comfort or gratification." Reiterating his view that reductions in working hours were opening the way for the mental and spiritual development for everyone, Channing asked, "Can anything be plainer than . . . that the application of science to art is accomplishing a stupendous revolution?"[53]

An elite few, holding privileged claims to education and culture, resisted this "stupendous revolution." These were the true believers in exclusion and inequality. Just as some excelled in earning and collecting wealth, others were gifted with intellect, creativity, artistic abilities, and admission to the schools of the privileged. Too often, as in the feudal past, these gifted few misused their learning and good fortune. Seeking distinction and status, such people, while living in a democracy, isolated themselves in privileged classes ("rank and caste"), in exclusive enclaves protected by churches, universities, and wealth. Channing charged, "Of all treasons against humanity, there is no one worse than he who employs great intellectual forces to keep down the intellect of his less favored brother."[54]

Envisioning a democratic culture in which all participated, Channing denied

to any individual or class this monopoly of thought . . . as well might a few claim a monopoly of light and air, of seeing and breathing, as of thought. Were the mass of men made to be monsters? To grow only in a few organs and faculties, and to pine away and shrivel in others? . . . But suppose the intellectual and the religious to cut themselves off by some broad, visible distinction from the rest of society, to form a clan of their own, to refuse admission . . . to people of inferior knowledge and virtue, and to diminish as far as possible the occasions of intercourse with them; would not society rise up as one . . . against this arrogant exclusiveness? And if intelligence and piety may not be the foundations of a caste, on what ground shall they, who have no distinction but wealth, superior costume, richer equipages, finer houses, draw lines around themselves and constitute themselves a higher class?[55]

Truly superior individuals would not try to reserve the things of the mind and spirit for themselves. On the contrary, the real elite in society would distinguish themselves through disinterested benevolence—by their selfless devotion to the elevation of others to "higher modes of existence."[56] This was not simply a matter of educating and selecting a few from among the less favored classes but of making it possible for everyone to take part in an egalitarian, democratic culture: "Great minds are to make others great. Their superiority is to be used, not to break the multitude to intellectual vassalage, not to establish over them a spiritual tyranny, but to rouse them from lethargy, and to aid them to judge for themselves."[57]

Concerned primarily with the equality possible in "higher modes of existence," Channing nevertheless presented a novel insight about the redistribution of material wealth. Having no interest in governmental efforts to achieve a more equitable distribution of wealth, in a move to be rehearsed by others such as Monsignor John Ryan, he turned instead to the reduction of working hours.[58] Explicitly disavowing "any special prophetic gift," Channing made a hypothetical case: If the set of unselfish community virtues derived from disinterested benevolence made progress, the wealthy would naturally become less concerned with those things that disturbed civility and promoted exploitation—status, position, power, and excess wealth. They would be more charitable indeed. But they might also become progressively less interested in acquiring more material goods than they needed, naturally finding it more rewarding to spend more of their lives in "higher modes of existence," leaving the marketplace along with the workers who were winning shorter hours.

Others in Channing's day imagined the future in terms of the growth of technology and wealth, predicting flying machines, glorious cities, and other technological marvels, much of which of course has come true. But Channing's progress in "higher modes of existence," in mental and spiritual development, and in conviviality remains largely in the realm of imagination and is often dismissed as utopian. However, Channing offered a prescient, critical evaluation of what has grown to be modern economic dogma—of progress defined only by economic growth and by the creation of new work forevermore:

> We do not find that civilization lightens men's toils: as yet it has increased them; and in this effect I see the sign of a deep defect in what we call the progress of society. It cannot be the design of the Creator that the whole of life should be spent in drudgery for the supply of animal wants. That civilization is very imperfect in which the mass of men can redeem no time from bodily labor for intellectual, moral, and social culture. . . . [R]ich and poor seem to be more and more oppressed with incessant toil, exhausting forethought, anxious struggles, feverish competitions.[59]

Labor and the Ten-Hour System

> The realm of freedom actually begins only where labour
> which is determined by necessity and mundane considerations
> ceases; thus in the very nature of things it lies beyond the
> sphere of actual material production. . . . Beyond begins that
> development of human energy which is an end in itself, the true
> realm of freedom. . . . The shortening of the working-day is its
> basic prerequisite.[1]
> —KARL MARX, *Capital*

America's educated elite initiated and led the antebellum period's reform causes: temperance, peace, women's rights, prison reform, and the abolition of capital punishment and slavery. Shorter working hours was the exception. While receiving vital support from people such as William Ellery Channing and Horace Greeley, workers began pressing for limits to their workday on their own. Prompted by their own motives and led by their own visions, workers also provided the organization and political will necessary to sustain their cause for over a century.

As the labor movement began, middle-class reformers who envisioned progress as the gradual reduction of working hours generally took their cue from workers' successes, often employing labor's rhetoric, such as "elevation," "higher life," and "larger liberty." After 1830 the vision of progress as the increase of freedom beyond the marketplace and courthouse, in what Karl Marx would call "the realm of freedom," was grounded in the reality of steadily decreasing work hours.

The century-long struggle for shorter work hours was part of workers' response to the modern changes in jobs and the work place. It is only in the late eighteenth and early nineteenth centuries that "work" in its modern form may be said to have begun. A good case has been made that "work" simply did not exist until the mid- to late eighteenth century.[2] Of course, the words *work, travailler, trabajo, labour, arbeit,* and so on, have been around much longer. Activities necessary to sustain life are primordial; humans have always had to eat. Nevertheless, "work" as we now understand it as a general, abstract category, independent of its particular forms (such as farming, manufacture, trade) and its age-old locations (primarily in private patriarchal households), has a modern origin.[3]

As large-scale labor markets began to function with some efficiency and regularity, workers were increasingly able to leave farms and households to sell their labor in public. Able to exercise close supervision, business owners began to purge nonproductive activities from the job, severely limiting worker control, "rationalizing" and revolutionizing the way that people had always gone about their business. The traditional workday had always included generous measures of nonwork activities: leisurely meals with the family, naps, conversations, stories, side trips, social drinking, games, and so on. The workweek included frequent breaks: festivals, fairs, marriages, frolics, and wakes. In Europe the church calendar marked as many as 156 holidays before the Reformation. Modern work discipline began with the systematic elimination of such nonproductive uses of time.[4]

In Europe workers initially resisted the coming of modern work discipline. However, E. P. Thompson explained, workers reluctantly accepted work's modern forms even though they were demanding as never before. In exchange for surrendering their traditional ways of working, workers began "to fight . . . about time," insisting that their workday be shortened for them to have some time to call their own and to return to those kinds of nonpecuniary activities and associations that had once been integral parts of their lives.[5]

In the United States a similar scenario played out but on a smaller scale and in different settings. Instead of the European large factory, the American small artisanal workshop witnessed work's metamorphosis.[6] David Saposs described how the newly emergent "merchant-capitalist" initiated a chain of events that ended in the institution of timed work and new forms of work discipline similar to those Thompson described. Because of the expanding trade opportunities opened up by roads, canals, and new shipping facilities and technologies, American merchants were able to exploit larger markets. Able to contract sales on a large scale, the merchant-capitalists then approached the masters of traditional workshops, seeking subcontracts. With sale price determined by competitive market forces beyond local control, the master was forced to economize in one of the few ways available—by reducing labor costs. Thus masters set about making their own work and the work of those they controlled as efficient and productive as possible.[7]

Infected by the merchant-capitalist desire to sustain and increase profit margins, masters intensified the pace of work and began creating work teams and subdividing tasks in order to lessen dependence on skilled labor and increase speed of output. Increasingly able to employ unskilled workers, children, women, and newly arrived immigrants, masters began to exercise close supervision similar to that already instituted in European factories, systematically eliminating all nonproductive activities from the workday and workweek. Saposs reasoned that because the masters' "profits were thus 'sweated' out of labor," the results were called "sweatshops."[8]

Interrupting the ancient blending of work and life, the new market realities also interrupted the traditional, reciprocal social relations between master, journeyman, and apprentice. In the place of the masters' traditional household, new kinds of "putting-out" systems (subcontracting) and impersonal workshops shorn of the masters' custom-bound responsibilities to their apprentices and journeymen appeared.

Traditionally, masters, journeymen, and apprentices had claimed to share a set of values that included craftsmanship, familial duties, and community and civic responsibilities. Such republican virtues often met and flourished in the workplace. But by the 1830s the traditional workshop settings were well on their way to being replaced by what Sean Wilentz called the "bastard workshop."[9] Apprentices and the new unskilled "operatives" were less and less a part of the master's household. Journeymen had fewer realistic expectations of starting their own shops. As manufacturing was increasingly rationalized, the "motley feudal ties" that had connected owner to operative and community fell away, replaced by impersonal market relations—a kind of wage slavery that the early labor press frequently compared to slavery in the American South. Republican virtues attached to the workshop and fair trading began to give way to the ethics of modern marketplaces—private profit and caveat emptor.

As work and the workplace changed, so too did the workers' understanding of their jobs. Doubts emerged that the job remained the place for selfless craftsmanship and duty, mutuality and community. Expectations about social mobility, of working diligently in order to have the chance to build a business for themselves, were less and less credible. Even though the Western frontier was a safety valve for some, an urban working class developed with fewer hopes for advancement, became increasingly stable, and showed signs of becoming permanent by the middle of the nineteenth century.[10]

The Fight about Time

As in Europe, the coming of modern work discipline together with work's new social and economic contexts prompted workers to initiate a century-long struggle for shorter hours in the United States. As in Europe, workers in America began to "fight about time,"[11] attempting to reclaim some measure of control over their lives and to return to those free associations and activities that had always been parts of their days. Early in the nineteenth century, at the beginning of the labor movement, workers "valued leisure for traditional pre-industrial reasons."[12] Subsequently, throughout the shorter-hours campaigns, workers claimed the right to spend more of their time in customary ways with family and friends, in community and civic activities, in rituals and celebrations, at schools and churches, and simply doing "what [they] will."[13]

As the ethics of laissez-faire capitalism increasingly governed economic life, the republican virtues that once attached to the workshop began to migrate to times and places outside work and the marketplace. Selfless service to the community and to the state was one such virtue. Personal wealth had long been seen as vital for the Republic because it allowed some the leisure necessary for public service. The link between leisure and political participation for the wealthy was firmly established in the United States by the end of the American Revolution.

With the coming of the "bastard workshop," the link was democratized. David Roediger and Philip Foner pointed out that the desire for "citizenship time" was among the causes of the beginning of the labor movement in the United States. Claiming the right to participate in elections, canvassing, rallies, and political discourse, workers complained that long hours and close supervision on their jobs deprived them of such basic liberties.[14]

During the Age of Jackson (1830–1842), organized tradesmen and operatives began to claim that increased leisure for workers might revive the Republic. They feared that republican virtues, founded on selfless concerns for state and regard for community, were being discarded by self-seeking merchants and greedy owners who were manipulating government in furtherance of their economic self-interests. Moreover, the Revolutionary generation that had championed republican virtue was dying away. One of the most frequent arguments made in support of the ten-hour day was that by introducing the time and energy of ordinary citizens into the political process, the old founding virtues, essential for the future of the Republic, might be redeemed and the new selfish, market-based morality challenged.

As divisions between the economic sphere and all other aspects of life began to solidify, becoming sharper through the nineteenth century, workers also turned to times and places outside the job and workplace to revive their families and local communities that were being overtaken by large-scale, impersonal economic forces. Old institutions and new establishments such as churches and saloons, bowling allies and poolrooms, benevolent associations and ethnic societies, and clubs and social centers became more important than the workplace in providing opportunities for simple convivial gatherings—for ordinary conversation, debate, and community activities. Indeed, those places that served workers' leisure became the locations for labor's nascent organization and the beginnings of working-class identity. For example, the historian Stephen Ross concluded, "Although work was a central focus of daily life, it did not produce a single working-class experience" for workers in nineteenth-century Cincinnati.[15]

Leisure provided the opportunity to address other problems brought on by modern changes in work and the economy. Historians agree that the desire for shorter work hours was the cause of the awakening of labor and of the working classes in the early nineteenth century. Roediger and Foner added that during the "Age of Jackson . . . increasing attention to the hours issue was the key element in the transformation of labor's consciousness and organization." They argued that because of its popularity, the issue became the "common denominator for American control struggles . . . around which workers from various craft and various cities could discuss their fears and register their protests against a myriad . . . of grievances."[16] Shorter hours thus came to "symbolize health, education, steady employment, and political participation."[17]

But it may be argued that the hours issue did more than supply a symbol to call attention to other related issues. Shorter hours provided the one necessary resource, free time, that could remedy problems emerging with industrialization and modern work discipline. Roediger and Foner argued that "the issue of education intertwined with that of hours."[18] But leisure did more than intertwine with education—it provided the medium in which education might increase.

The recovery of traditional cultural practices and activities and the addressing of new, pressing problems such as health and education were critical concerns motivating workers during the early years of the century-long shorter-hours process. But of equal and perhaps greater importance were their aspirations for the future—aspirations shared by workers in other industrializing nations.

Workers' Nights

In *La Nuit des Prolétaires*, Jacques Rancière presented an evocative account of a few hundred Parisian artisans and shop owners whose fates and hopes for the future were similar to American workers' at the time (the 1830s and 1840s).[19] Their example may offer some direction for historians trying to understand the shorter-hours movement in the United States. Seeking to illuminate "something as broad as freedom" from a historical perspective, Rancière, whose primary discipline is philosophy, focused his study on how workers understood, yearned for, and experienced freedom in the modern world.[20] Thus, he attempted to ground his philosophical meditations about freedom in the lived experiences of ordinary people, identifying their successful quest for leisure with freedom's modern advent. Turning from historical generalizations and philosophical theorizing, Rancière defined freedom in terms of workers' concrete, daily activities and perceptions.

As had E. P. Thompson, Rancière noticed that as his workers experienced the new, "severe" kinds of constraints brought about by the beginning of modern work discipline, they resisted its "unyielding predetermination."[21] Because the contrast between their work and the rest of their lives had become so stark, they began to cherish their free moments as never before and to envision their freedom in new ways. They began to imagine what might be possible in the interstices of free time emerging in their lives.[22] A Parisian carpenter and floor layer, Louis Gabriel Gauny, set about to describe "an entire vision of life, an unusual counter-economy which sought ways to reduce the worker's consumption of everyday goods so that he would be more independent of the market economy."[23]

Living into the bits and pieces of free time they were able to carve out of their workdays, Rancière's workers experimented with new possibilities, revising and enlarging their vision of what their new freedom meant for them and might mean for future generations. Thus, like American workers who fought for the ten-hour day, they were vitally concerned with appropriating the time they did not have . . . by giving up their own night of rest to discuss or to write, to compose verses or to work out philosophies. These hard-won bonuses of time and liberty were not marginal phenomena, they were not diversions from the building of the worker movement and its great ideals. *They were a revolution . . . and they made [the labor movement and the formation of working-class identity] possible.* [Such free hours made possible] the *work* by which men and women tore themselves away from an identity forged for them by a system of domination and affirmed themselves as independent inhabitants of a common world, capable of all the refinements and self-denials that previously had been associated only with those classes that were released from the daily concern of work and food.[24]

Conversing in cafes, composing verse, wandering around the city, and envisioning the future of the laboring classes, these Parisians began to engage in the sorts of free activities that the leisured aristocracy had always before claimed as its special privilege. During "those nights snatched from the normal round of work and repose" they began to erode the feudal barriers between the literate elite and the rest of the nation. Rancière's workers began to struggle with fundamental questions of their being—with meaning, purpose, identity, destiny, community—using the language and techniques available to them, claiming to do literature, poetry, painting, and philosophy as their natural rights.[25]

Moving within the newly fluid margins of both class and the new work settings, they began developing a working-class consciousness in pre-1848 France, coining the idioms and slogans that circulated widely enough to help fix a national language of class in that country by the turn of the twentieth century. Moreover, galvanized originally by the "absurdity of having to go on begging, day after day, for this labor in which one's life is lost," workers mounted a vigorous critique of work's new industrial forms and of capitalism in general.[26] Dreading the return to their jobs each day, most also rejected bourgeois attempts to glorify work's new modern forms.

Thus Rancière challenged the conventional understanding that such workers as these were "labor loving" craftsmen. He assailed Marxist assumptions that human beings are in essence *Homo faber* and that our fundamental desire (and history's motive and direction) is to find freedom and meaning in work over which we have regained control—in work with which we transform nature into useful products, through which we express ourselves and impart our personhoods to creations that we exchange, and by which we create ourselves by inventing new necessities, utility, and work.

Rancière juxtaposed the experiences and discourse of workers who were exposed for the first time to the rigors of modern work discipline against the widely accepted modern myths about the "glory of work," showing that their leisure rather than their jobs represented freedom and was central to their hopes for personal advance and the progress of liberty. It was in leisure, not work, that they expected to realize their humanity. He demonstrated that workers who found their new jobs painful and constraining as never before placed their hopes for their future in "the night of the proletariat"—in *escaping*, as much as possible, the new forms of work discipline that capitalism required and in imagining an *alternative*, free social order outside the emerging market economy.

Rancière observed that according to historians' "grand modernist narratives," his "little stories of workers taking an afternoon walk, or straying far from the solid realities of the factory and the organized struggle, have no historical importance."[27] He countered that discounting workers' experiences and discourse privileges the knowledges of an elite, articulate few over the perceptions and aspirations of those whose voices are rarely heard directly. Claiming to be able to discern the workers' real intent hidden by false consciousness, modern historians tend to

> confirm the [existing] social order, which has always been built on the simple idea that the vocation of workers is to work—"and to struggle," good progressive souls add—and that they have no time to lose in wandering, writing or thinking. . . . [T]his is the reason why our severe theorists and historians decided that [*La Nuit des Prolétaires*] was literature rather than history.[28]

Suggesting that Socrates represented an early version of the sophistry he detected in historians' "grand modernist narratives" glorifying work, Rancière recalled that in the third book of Plato's *Republic* Socrates advanced the notion that humans were naturally divided into two classes: those who have to work and those who have leisure to govern and search for truth. Socrates reckoned that little could be done about such a condition and that the latter would always have to guide the former because the gods had mixed gold with the souls of the philosopher-rulers but iron with the souls of workers.

Rejecting this "outlandish tale," Rancière insisted that "there is no popular intelligence occupied by practical things, nor a learned intelligence devoted to abstract thought. There is not one intelligence devoted to the real and another devoted to fiction. It is always the same intelligence."[29] He offered as proof his Parisian artisans who, claiming the leisure to read, write, and philosophize, laid claim to golden souls.

Rancière's book may be something of an idiosyncratic historical account, limited to what he admitted were a few ordinary individuals for whom extraordinary records had been found. However, his claim that leisure, those "hard-won bonuses of time and liberty," constituted "a revolution" by offering a new experience of freedom and his assertion that modern work was originally understood and experienced in ways quite different from today's "grand modernist narratives" may to some extent be substantiated, and the content of the leisure revolution elaborated in greater detail, by the history of labor in the

United States. Most importantly, Rancière's re-presentation of workers' "vision of life . . . independent of the market economy," transcending what he called the "kingdom" of modern work, provides a vital insight about how to read first-hand accounts of American workers' struggle for shorter hours.[30]

A "Vision of Life . . . Independent of the Market Economy"

Workers in the United States, as capable as French workers of understanding their new experience of freedom without the guidance of academic interpret-ers, shared the belief that theirs were golden souls. Many wanted as much as Louis Gabriel Gauny to use their new freedoms to find community, meaning, purpose, and their identities by searching outside the new iron cages of work and the capitalist marketplace. Perhaps the best-known example of workers' in-tellectual accomplishments and aspirations in the United States is the "learned blacksmith" Elihu Burritt. A controversial figure, prone to self-promotion and exaggerated claims about his intellectual prowess, Burritt became something of a worker-mascot for the bourgeoisie by mid-nineteenth century, appearing to confirm its mythology about self-made men and the glory of manual work that made meals taste so good and sleep so blissful.[31]

But less controversial examples of workers who laid claim to the right to think and speak are plentiful. As they were pressing for a ten-hour workday in the 1840s, some of the women employed at the Lowell mills in Massachusetts demonstrated that they were just as interested as Rancière's workers in reclaim-ing fragments of their life time. In a letter to the *Voice of Industry* dated May 4, 1847, from Lowell, a woman signing herself "Juliana" railed against a few of her sister workers who, accustomed to an earlier starting time, had been standing at the plant gates, waiting as long as ten minutes to be let in:

> Have they common sense, or any minds at all? If so, why are they seen wasting their precious moments . . . ? Have they become so accustomed to watching machinery that they have actually become dwarfs in intellect— and lost all sense of their own God-like powers of mind . . . ? Why are they not in their rooms storing their minds with . . . knowledge which shall fit them for high and noble stations in the moral and intellectual world?[32]

Huldah Stone's was another articulate voice that emerged from among the operatives at Lowell. Jama Lazerow observed that "Stone typified antebellum laborites who demanded more time to cultivate their 'higher sensibilities.'"[33] She was secretary of the Female Labor Reform Association (FLRA) in the mid-1840s and corresponded regularly with labor newspapers.[34] Writing in support of the ten-hour day, she asked:

> Is it necessary that men and women should toil and labor twelve, sixteen and even eighteen hours, to obtain mere sustenance of their physical

natures? Have they no other wants which call as loudly for satisfaction ... ?
Call ye this *life*—to labor, eat, drink, and die without knowing anything ...
of our mysterious natures—of the object of our creation and preservation
and final destination. ... [Life is] *earnest* in procuring the riches of enduring, unfading and *ever increasing* goodness and true wisdom.[35]

She shared the Parisian workers' aspirations for a literate existence—a life
of the mind that the ten-hour day might bring closer to her and her sisters'
reach—and she had begun to realize that

> a portion time must be devoted to moral and intellectual culture corre-
> sponding with the importance of the object. When I hear people say they
> have not time to read—O, how does the thought come home to my heart—
> "in heaven's name what do they live for." What in mercy's name do they do
> for thoughts, for the ever active and restless mind to feast upon from day
> to day! What do they do with the starving intellect ... ? Is it possible that
> *any* can be satisfied to exist only in a physical sense, entirely neglecting the
> cultivation of the noblest powers which God has given them?[36]

William Young, the first editor of the *Voice of Industry*, arguably the most
influential labor newspaper before the Civil War, consistently referred to himself as a "mechanic turned editor."[37] His were practical efforts to "elevate labor,"
by offering his newspaper as a forum for workers, soliciting and publishing
their letters and poetry, and making it possible for others to tell their stories and
articulate their complaints, criticism, plans, and dreams. Young and the editors
of other labor newspapers, building on the issue of ten-hour days, played vital
roles in the formation of labor organizations, establishing an ongoing local discourse in cities such as Lowell and Fall River, Massachusetts.

One of the most frequent reasons that workers gave for demanding shorter
hours was education.[38] Historians have tended to emphasize the importance
workers attached to *practical* education: night schools for learning new skills,
trades, and basic reading skills for getting ahead in the business and professional worlds. However, the kinds of education that workers had in mind for
their children and themselves was often that of preparing for and pretending to
a literate existence.

Certainly workers' educational aims and literary endeavors often con-
formed to what the educated elites of the day expected. However, workers'
claims to a life of the mind involved more than conforming to middle-class
notions about proper culture. Instead, laborites demonstrated a more authentic
participation in and creation of local communities of word and sign, drawing
on, but nevertheless partly independent of, the dominant culture. Most of the
letters, poems, advertisements, and editorials in labor newspapers were addressed primarily to fellow workers and local communities.

There are important elements of personal reflection and sharp social criticism present in Stone's letters and Young's editorials. Historians have long recognized the emphasis leaders such as William Heighton and others put on education as a way to acquaint workers with their rights, expose their oppression, and strengthen their organizations.[39] However, American workers' pursuit of educational reform is also explained by their desire to articulate a vision of a social and economic order alternative to capitalism's "selfish system" and to maintain and enliven a community of literate fellows—to participate more fully in what might reasonably be described as a "lifeworld and system" of "communicative discourse."[40]

Rancière's workers lived before the emergence of the Left Bank as a symbol of the Bohemian artistic and intellectual world for which Paris became renowned. Famously, the city's avant-garde gloried in separating from the common herd to revel in its genius. By contrast, workers such as Stone, "Juliana," and Rancière's Parisians, with fewer pretensions to genius and history making, sought mainly to share a literate existence within their communities, writing and speaking to others around them about their oppression and attempts to organize and influence legislation—but also about their daily experiences and thoughts, dreams and visions, and experiences of tragedy and beauty. These fledgling "communities of discourse" were founded on the expectation that democratic culture might progress and the use of language and sign in dramaturgical, communicative, and moral expression would increasingly become the daily, free occupations of ordinary citizens.

For such workers as Young and Stone, culture could no longer be reserved for an aristocracy of birth or genius (or what were to become the literate professions and academic disciplines). Indeed, worker identity founded in the experience of community, what would be called "solidarity" in the twentieth century, had at its source the hope for democratic literate exchange in an authentic "lifeworld" that laborites tried to construct during their new leisure.

The Revolutionary Heritage and the Pursuit of Happiness

In addition to what Rancière claimed may be universal longings for meaning and expression, for "golden souls," American workers experienced and began to understand their new bits of freedom from the workplace in the particular context of their new nation—its Revolutionary heritage and embrace of natural rights, republican virtue, and the kingdom of God. At the beginning of the labor movement, American workers believed that shorter working hours offered them a practical way to make real the freedoms promised by the Declaration of Independence and argued that some freedom from work was a natural right. Employing the language of the preceding Revolutionary generations, laborites spoke and wrote of liberty's new frontier—of a "larger liberty" to be found beyond the factory gates and marketplace that would fulfill the hopes of the nations' founders. After castigating her sisters for waiting ten minutes outside the plant to go to work, "Juliana" asked:

> What, has a *beneficent Creator bestowed upon us* faculties and powers of mind which are capable of being improved and cultivated *ad infinitum*, and which if trained aright assimilate us to God and the Angels . . . ? [S]hall we suffer them to wither and perish for lack of proper time and attention on our part? Forbid it righteous God! Let it not be said of us here in this land of boasted liberty and equal rights, that thousands are bound down in ignorance and worshiping at the altar of the god of mammon! Awake! Daughters of America to a realization of the evils which follow in the train of ignorance and selfishness! Awake and arise from the low groveling charms of dollars and cents, to a knowledge of your own high and holy duties and destinies. Awake and resolve from this time forth to live, not merely to gain a bare subsistence, but to live for nobler, worthier objectives. Live, not to wear out and exhaust your physical energies in obtaining a few more paltry shillings, but to adorn and beautify the minds and intellects which a kind Father hath conferred upon you.[41]

Such was the contrast between industry's new work discipline (which had become more rigorous in Lowell during the 1840s) and the few hours she had off work that "Juliana" recognized in those "wasted" ten minutes the liberty her nation had proclaimed from the days of its Revolution, using some of the most militant of Thomas Jefferson's rhetoric.[42]

Demanding the right to sell as much of their own time as they wished, New England workers often spoke and wrote of the dependency and "despotic servitude" into which they were forced by new would-be King Georges—the merchant-capitalists and shop owners who seemed to live as idle parasites, feeding on the labor of those they oppressed. Contrasting the selfless virtue of their productive work with the greed of the idle pretenders to an American aristocracy, workers claimed the nation's Revolutionary legacy as their own.

William Young, reporting in the *Voice of Industry* about his visit to Manchester and the "Great Meeting at the Town Hall," which he called "one of the most rational and enthusiastic meetings ever held in New England," recorded the workers' proclamation:

> In view of the alarming increase of the evils of factory labor . . . [to] gradually subvert the republican institutions of our country and fill the land with a dependent, overworked and much oppressed populace. . . . RE-SOLVED: That the fourth of July 1846, shall be the day fixed upon by the operatives of America to declare their INDEPENDENCE of the oppressive Manufacturing power, which has been imported from Old monarchial England, and now being grafted upon the business institutions of our country.[43]

The resolution was in the form of an ultimatum in clear revolutionary language. If the manufacturers were to *"practically* signify an unwillingness to mutually adopt the Ten Hour System," then, come the next July 4, workers throughout New England would "declare their INDEPENDENCE" from owners and the capitalist system, just as the colonies had declared their independence from Great Britain exactly seventy years before.[44]

Labor newspapers were replete with such revolutionary language. In a letter to the *Workingman's Advocate* from Chester Creek, Connecticut, dated September 2, 1835, "An Operative" observed, "The Lord has raised to us another Washington under the name of the Trades' Union: hear ye its voice; enlist under its banners; it is it that is destined to crush the head of oppression."[45]

House carpenters, masons and stone cutters, assembled in Julien Hall, Boston, May 4, 1835, swore allegiance to the ten-hour cause "by the blood of our fathers, shed on our battle fields in the War of the Revolution, the rights of American Freemen."[46] Journeymen cordwainers of Lynn issued a circular declaring their intent to "show the shoe manufactures of New England, that we have not degenerated, but are true representatives of those noble spirits that so fearlessly denounced the usurpations and tyranny of a British king!"[47] Workers in New York City's shipyards had a "Mechanics' Bell" built to help keep track of their working hours, prompting one of their leaders to write, "As the 'Liberty Bell' rang out the proclamation of liberty from monarchial control, so the 'Mechanics' Bell' proclaimed the liberty of leisure for the sons of toil."[48] The New England Workingmen's Association in convention in 1846 resolved, "That the long hour system of labor is inconsistent with the law of nature implanted in every human being by the author of our existence. . . . [Therefore] the great prominent object of the workingmen of N.E. is the reduction of the hours of labor."[49] The *Voice of Industry* editorialized:

Let the ten-hour system be adopted universally . . . and what a change would be brought about. Now let that class [laborers] arise, and in unison assert their rights, their right to enjoy with others all the blessings of life— the right to possess the means of moral, social, intellectual and physical improvement.[50]

The *Mechanic* concluded:

Social tyranny and oppression [that result from long working hours] are a worse evil for the poor working man to endure, than political despotism, because they stare him in the face every day of his existence, grind him into the dust, wither his hopes and happiness of his family, and poison the domestic endearments of his conjugal life.[51]

Struggling for the ten-hour day, the New England worker extended the concept of natural rights to include freedom from work and bosses, recognizing freedom in the most down-to-earth terms: as a daily liberation from "social tyranny and oppression" that "stare[d] him in the face every day of his existence." In Fourth of July orations throughout the Northeast, speakers reiterated what they understood as the Declaration of Independence's sanctioning of the ten-hours struggle: "But what has the ten hour system to do with this day? Why, it is a part of the Declaration of Independence, 'the pursuit of happiness.'"[52] In support of the "Ten Hour System," the "female operatives" from Lowell presented a report to the National Industrial Convention in 1844 proclaiming

> the great principles which pertain to human rights and human duties. . . . The Female Labor Reform [Association] . . . is seeking to increase the intelligence and improve the condition of this down-trodden . . . mass of defenseless females, who are imprisoned within the pestilential walls of cotton mills thirteen hours [a day], deprived . . . of all means of mental or moral improvement—compelled to trample under foot the great physical laws of their being.[53]

As a first step to accomplishing their goals, the FLRA attempted to help "the operative to understand his and her great and inalienable rights" to live free.[54] In 1846 a petition signed by nearly five thousand "operatives and citizens" of Lowell and ten thousand "petitioners in other towns in the state," calling for ten-hour days and "addressed to the Senate and House of Representative of the State of Massachusetts," charged that long hours enriched "the capitalist and depress[ed] the laborer," allowing "wealth and monopoly to feed upon the natural rights of the working classes."[55]

In 1821 Jefferson observed that the "flames kindled on the fourth of July 1776 have spread over too much of the globe" to be extinguished by the return of despotism and tyranny.[56] For workers who organized to initiate and sustain the shorter-hours campaigns throughout the nineteenth and early twentieth centuries, that same fire lit a vision of freedom as leisure—a new, refined, and open-ended liberty beyond industrial work discipline and laissez-faire capitalism. Together with Louis Gabriel Gauny in Paris, they defined modern freedom by means of the sharp contrast between the new constraints of their jobs (that stared them "in the face every day of their existence") and their new experience of leisure. They too were led by a "vision of life . . . independent of the market economy," transformed as the original American dream.

Together with Rancière's Parisians, laborites who demanded the ten-hour day in the United States saw little intrinsic value in the deskilled work they had to do. Calling themselves "wage slaves" they often shared the French workers' dread of having to return to the job each day.[57] In a letter to the *Voice of Industry*, "The Ten Hour System, and Its Advocates," "SGB" observed:

> There is no subject that agitates and interests us as a people more than the subject of a reduction of the hours of labor. . . . As the day dawns upon

[mill workers], they regret that it is not past, and as the evening closes, and they retire, they wish that it would not so soon be morning.[58]

A Dr. Tewkesbury, editor of the *Temperance Review* (Concord, Massachusetts), criticized the New England Labor Reform League (NELRL) in March 1847 for demanding that their work hours be reduced. He pointed out to their meeting that in his experience the workers at the Lowell mills were among the happiest groups of women in the nation, taking pride in work they enjoyed. In reply, a letter from a "mill girl" (as most women working in the textile mills were then called) was "read to the [next NELRL] convention and accepted." She wrote:

It is not because they are shut up in a factory that they are happy.... I once heard a runaway slave [say] that it was [the same] with the negroes at the South. He said that when a stranger wished to know how they liked their master, "Oh, massa bery good: kind massa." But when they were alone, it was then that real opinions were to be heard.[59]

Nevertheless, workers in Fall River and other industrializing cities in the United States might have been somewhat more willing than Rancière's Parisians to view their work—as difficult, constraining, and life consuming as it had become—in positive terms. Laborites such as Young and Simon C. Hewitt and middle-class reformers such as the Channings, who claimed to speak for workers, were among those nineteenth-century voices that praised the industry of workers most enthusiastically. Among the *Voice of Industry*'s favorite themes were the virtues of labor and the curse of idleness.[60]

Workers appear to have been most responsive to attacks aimed at the "idle non-producer" who was able to escape the "curse of work" under which the workers toiled. Few other themes were applauded as loudly at rallies and conventions or reiterated more often in letters, speeches, editorials, memoirs, and circulars as that of reprehensible owners and merchants and their families who cultivated the vices of extravagance, greed, and sloth.[61] For example the *Star of Bethlehem* observed that "the few roll in luxury, and enervate and destroy themselves by indolence and sensual indulgence.... Labor [is] branded with disgrace, and idleness crowned with honor."[62]

Laborites were sensitive to countercharges that they were the ones susceptible to idleness. John R. Commons noted, "When [workers] first asked for more leisure, the employers scoffed at the idea and said that the time thus taken from work would only be spent in idleness and debauchery. The workingmen resented this charge and spent more oratory on it than on any other of the arguments."[63]

Workers claimed the virtue of hard work as their own. Labor leaders and their supporters agreed that honest labor represented workers' unselfish willingness to fulfill the responsibilities to society that everyone shared. Labor newspapers and circulars, orators, and letters from workers reiterated the demand that all should do some kind of "real" work. The *Workingman's Advocate* observed that part of the value of public education was that it would reveal "the radical error . . . that has made it necessary to regulate the hours of labor, [that] in a country where, if all performed *their share* of *useful labor,* six-hours labor a day from each would be amply sufficient to provide *all* with plenty of the necessities and comforts of life."[64] Simon Hewitt wrote, "[Labor is] the birth-right of Humanity. It is one of the greatest blessings ever vouchsafed to man."[65] The next week he observed that in owners and merchants "is seen the narrow contracted, selfish Aristocrat, and in [workers] the whole souled Republican."[66] William Young editorialized, "Labor is honorable, aye divine."[67]

Such positive views of work were founded largely on a traditional republican understanding of virtue as self-sacrifice for the good of the community—workers shared few of the other new claims about the intrinsic "blessings of work" that filled the bourgeois press at the time. Having seen the cornerstones of the "work ethic"—self-reliance and control, creativity, self-expression, and social mobility—crumble at their jobs, they were as hesitant as their Parisian sisters and brothers to embrace the widespread cant about the glory of work.[68] They were dubious about work's supposed intrinsic rewards and those delicious meals and that blissful slumber that Burritt, the "learned blacksmith," claimed made long working hours worth it.

Labor's Vision: The Original American Dream

Certainly, workers were interested in improving their workplaces and making their jobs as pleasant as possible. But the modern expectation that progress might transfigure jobs into the vital center of existence is virtually absent from the historical record. Instead, one finds widespread claims that work's perfection, and the redemption of capitalism, was to be found in *progressively* shorter work hours—in expanding leisure that gradually liberated all, worker and owner alike, from the discipline and demands of modern work and from the ethical jungle that was laissez-faire capitalism. Labor was honorable, "aye divine," primarily because it decentered work and led to a better, freer life beyond the job.

The visions that animated the early labor movement were of gradual liberation from the marketplace and of jobs tamed and made subordinate to the more important business of living free—of leisure rather than work as the time to realize human potential. The "mill girl" who contradicted Dr. Tewkesbury and his bourgeois effusions over happy workers eloquently expressed her and her sisters' daily longings and labor's original vision:

> It is not because they are shut up in a factory that they are happy, but because they are blessed with a happy and hopeful vision which can pierce those thick walls, and looks beyond to that coveted, but slow-coming hour, that shall place them beyond the influence of factory bolts and locks, and factory oppression.[69]

Based on the expectation of progressively shorter hours and the gradual escape from the "selfish system," labor's vision had several components. Labor historians have consistently stressed the importance of wages. Indeed, some still claim that higher wages is the essence of the history of labor. However, even John R. Commons and his associates at the University of Wisconsin recognized the preeminence of shorter hours at the beginning of the labor movement. Helen Sumner wrote of the "cause of the awakening" of American wage earners: "Around two chief grievances . . . the workingmen of this period rallied. First was the demand for leisure . . . second was the demand for public education. . . . The most frequent cause of complaint among the working people was the lack of leisure."[70] However important worker concerns about wages might have been, originally they were subordinate to other issues. Moreover, in contrast to their hopes for leisure's open-ended increase, workers' original expectations about wages were more conventional for the time and less visionary.

Among the workers' most common complaints about their pay was that owners and the well-to-do were living not only as idle parasites but in extravagance, buying things and amassing property far beyond any rational understanding of human need. By contrast, workers, living in the midst of a prosperous nation, were being forced to live on a pittance, often unable to buy essentials. A basic moral defect in the capitalist system was that the rich were able to buy things they did not need, depriving the working classes of life's necessities. At the beginning of the labor movement, higher wages was fundamentally a moral issue.[71]

Assuming that if everyone did their fair share of productive work, ten hours a day or less would be sufficient to produce more than enough "necessaries" for everyone, laborites maintained that higher wages were needed for everyone to share in the existing abundance—higher wages were a necessary means to a clearly defined end. With future advances in labor-saving machinery, wages would have to get even higher as the hours of labor got shorter. Labor's original vision was of what may be called a stable-state, or mature, economy, in which enough for all continued to be produced and fairly distributed as economic progress gradually liberated human beings from dependency on the new capitalist marketplace. Branded the "lump of labor" theory by economic textbook writers in the twentieth century, labor's early view of economic progress was not that total production was limited by a set of basic, unchanging human needs but that economic progress *ought* to first produce the necessities of life for all and then free humans to do better things.

The *Northampton Democrat* reported that Benjamin Franklin's predictions of a four-hour workday were well known. Franklin had written:

> If every man and woman would work for four hours each day on something useful, that labor would produce sufficient to procure all the necessaries and comforts of life, want and misery would be banished out of the world, and the rest of the twenty-four hours might be leisure and happiness.[72]

After paraphrasing Franklin's words, the paper added, "Now, in consequence of the great improvement in labor saving machinery, as much labor can be performed in three hours as could then [in Franklin's day] be produced in four."[73]

Franklinesque declarations of abundance ("all the necessaries and comforts of life") coupled with predictions of "much shorter periods of labor than ten hours,"[74] were widespread during the antebellum period, particularly in labor publications. Having predicted that "eight, and six-hour" systems would naturally follow "your ten hour system,"[75] Simon C. Hewitt observed:

> [Even] our opponents [admit that] if men will apply themselves to labor for ten hours in the day, sufficient may be produced to supply all the necessary wants of life. [Since working for ten hours will supply] ALL my wants; . . . to labor for more than this, is to be ungrateful for enough and to act the part of an idol worshiper in being covetous; according to the New Testament, covetousness is "idolatry."[76]

The *Sentinel*, in an article reprinted by several labor newspapers, observed that if the hours of labor "from Maine to Georgia, were restricted to nine, or even to *eight* . . . there would still be no deficiency of any article. The difficulty is not in producing, but in getting rid of superabundant produce. . . . Excessive labor produces superabundance . . . beyond the demand or wants of the people. . . . How is this surplus to be disposed of? Evidently by tempting us to buy what we do not want."[77] In an address before the General Trades' Union of New York in 1835, its president, John Commerford, declared that machines were daily replacing labor:

> Machinery must be viewed as one of the most energetic agents in hastening the political Millennium, so confidently predicted. [The result] must be revolution and reform . . . for when Machinery arrives at the point, which will give to the world those necessary commodities for consumption . . . the contest of capital will cease, because the supply will be furnished in such vast quantities that competition between individuals will be destroyed. Machinery will not then be used, as it now is, for the benefit of the few, but for the masses. Governments will become the legitimate guardians of its improvements.[78]

Abundance coupled with the principle of progressively shorter work hours was a favorite editorial topic for the *Voice of Industry*.[79] When abundance was fairly distributed so that all had enough, bosses would begin to lose their grip on individual workers and the capitalist marketplace (the "selfish system")[80] would begin to lose its grip on the nation. The widespread demands for liberation and independence in the labor press were frequently paired with condemnations of workers' dependence on industry's new jobs and on the developing system of laissez-faire capitalism. Such dependency was frequently portrayed as a great evil, comparable to the colonies' dependence on Great Britain. Just as the American colonies had won their liberty from England, American workers were seeking liberation from the "selfish system" by demanding shorter hours.

The avarice and extravagance of the rich were often seen to contrast with the virtuous frugality and simple living of workers. Not only did workers claim to know the true value of an hour's free time; they also claimed to know the value of a dollar. The classical Stoic and Epicurean virtues of self-sufficiency, simplicity, and frugality that had informed the previous Revolutionary generation also had their champions among ten-hour advocates. Charles Douglas, president of the New England Association of Farmers, Mechanics, and Other Workingmen, called on their convention to "exchange . . . aristocratical and antisocial usages for *republican* institutions [and virtues]." He pointed out that in their disregard for republican virtue "the aristocracy are not so *disinterested* as to sacrifice one of their acquired privileges for the benefit of others. No—they will cling to them . . . so long as . . . money continues a powerful instrument in the hand of the few." To overcome this power and selfishness, he advised the conventioneers that they must strive to be as independent as possible from the "selfish system" and "not ape the manners of the rich, by substituting external show for internal excellence, but avoid extravagance and its attendant evils, debt and degradation; encourage frugality and simplicity in dress and in manners."[81]

In Paris, Louis Gabriel Gauny described an "entire vision on life, and unusual counter economy which sought to reduce the worker's consumption of everyday goods so that he would be more independent of the market economy."[82] In Lowell, Huldah Stone called on mill workers to give priority to the needs of the community and their own mental and spiritual development and, if need be, sacrifice essentials:

> Let the old tabernacle of clay be clothed in *rags*, and enjoy but two meals a day, [rather] than suffer the intellect to dwindle—the moral and religious capacities to remain uncultivated—the affections unfurnished, the charity limited—the mind contracted with blind bigotry and ignorance.[83]

Such calls to simplicity, generosity, republican virtue, and frugal living may be contrasted with bourgeois attempts to blunt worker consciousness by advising laborites to be satisfied with the wages they were paid. What Huldah Stone envisioned was that the less her sisters participated in the new marketplace, working less and buying less, the more they would be liberated from its bondage. With Gauny, American workers such as Stone envisioned a counter-economy, an alternative to laissez-faire capitalism, based in leisure, in which selflessness, mutuality, and free gift might come to govern human interaction instead of selfishness, control, and competition.

The Selfish System

Since "labor-saving machinery is . . . half-repealing the decree: 'in the sweat of his brow shall he eat bread,'" the *Workingman's Advocate* questioned why workers were seeing so few of the benefits of increased productivity. The problem was that "the present arrangement of society" was an irrational, "selfish system" that needed to be reformed.[84]

Labor publications denounced the "selfish system" and its lack of republican virtue as often as they condemned the avarice and extravagance of rich individuals. William Young observed:

> Selfishness predominates over charity and benevolence; [New England's] mad avariciousness is swallowing up and poisoning all her philanthropy and love for the good. . . . [T]oiling thousands are reared by avarice. . . . In fact our whole political and social organization are full of the seeds of avarice and selfishness, which are fast developing themselves every year, in the various forms of vice, wickedness, poverty, strife, and bitterness, which we daily witness around us.[85]

Laissez-faire capitalism was daily teaching people to be selfish. Instead of advancing morally toward republican virtue, the country was retreating toward greed, pride, extravagance and all the other progeny of selfishness. Simon Hewitt concluded, "Avarice cannot long be allowed to run riot in its present oppressive course."[86]

D. S. Pierce, representing the Fall River Mechanics' Association, addressed the New England Working Men's Association convention in 1846, pointing out that the "first lesson taught the boy" when he leaves home was "to get gain—gain wealth." In keeping with what was coming to be accepted morality, "the boy" made gain the guiding principle of his life. He then entered the competitive fray, "forgetting all but self in the furthering of this object." In this climate of competition, individuals were isolated, their affections stunted and their native generosity and ability to live with each other compromised: "They are arrayed against each other—strife and discord are the legitimate offsprings of such a state of things." Pierce concluded, "We should have some object in view—something higher and nobler . . . [some] universal principles which embrace all humanity." Only in the service of "higher and nobler . . . universal principles" did capitalism make sense. Without them, serving no other purpose except the perpetual increase of wealth, the "selfish system" was monstrous.[87]

Speaking next, Seth Luther agreed, going even further and "speaking in censure of the selfish spirit of the workingmen" who had been infected by the new morality. Even the educational system had been contaminated. Education was no longer "calculated to ennoble the mind—the student who is sent to college is educated so as to take advantage of society by his knowledge." He then elaborated on Pierce's "higher and nobler" objective, describing "the encouraging success of the TEN HOUR SYSTEM" that represented the selfless alternative that might yet harness the "selfish system" in the service of republican virtue and Christian disinterested benevolence.

The Ten-Hour System

Arrayed against capitalism's new "selfish system" stood labor's "TEN HOUR SYSTEM"—the term was frequently set in uppercase letters or between quotation marks before the Civil War. The ten-hour system was more than just a single reform. Certainly, as historians have recognized for decades, it "represented," "symbolized," was "entwined with," or was "the prelude to" labor's other causes and issues and was the basis for union recruitment and organization. But for many of its original supporters, it offered a complete alternative to laissez-faire capitalism: an original American dream that, in the unnamed "mill girl's" words, "shall place them beyond the influence of factory bolts and locks, and factory oppression."[88]

In the opening "realm of freedom" that might begin with the ten-hour day, humans would gradually be weaned from the "selfish system" that perverted human nature and nurtured dissension and discord. However, the "selfish system" need not be replaced. Instead, it might be tamed and used as a stepping-stone—a preparatory stage of human development. Gradually, having more and more time free from work and economic concerns, humans would be able to progress morally, cultivating their natural bent toward "benevolence," developing abilities to freely and virtuously live together in families and communities "beyond the influence of factory bolts and locks." Public education was a prime necessity for such "elevation"—as were the newly instituted Sunday schools. In school and then in the cultural space opened by shorter hours, owners and workers might find true equality and mutuality, even "solidarity," progressing together—making "moral, social, intellectual and physical improvement."[89]

Simon C. Hewitt, one of the best-known and most successful labor organizers of the 1840s, explained that a "radical *reform*" of capitalism was necessary. The "ten-hour *system*" represented that radical alternative:

> The ten hour system goes beyond the idea of merely working ten hours in the day. It looks to human elevation—the progress and redemption of society from the social hell into which it is now so deeply plunged. We therefore propose a plan of union, which will not only reduce the hours of labor to ten, and indefinitely lower,—which will not only give time for relaxation . . . [and] for general mental improvement, but present infinitely greater inducement for such improvement [in the arts of living together in community], and give more of the necessary means for its attainment, that can be found in any other method.[90]

Hewitt shared Young's hopes for equality and mutuality. He claimed that he had always tried to bring people together in the towns he visited: "I have invariably tried to fill up an awful chasm . . . between the laborer and the capitalist." Taking his ten-hour message of cooperation and equality, growth and progress, to workers in small towns throughout the region, he claimed to have met with success virtually everywhere he went.[91]

The ten-hour system would begin to open a "realm of freedom" in which equality and genuine progress were *practical* possibilities for all. In an editorial defending the ten-hour system against attacks accusing workers of selfish motives, Young wrote:

> We do not wish to benefit the laborer [with the ten-hour system] at the expense of the employer, but to benefit both, not so far as dollars and cents are concerned but in point of true human elevation, that all men . . . may live out what they were designed to, and realize that degree of happiness they are capable of enjoying.[92]

Shorter work hours would free both laborer and owner to live together with mutual regard. Young explained:

> Our reform is broad and universal, excluding none . . . [and] it is based deep down upon the eternal principles of truth and justice, which we believe should and will be acknowledged and made *practical* [before] men will live at peace with each other. Unfortunately the Capitalist "selfish-system" and New England society and polity are at war with these principles.[93]

The *Factory Girl's Album and Operatives' Advocate* of Exeter, New Hampshire, advised:

> Let the ten hour system be adopted universally . . . and what a change would be brought about. Now let that class [workers] arise, and in unison assert their rights, their right to enjoy with others all the blessings of life— the right to possess the means of moral, social, intellectual and physical improvement. . . . If the ten hour system were adopted and practiced,— then if labor were rewarded as it should be, all might gain and more than gain subsistence, while time and means would be placed within the reach of all for improvement in all other respects.[94]

In the United States, class struggle originated more in labor's desire to use conflict to bring laissez-faire capitalism under control rather than replace it. Labor's ten-hour vision involved using the capitalist system as a stepping-stone to freedom within the framework of American constitutional democracy. The ten-hour system's primary "institutional change" was progressively shorter hours—well within the purview of the American Constitution and the free market. Nevertheless, a more fundamental societal change is hard to imagine.

Shorter hours represented a shift in the basic human resource, time, from the new institutions of the capitalist marketplace back to traditional institutions that were losing their economic functions: the family, community, and civic and religious organizations.

To support such a reform, the labor press advocated building the infra-structures of freedom: public schools, parks, promenades, gardens, libraries, "public drawing rooms," theaters, and benevolent associations.[95] Such public spaces needed to be built to provide for "moral regeneration," "spiritual devel-opment," and community living—for the practice of republican virtue and "the cult of benevolence."[96]

Like Stone, Hewitt, and Young, ten-hour supporters generally held opti-mistic views of human nature, as evidenced by their vehement rejections of ac-cusations that workers would misuse their free time. Some also hoped that the new epidemic of greed and selfishness could be controlled, gradually curtailed by the careful nurture of innate civility and benevolence. Well into the twen-tieth century, laborites continued to trust that the center of republican virtue, selflessness, might hold and be cultivated even in the face of the "selfish sys-tem's" ascendancy.

Conclusion

Ten-hour supporters claimed that theirs was the cause of generosity, commu-nity, and republican virtue. Their cause, by gradually abridging labor and hold-ing the new impersonal marketplace in check, would advance the freedom of all. Labor's opponents argued their case on the new moral grounds of laissez-faire capitalism—defending the "selfish system" as based on a realistic assess-ment for human nature and their view of progress as the open-ended increase in wealth. They were interested not in sharing the abundance industry was pro-ducing but in providing profitable investments that would eventually produce more for both the wealthy and poor—the greatest good for the greatest num-ber. The ten-hour system provoked a clash of moralities, in which traditional republican selflessness contended with bourgeois prudence, and a collision of views of progress, in which traditional hopes for abundance (enough for all) coupled with expanding freedom and equality contended with new visions of the perpetual advance of wealth and the transfiguration of work to the center of life as a moral good in and for itself.

3

Walt Whitman

Higher Progress at Mid-century

In 1855 in his first preface to *Leaves of Grass*, Walt Whitman's democratic vision was clear, bold, and optimistic, not yet clouded by events and democracy's rude growths. But after the Civil War and with the publication of *Democratic Vistas*, he had become painfully aware of freedom's failures: rampant hypocrisy in literature, political corruption and business frauds, and social posturings and overreachings, among others. Most troubling was the widespread failure of belief:

> Never was there, perhaps, more hollowness at heart than at present, and here in the United States. Genuine belief seems to have left us. The underlying principles of the States are not honestly believ'd in . . . nor is humanity itself believ'd in. . . . The spectacle is appalling. We live in an atmosphere of hypocrisy throughout. The men believe not in the women, nor the women in the men.[1]

The widespread loss of faith had resulted in a disappointing lack of progress toward democracy's "higher," better promises that originally animated *Leaves of Grass*. Instead of experiencing a rebirth of its multiform freedoms, democracy had been sidetracked after the war. The nation had become overconcerned with national power and empire, "materialistic development," and "popular intellectuality." The certainty of progress was in question—Whitman's hope was now "desperate":[2]

Portions of this chapter were previously published in Benjamin Kline Hunnicutt, "Walt Whitman's 'Higher Progress' and Shorter Work Hours," *Walt Whitman Quarterly Review* 26, no. 2 (2008): 92–108. The author gratefully acknowledges permission granted by the *Walt Whitman Quarterly Review* to include portions of the article in this chapter.

I say that our New World democracy, however great a success in uplifting
the masses out of their sloughs, in materialistic development, products . . .
is, so far, an almost complete failure in its social aspects, and in really
grand religious, moral, literary, and esthetic results. In vain do we march
with unprecedented strides to empire. . . . It is as if we were somehow being
endow'd with a vast and more and more thoroughly-appointed body, and
then left with little or no soul.[3]

Nevertheless, Whitman persevered, reaffirming his original vision with
Democratic Vistas, willing his optimism to endure, believing that his nation,
having "appointed" and satisfied the "body," would again pursue democracy's
Higher Progress.[4] Reread sympathetically rather than queried or interrogated,
as many scholars now prefer, Whitman's texts reveal replies that he might offer his present-day critics. Such a reading might also re-present his critique of
modern developments, reexposing undemocratic growths that yet entangle individuals and confound the nation.[5] Such a reading might reaffirm Whitman's
vision of the "underlying principles of the States" as an eminently practical and
inspiring alternative to what he despised but now has nearly triumphed.

Whitman would almost certainly have approved such a project, for his
prospect was always the future, his voice prophetic. He expressly intended to
speak to the generations to come, confident that his words and vision would
speak to the future even more than his contemporaries. He believed that we
would understand and embrace him to renew belief. Believing, we then would
find practical ways to realize democracy's vision, which he re-presented.

The Progress of Freedom in Three Stages

Like many of his countrymen and European philosophers he admired, Whitman believed that progress meant the advance of freedom. With *Democratic
Vistas* he attempted to explain more fully than he had before how one liberation encouraged the next and how civilizations advanced in stages, each stage
founding the next higher and freer level.[6] Whitman also believed that the
United States was leading the way, continuing to spread basic political rights to
disenfranchised, exploited, and enslaved groups.

However, progress was not simply the expansion of human rights, vital
though such a widening might be. Freedom's progress also entailed a qualita-
tive change, an advance from fundamental political rights and basic economic
freedoms and opportunities to higher physical, mental, and spiritual possibilities, an advance Whitman called "higher progress":

The world evidently supposes, and we have evidently supposed so too,
that the States are merely to achieve the equal franchise, an elective
government—to inaugurate the respectability of labor, and become a nation of practical operatives, law-abiding, orderly and well-off. Yes, those
are indeed parts of the task of America; but they not only do not exhaust

the progressive conception, but rather arise, teeming with it, as the mediums of deeper, *higher progress.* Daughter of a physical revolution—mother of the true revolutions, which are of the interior life, and of the arts. For so long as the spirit is not changed, any change of appearance is of no avail.[7]

Whereas Lincoln and the war extended the Declaration of Independence's guarantees of basic human rights to begin to include African Americans, reaffirming freedom's promise of similar liberations to come and reiterating the necessity of continued belief, commitment, and struggle, Whitman hoped to champion freedom's final frontier with *Democratic Vistas.*[8] Similar to the nation's attempts to spread human rights, Whitman's Higher Progress was less a naively optimistic, uncritical metanarrative than a project; it was a vision that might be realized—its consummation, however, contingent on the belief and commitment of future generations. Belief, will, affection, and vision were essential for liberty's advance but were also free human qualities that might be forgotten or neglected.

Whitman, steeped throughout his life in this vision, embraced Higher Progress as the pursuit of "higher forms of human achievement." Walking wellworn rhetorical pathways, he nevertheless offered unique insights, dilating and *democratizing* the old republican dream and millennial hope as few had done before. David Anderson agrees that Whitman's poems and prose reflect the beliefs in progress characteristic of his age, concluding, "The greatest significance of . . . advances in technology was, for Whitman, the fact . . . that out of these advances, a new world would emerge, based upon his principles of comradeship."[9]

During his editorship of the *Brooklyn Daily Eagle* from March 5, 1846, to January 18, 1848, Whitman made frequent references to America's "experiment of popular freedom" and described the "progress in simple happiness" as freedom's crowning achievement, which signaled the coming of "'*the holy millennium of liberty*' when the 'Victory of endurance born' shall lift the masses of the down-trodden of Europe, and make them achieve something of that destiny which we suppose God intends eligible for mankind."[10]

In *Democratic Vistas* Whitman reaffirmed the "under-lying principles of the States." The American Republic would flower in freedom—in occasions for song, poetry, play, festival, celebration, and comradeship—as it built on "two grand stages of preparation-strata":

> For the New World, indeed, after two grand stages of preparation-strata, I perceive that now a third stage, being ready for, (and without which the other two were useless,) with unmistakable signs appears. The First stage was the planning and putting on record the political foundation rights of immense masses of people—indeed all people—in the organization of republican . . . governments. . . . This is the American programme, not

for classes, but for universal man. . . . The Second stage relates to material prosperity, wealth, produce, labor-saving machines, iron, cotton, local, State and continental railways.[11]

Abundance

Whitman believed as strongly in the coming of material abundance ("material prosperity") as he did in the advance of political freedoms—his doubts were mainly about the fate of Higher Progress.[12] Like many of his generation, such as Huldah Stone and William Young, Whitman fully expected that America would soon solve its "economic problem."[13] A "triumphant future" when technology had conquered nature and "all life's material comforts" were vouchsafed at last for everyone, "the dream of the ages," "is certain": "Not the least doubtful am I on any prospects of their material success. The triumphant future of their business, geographic and productive departments, on larger scales and in more varieties than ever, is certain."[14]

Leadie Clark observed, "The 'someday after many days' would arrive for Whitman when no man would be rich nor any man poor, but all would be financially secure."[15] Whitman remarked that "the final culmination" of American progress would be the "establishment of millions of comfortable city homesteads and moderate-sized farms . . . *life in them complete* but cheap, *within the reach of all.*"[16] Alan Trachtenberg concluded that with these words Whitman expressed "the prevalent aspirations of factory workers, farmers, small merchants, and manufacturers."[17]

Whitman had few objections to wealth per se, assuming that economic inequality was not only inevitable but relatively unimportant once everyone had enough. Equality would be found in Higher Progress, not in the marketplace. Nor was he interested in the state's redistributing wealth. On the contrary, excessive concern on the part of the state or the individual about material wealth once abundance had been achieved might retard Higher Progress.

Ken Cmiel observed:

> Far from being a protosocialist, Whitman praised the "true gravitation hold of liberalism in the United States," which he described as "a more universal ownership of property, general homestead, general comfort— a vast intertwining reticulation of wealth." While he might decry the "yawning gulf" that was the "labor question," Whitman still "hailed with joy" the "business materialism of the current age." If it could only be spiritualized, all would be well.[18]

Whitman did fear that the third, the culminating and defining stage—the whole point of progress, without which the first two stages were incomplete— was being sidetracked by a people overly enamored of their material successes.

The nation, like Nathaniel Hawthorne's traveler in "The Celestial Railroad,"[19] was being tempted to settle for humanity's penultimate destination and make its dwelling in Vanity Fair:

> *Allons! we must not stop here,*
> *However sweet these laid-up stores, however convenient this dwelling we*
>   *cannot remain here.*[20]

Higher Progress was not inevitable; a people deficient in belief or affection might settle for lesser things. Substituting the selfish idols of comfort and convenience, reputation and position, wealth, power, and "security," they might forget that life offered infinitely more. Such apostasy alienated and diverted individuals from their destiny and led to spiritual famine in the midst of material abundance—to unnecessary depravations of the soul that eventually spawned "a secret silent loathing and despair."[21]

Higher Progress

But a true poet might yet lead the way beyond the allures and despair of Vanity Fair, offering himself as a foretaste, a specimen of what might be in store. Over and again Whitman offered his particular vision of Higher Progress to spur his readers on to realizing liberty's promise, promoting himself as exhibit one.

For Whitman Higher Progress presented an open road on which individuals might come fully into their own. Less and less encumbered by political oppression, social custom, the demands of the job, and economy, each person would have equal chance to more fully engage his or her humanity, delighting in nature, the body, and comradeship and struggling with life's tragedies and the challenges of the spirit and of the day. Only in this refined freedom was true equality to be found.

Beyond want and necessities, ordinary purposes and convention, obligation and reward, Higher Progress presented liberty's ultimate challenge to citizens to fill the purest of freedoms with activities that were complete in themselves—that, containing their own meaning, were their own reward. Together with Jonathan Edwards, Samuel Hopkins, William Ellery Channing, and European philosophers such as Friedrich Hegel, Whitman recognized the modern challenges of the *autotelic*, questioning and exploring what a fullness of free-being might look like and proposing a variety of metaphors and practical possibilities that might prepare for freedom's final test in the "greater struggle" to come.[22]

Whitman's Activities of Freedom

How then does Whitman answer the challenges he sees facing us at the end of history? What free activities does he add to the lists already drawn up by people such as Edwards, Channing, Huldah Stone, and William Young? Whitman begins in tranquility, offering, first, as did Frederick Hegel, the purest free act of being-for-itself: self-awareness.[23] Consciousness of consciousness, awareness of the freedom of awareness astounds and delights the soul, offering it infinite employment:

> *I exist as I am, that is enough . . .*
> *One world is aware and by far the largest to me, and that is myself . . .*
> *I dote on myself, there is that lot of me, and all so luscious*[24]

However, the soul aware is quickly the soul in motion. Self-awareness leads directly to a new consciousness of and relationship with the material and social worlds. The "Self," aware, leaving behind it age-old struggles and conflicts, recognizing kinship with the body, other potentially free beings, nature, and the city, is drawn to reimmerse itself in the world in new, free kinds of experiences: wrapping arms around in embrace, rolling around in the woods, naked:

> *A few light kisses, a few embraces, a reaching around of arms . . .*
> *I will go to the bank by the wood and become undisguised and naked,*
> *I am mad for it to be in contact with me.*[25]

Whereas Hegel and other German philosophers spoke abstractly about the "Spirit's" freedom in terms of *thymos* (desire for recognition and respect) and art for art's sake, Whitman used the familiar experiences of daily life to represent the reunions that democracy was making available to all. Thus, he celebrates, sings, touches, and plays.

He wrote often of "celebrations" as activities of joyful awareness and appreciation of the self, the world, and others—of activities valuable in and for themselves rather than for some need they met or utilitarian function they served. To celebrate is also to be keenly aware of and in the moment, the eternal, fleeting, quotidian present—an awareness that amazes the soul as much as self-consciousness: "Each moment and whatever happens thrills me with joy."[26]

Whitman also would "sing" in an unusual way (e.g., "I . . . sing myself") to suggest how a poet inspires the world and others. Hearing the music inherent in creation and recognizing the latent beauty, he joins his voice, making the eternal song ring clearer, helping transfigure the physical world into meaning and beauty.[27]

The free activities of Higher Progress were also tactile. For Whitman the body has its reasons, its own kinds of awareness and its own kinds of rejoinings with the world and others. Thus touch, the most fundamental of the senses, as well as taste and smell, figure prominently in his poetry as metaphors for very tangible reunions. Some of his sexual imagery served a similar purpose. Rejoining with others in mutual caress and penetration, the vigorous plunging into nature and into an anthropomorphic nation are vivid images of the new free relations available in Higher Progress. Such bodily reunions infuse the material and social worlds with Eros as well as a kind of consciousness:

> Divine am I inside and out, and I make holy whatever I touch or am touch'd
>   from;
> The scent of these arm-pits is aroma finer than prayer . . .
> I merely stir, press, feel with my fingers, and am happy,
> To touch my person to some one else's is about as much as I can stand.
> Is this then a touch? quivering me to a new identity,
> Flames and ether making a rush for my veins[28]

Whitman also used play as a metaphor for the free activities of Higher Progress. He begins playfully. Celebrating, loitering, and loafing, in perhaps his best-known words he sets a poet's way in sharp contrast to the workaday, serious world:[29]

> I celebrate myself, and sing myself,
> And what I assume you shall assume,
> For every atom belonging to me as good belongs to you.
> I loafe and invite my soul,
> I lean and loafe at my ease—
> Observing a spear of summer grass.[30]

Whitman understood that, like consciousness, play is usually of something or with something or someone, involving either an exuberant outpouring of being ("the play of shine and shade on the trees as the supple boughs wag") or intersubjective, transformative kinds of experiences.[31] For Whitman, play demonstrated the transformative relationships of freedom. Play, like poetry, creates a new kind of alternative, free reality, willed into being and consisting of activities that are changed in their essence by new game rules freely accepted, and a place, a playground or open road, deliberately set apart from ordinary life. He recognized play as an arena of freedom in which consciousness reimmersed ("pour'd into") with the material world, transforming bits of it into playthings and playgrounds and others into playmates.[32] Play also usually exhibits what Eugen Fink called "the color of joy": the properties of fun, exuberance, enthusiasm, transitoriness (for the time "being"), willing belief, experimentation, and fellow feeling—the virtues Whitman associated with Higher Progress:[33]

> That, I alone among bards in the following chants sing. . . . One's self—
> you, whoever you are, pour'd into whom all that you read and hear and
> what existent is in heroes or events, with landscape, heavens, and every
> beast and bird, becomes so only then with play and interplay.[34]

Celebrating, singing, touching, and playing the soul transfigures the commonplace, infusing it with meaning. Instead of the age-old human experience of the natural and social worlds as places of resistance and confinement (Hegel's second historical stage), the poet realizes a new relation by reimmersion, still free, still self-aware. Rather than experiencing places, things, and people as objects to be challenged, subdued, or changed to satisfy some need, some lack, the poet achieves a higher purpose, saturating all with Eros and awareness.[35]

Such reimmersions opened up a world of possibilities for individuals to reconstruct themselves. Whitman envisioned democratic individuality, or "personalism," as a project available to all.[36] In progress's final stage, freedom might be experienced as individual potentiality realized in open-ended construction and reconstruction. No longer identified in advance by caste, wealth, or conventional social place, individuals might take responsibility for their selves, becoming the architects of their identities, playfully constructing composite selves out of the fabric of daily life in an ongoing project of discovery and reinvention. Whitman expected that progress would lead at last to the democratization of "human self-conception."[37]

George Kateb points out that, for Whitman, all of us have the potential to become infinitely more than we realize. It is possible for us to become something like everyone we meet, a fact that establishes the ground for the most profound and surest forms of human connectedness—what Whitman called "adhesiveness." Kateb concludes that "Whitman's poetic aim is to talk or sing his readers into accepting this highest truth about human beings."[38]

Expanding freedom need not set each against all as so many, including Thomas Carlyle, feared. Rather than stranding men and women as isolated selves, in social chaos, freedom could be the arena in which humans might rejoin each other in the most powerful of ways, beginning with "human self-conception."

Writing of comradeship, manly love, and of intercourse of all kinds, Whitman gives some of his best answers to freedom's autotelic challenge. Celebration, song, touch, and play are each modes of "adhesiveness," of free human interrelations that transcend the marketplace and courthouse. Because individuals are valuable in and for themselves, the epitome of the autotelic, their joining in free *activities* constituted the acme of progress and liberty's final achievement.[39]

Whitman was not overly shy by the standards of his day about overt sexual expression. He also had an unusually broad concept of Eros, even by current standards, that was central to his poetry and democratic hopes. His major concern was a thoroughly diffuse pleasure-in-being, liberated from the standard places, moments, or traditionally erotic parts of the body. His homosexual images were steps along the way, opening erotic expression to more people in more varied ways in a larger project of saturating and transfiguring all human relations, the total body, and even the natural world with the energy of "pure and sweet . . . adhesive love" too long confined and constrained by convention.[40]

Whitman frequently upset polite gatherings by boyishly horsing around with his pals. His playfulness and bawdy pranks not only confused those around him but have been mistaken by overly serious modern readers, who see his erotic exuberance as passion driven rather than as the expression of an open-ended, playful sexuality, liberated and complete in itself. A good deal, perhaps the majority, of Whitman's erotic nature was expressed playfully—his sexual experimentation a high-spirited, suggestive what-if closely related to celebration.

The Erotic, Joining Word

The word transfigured by consciousness and love is "poetry." The poet's new creation exemplifies the erotic rejoinings Whitman envisioned: rejoinings that transcended traditional connections based on wanting, rejoinings that produced a transfigured world newly saturated with imagination and affection, made lucid by awareness. The poet uses words to infuse meaning, beauty, pleasure, and joy into ordinary objects and human associations, opening up new worlds of shared meaning—intersubjective spaces that like play created a reality "for the time being," and promoted the new, vigorous activities of "adhesiveness."[41]

However, the poet of democracy would not simply refocus the traditional art from the heroic topics of the feudal past to democratic themes. Rejecting the European feudal model of a literary caste particularly blessed with genius or some rare insight, commitment, or gift, the poet points beyond him- or herself and his or her words to an egalitarian literature and democratic culture— arenas in which equality was not so much a topic to be written about as it was a project to be realized in practice.

Whitman did not imagine himself to be one of the first in a lineage of American aristocrats of literature. Indeed, such a notion remained foreign in the United States until academics devised the Golden Day of American literature trope in the 1920s.[42] On the contrary, he presented a thoroughgoing critique of the literature of feudalism in its forms, themes, and deference to literary genius. Departing from the European model, Whitman understood his genius simply as a place at the apex of a democratic pyramid that would spread the free use of language to ever more people and finally to all.

He intended to propagate his experience of poetry as the act of free consciousness transfiguring ordinary reality. He was intent on promoting the quotidian word, looking to a future in which ordinary people, the "high average of men," regularly lifted their experiences into meaning with their words and, rejoining their fellows in common discourse, created intersubjective, "discussional" communities locally and on their own.[43]

Not everyone would be a poet per se, of course. Instead, a legion of poet-priests might spring up throughout the nation to take over from pioneers like Whitman, using the "gray detail" of discourse (stories, legends, myths, conversations, gossip, speeches, sermons, disputes, pageants, parades, and festivals) that flowed around them locally as the subjects of their poetry, thereby encouraging, validating, and promoting the democratic, creative use of every-day language and sign.[44]

In freedom's final frontier, everyday discourse might become, like poetry, autotelic, "communicative action"[45] to form adhesive communities in which individuals could explore and create meaning and identity together:

> I should certainly insist . . . on a radical change of category. . . . I should demand a programme of culture, drawn out, not for a single class alone, or for the parlors or lecture-rooms, but with an eye to practical life, the west, the working-men, the facts of farms and jack-planes and engineers, and of the broad range of the women also of the middle and working strata, and with reference to the perfect equality of women, and of a grand and powerful motherhood. I should demand of this programme or theory a scope generous enough to include the widest human area. It must have for its spinal meaning the formation of a typical personality of character, eligible to the uses of the high average of men—and not restricted by conditions ineligible to the masses. The best culture will always be that of the manly and courageous instincts, and loving perceptions, and of self-respect—aiming to form, over this continent, an idiocrasy of universalism, which, true child of America, will bring joy to its mother, returning to her in her own spirit, recruiting myriads of offspring, able, natural, perceptive, tolerant, devout believers in her, America, and with some definite instinct why and for what she has arisen, most vast, most formidable of historic births, and is, now and here, with wonderful step, journeying through Time.[46]

Whitman's vision of democratic culture is astonishing—undoubtedly more so now than when he published it. Whereas Hegel envisioned the end of history as the advent of constitutional democracies, Whitman hinted at a more profound and still unacceptable terminus. Just as democracies were outgrowing the heroic political themes and rigid poetical forms of the feudal past, the literary genius with special gifts who made unique contributions to literature of permanent historical significance was disappearing, less and less credible as the democracy of the word spread.

Whitman had little interest in elevating the literary tastes of ordinary readers in a kind of great-literature-appreciation crusade. Rather than jettison the literary milestones of the feudal past, however, he conceived an alternative, democratic use:

> The New World receives with joy the poems of the antique, with European feudalism's rich fund of epics, plays, ballads—seeks not in the least to deaden or displace those voices from our ear and area—holds them indeed as indispensable studies, influences, records, comparisons.[47]

The works of Shakespeare, Milton, Cervantes, "and the rest" would serve the nation as they served Whitman, as a kind of compost that fertilized "the democratic average and basic equality." The democratic yield then might be "the Human Being, towards whose heroic and spiritual evolution poems and everything directly or indirectly tend Old World or New."[48]

Rooting their democratic project in the seedbeds of the Old World masters, the first poets of the New World would lead forthrightly, modeling, instructing, encouraging, and engaging their readers, propagating the quotidian word. To this end Whitman deliberately blurred the boundaries of conventional literary texts. Rather than intending that his readers find some stable meaning in his poems, he offered a poetic field, a kind of playground in which his words could be *actively* played out in arrays of novel readings:[49]

> A great poem is no finish to a man or woman but rather a beginning. Has any one fancied he could sit at last under some due authority and rest satisfied with explanations and realize and be content and full? To no such terminus does the greatest poet bring . . . he brings neither cessation or sheltered fatness and ease. The touch of him tells in action. Whom he takes he takes with firm sure grasp into live regions previously unattained . . . thenceforward is no rest . . . they see the space and ineffable sheen that turn the old spots and lights into dead vacuums. . . .
>
> There will soon be no more priests. Their work is done. . . . A superior breed shall take their place . . . the gangs of kosmos and prophets en masse shall take their place. A new order shall arise and they shall be the priests of man, and every man shall be his own priest.[50]

Thus Whitman's words often seem paradoxical, warning us against taking them too seriously as a repository of truth ("sit[ting] at last under some due authority") or mistaking his poetry for a continuation of the history-making feudal project, yet insisting that we share his authentic, "serious," and enduring visions of freedom and democratic culture.

Kerry A. Larson objects to Whitman's prescriptive use of "you," concluding that Whitman demands assent rather than encourages dialogue. Several writers make similar objections to Whitman's insistence on a poet's authority.[51] However, the fundamental imperative the poetical authority is based on is Whitman's demand that the reader embrace the freedom of Higher Progress and engage the poet and the world in that freedom—a demand that Whitman recognized as paradoxical. The last "history making," "privileged" text would point beyond itself to the end of the feudal project and history-making art and to the "decentering" (democratizing) of what Jürgen Habermas called "communicative action."[52] Robert Olsen noted:

> [*Leaves of Grass*] must solicit the willing participation of its readers in order to realize the project that it undertakes. Whitman's poetry requires that the reader constantly renew its discourse by reinvesting it with new poetic meaning and, as a result, reaffirming it as the poetry of a flourishing, liberal American state.[53]

Whitman invites us to compose with him as we read—to be become his co-poet or novice playmate, taking our first halting steps safe in the embrace of his words.[54] He demystifies poetry, insisting again and again that poetry is not just the business of a special breed of humans. Rather, at the pinnacle of freedom, it is available to all. Thus Whitman offered himself as a model, a specimen, for the coming legion of poets of democracy who would employ their talents to propagate and sustain the democracy of words:[55]

> The messages of great poets to each man and woman are, Come to us on equal terms, Only then can you understand us, We are not better than you, What we enclose you enclose, What we enjoy you may enjoy. Did you suppose there could be only one Supreme? We affirm there can be un-numbered Supremes, and that one does not countervail another any more than one eyesight countervails another. . . . The American bards shall be marked for generosity and affection and for encouraging competitors. . . . They shall be kosmos . . . without monopoly or secrecy . . . glad to pass any thing to any one . . . hungry for equals night and day.[56]

Whitman's Critics and Shorter Work Hours

Accused of being an idle dreamer, Whitman, with William Ellery Channing, has been routinely taken to task for his democratic vision. Betsy Erkkila agrees with Sean Wilentz that Whitman's political views were influenced from an early age by the republicanism of New York's artisan community. Whitman came to share both its suspicion of government and its dislike of the growing power of industry. Thus Erkkila argues that Whitman's position was increas-ingly untenable. His self-reliant individualism prohibited him from supporting governmental measures necessary to regulate the burgeoning forces of capi-talism that were choking out the very agrarian values, republican virtues, and artisanal culture he hoped to save. Hence, his work, along with the world of artisanal republican virtue, became increasingly ironic.[57] Arthur Wrobel, sum-marizing the criticism of a variety of Whitman scholars, concluded that Whit-man was "a bit short on practical suggestions."[58]

However, such critics ignore a vital part of Whitman's experience that grounded, and arguably gave rise to, his continuing hopes for Higher Progress. Whitman and many of his contemporaries recognized a practical opportunity emerging with the nation's economic successes and technological development. The reduction of working hours was then, as now, the obvious practical link be-tween increasing material wealth and Higher Progress. Common sense, as well as republican virtue, dictated that if people earned and saved enough to take care of necessities, they could reasonably expect to take time off to do other, more enjoyable, even more virtuous things.

Reductions in the demands of work and the marketplace on the individual, made possible by labor-saving machines, were at the core of Whitman's belief that economic success would make Higher Progress possible. Whitman shared the new experience of freedom as leisure with the workers he mingled with on Broadway and in the Bowery Theatre. With them he recognized the growing importance of the time freed from modern work. Like the Parisian Louis Gabriel Gauny,[59] he recognized freedom's advent in workers' new leisure. Hearing their complaints about "wage slavery," he embraced their hopes and expectations as his own. While he celebrated the variety of work's forms, he never idealized work as the site of freedom or romanticized the job as the place for individuals to realize their full humanity—such beliefs spread widely only in the twentieth century. Work, like economic progress and wealth, was ennobling primarily because it led to better things. With the majority of workers in the nineteenth century for whom work had lost much of its intrinsic virtue, Whitman recognized that a job was a means to an end rather than an end in itself—a sentiment captured by the doggerel repeated by generations of workers: "Work to live; don't live to work."

Whitman was aware that achieving shorter hours was the primary issue of the working classes in New York. He was also aware of the importance of increasing leisure as the way to preserve artisanal republican virtues that had once attached to work. His apprenticeship for the *Long Island Patriot*, his work as a compositor on the *Long Island Star*, and his editorship of the *Long Islander* put him in newsrooms that regularly covered workers' demands for the "Ten Hour System."[60] His support of and campaigning for Martin Van Buren put him in the middle of the political debates about ten-hour days that were centrally important to Van Buren's election and political success.

U. S. Grant's executive order of 1877 that established the eight-hour day for manual workers under government contract created a national debate that would have been hard to ignore. Such transitional moments would have been constant reminders to Whitman that economic developments and political struggles were steadily reducing work hours and laying a practical foundation for Higher Progress.

During Whitman's editorship from March 5, 1846, to January 18, 1848, the *Brooklyn Daily Eagle* carried editorials that came close to endorsing ten-hour legislation and published reports and letters that made explicit links between shorter hours and elements of what would come to constitute Whitman's Higher Progress.[61] For example, on April 6, 1847, the *Daily Eagle* reported that journeymen house carpenters in Nashville were striking for a ten-hour system to replace the traditional sun-to-sun workday. Reporting that "they have families and household affairs which claim a portion of their attention," the paper quoted the Nashville carpenters:

> We are flesh and blood; we need hours of recreation. It is estimated by political economists that five hours per day by each individual would be sufficient to support the human race. Surely then we do our share when we labor ten. We have social feeling which must be satisfied. We have minds and they must be improved. We are lovers of our country and must have

time and opportunity to study its interests. Shall we live and die knowing nothing but the rudiments of our trades? Is knowledge useless to us
that we should be debarred of the means of obtaining it? Would we be
less adept as workmen . . . less respectable or useful . . . because we were
enlightened?

Natural rights rhetoric—echoing the Declaration of Independence and
identifying shorter hours with the liberty to pursue republican virtue—was
widespread in the streets of New York and remained a fundamental part of
labor's struggles throughout Whitman's life. On September 22, 1847, Whitman
editorialized in the *Daily Eagle* that "although we belong to that school which
thinks that the less government or law interferes with labor, or with the contracts to do it, the better, we are fain to confess that if we should make any
exception at all, it would be in favor of such law as the one lately passed in New
Hampshire, called the 'ten hour law.'"

After his career as a newspaper editor, Whitman made numerous references to "labor-saving machines," leisure, and the importance of putting aside
work to accomplish finer, freer things. Signs of Whitman's concerns about excessive work hours ("wage slavery") began to appear in his fiction during the
1840s.[62] In the main body of his mature poetry and prose, Whitman suggested
that labor-saving machines would be history's agents for liberating humans
from wage slavery and for Higher Progress. Describing in *Democratic Vistas*
the "two grand stages of preparation-strata" that would found progress's final,
"third stage," he included labor-saving machines as part of the nation's material
infrastructure.[63] In his poem "No Labor-Saving Machine," he also listed labor-
saving machines as part of the wealth building up in the nation, together with
establishment of hospitals and libraries and performance of deeds of courage.[64]
He put "the better weapons," "labor-saving implements," in the hands of soldiers returning from the war. For Whitman, these soldiers were beginning to
fight "saner wars, sweet wars, life-giving wars" in the "true arenas of my race,
or first or last / Man's innocent and strong arenas":

Well-pleased America thou beholdest,
Over the fields of the West those crawling monsters,
The human-divine inventions, the labor-saving implements;
Beholdest moving in every direction imbued as with life.[65]

His description of a utopian community, read in the light of his confidence
in the advance of labor-saving machines, becomes much more than the nostal-
gic caricature that scholars such as Thomas Haddox draw:[66]

I can conceive a community . . . say in some pleasant western settlement
or town, where a couple of hundred best men and women, of ordinary
worldly status, have by luck been drawn together, with nothing extra of

genius or wealth, but virtuous, chaste, industrious, cheerful, resolute, friendly and devout. I can conceive such a community organized in running order, powers judiciously delegated—farming, building, trade, courts, mails, schools, elections, all attended to; *and then the rest of life, the main thing,* freely branching and blossoming in each individual, and bearing golden fruit. I can see there, in every young and old man, after his kind, and in every woman after hers, a true personality, develop'd, exercised proportionately in body, mind, and spirit. I can imagine this case as one not necessarily rare or difficult, but in buoyant accordance with the municipal and general requirements of our times. And I can realize in it the culmination of something better than any stereotyped éclat of history or poems. Perhaps, unsung, undramatized, unput in essays or biographies—perhaps even some such community already exists, in Ohio, Illinois, Missouri, or somewhere, practically fulfilling itself, and thus outvying, in cheapest vulgar life, all that has been hitherto shown in best ideal pictures.[67]

Whitman's Leisure

Not yet trivialized as it is today, through most of the nineteenth century "leisure" was an ordinary-enough word that meant simple opportunity, often only the privilege of the wealthy. Whitman, perhaps influenced by the workers he associated with in New York and by their ten-hour system, pointed to leisure's democratic potential, adding layers of new meaning to the word, new usages that he revealed in specific lists of what is possible in that refined freedom. In the process he continued to clothe the old republican dream of moral progress and humane freedom with very real kinds of human experiences.

He described the "wife of a mechanic" who is "physiologically sweet and sound, loving work, practical," who nevertheless "knows that there are intervals, however few, devoted to recreation, music, leisure, hospitality—and affords such intervals."[68] His "complete lover . . . the greatest poet . . . in . . . the presence of children playing or with his arm round the neck of a man or woman" whose "love above all love has leisure and expanse . . . leaves room ahead of himself."[69]

In his famous 1856 letter to Ralph Waldo Emerson, he cautioned his "Master":

We have not come through centuries, caste, heroisms, fables, to halt in this land today. Or I think it is to collect a ten-fold impetus that any halt is made. As nature, inexorable, onward, resistless, impassive amid the threats and screams of disputants, so America. Let all defer. Let all attend respectfully the leisure of These States, their politics, poems, literature, manners, and their free-handed modes of training their own offspring. Their own comes, just matured, certain, numerous and capable enough, with egotistical tongues, with sinewed wrists, seizing openly what belongs to them. They resume Personality, too long left out of mind.[70]

Finally, his clear calls to redeem the time, to understand the urgency of leaving work, shops, schools, the courthouse, and marketplace behind as soon as possible for the freedom of the open road, are expressions of his hope for a leisured future.

> *Allons! the road is before us!*
> *It is safe—I have tried it—my own feet have tried it well—be not detain'd!*
> *Let the paper remain on the desk unwritten, and the book on the shelf unopen'd!*
> *Let the tools remain in the workshop! let the money remain unearn'd!*
> *Let the school stand! mind not the cry of the teacher!*
> *Let the preacher preach in his pulpit! let the lawyer plead in the court, and the judge expound the law.*[71]

Whitman would have agreed with Emerson's punning lament, "Works and days were offered us, and we took works."[72] Thus he urged us—poets all if we were but to choose—to reconsider how we spend our time:

This is what you shall do: Love the earth and sun and the animals, despise riches, give alms to every one that asks, stand up for the stupid and crazy, devote your income and labor to others, hate tyrants, argue not concerning God, have patience and indulgence toward the people, take off your hat to nothing known or unknown or to any man or number of men, go freely with powerful uneducated persons and with the young and with the mothers of families, read these leaves in the open air every season of every year of your life, re-examine all you have been told at school or church or in any book, dismiss whatever insults your own soul, and your very flesh shall be a great poem and have the richest fluency not only in its words but in the silent lines of its lips and face and between the lashes of your eyes and in every motion and joint of your body. . . . The poet shall not spend his time in unneeded work. He shall know that the ground is always ready plowed and manured . . . others may not know it but he shall. He shall go directly to the creation. His trust shall master the trust of everything he touches . . . and shall master all attachment.[73]

Whitman's followers have been even more exact and explicit about the way that Higher Progress would be available to all. In 1919 David Karsner reported that Horace Traubel, Whitman's dear friend for the last twenty years of his life, "contended for the larger aspects of the labor movement." Traubel thought:

If the struggle of the working class hinged entirely upon the bread and butter question it might not be so furiously combated by those who hold the keys to the social storehouses. . . . But the granting of more wages and the lessening of the hours of labor presents an opportunity to the workman to read and to think and increase his social vision. That is more dangerous to the ruling class than increased wages. . . . [T]he spiritual aspect of the labor movement is the desire, not for more wages only, but for opportunity in which to reach out in quest for finer possessions and richer truths. The terrific industrial struggle may account for the materialistic doctrine, but does not allow for the equally intense ethical and intellectual discontent.[74]

Embracing labor's struggles as his own, Traubel wrote:

Our fight is a fight for leisure. . . . We want to do things. We need time and space to do them. We're fighting for that time and space. That time and space is what we call leisure. We need room to move around in. That's what we are fighting for. Not for meals and clothes and houses. That's only the incident. We're after life and more life. We're after expansion. . . . That's our fight. We don't fight to possess goods. We fight to stop goods from possessing us.[75]

Arguably, Whitman influenced discussion about the forgotten American dream more than any other writer. Champions of labor as well as leisure advocates, such as Fannia Cohn, Frank Lloyd Wright, Dorothy Canfield Fisher, and Robert Maynard Hutchins, repeatedly employed his words, images, and metaphors well into the twentieth century. Whitman's vision persisted even after World War II, together with the expectation that working hours would continue to decline. During a CBS radio broadcast in 1948, Lyman Bryson asked, "What is the essence of [Whitman's] revolutionism? . . . [W]e say he believed in a vision of greatness, that the people were not realizing it nor living up to his vision. . . . What kind of revolution?" Mark Van Doren responded:

Well, Whitman says in *Democratic Vistas* that there are stages in the development of America. First, there is the political, without which you cannot guarantee any other form of freedom. And second, there is the economic, the conquest of nature, the pioneer's dream, the epoch of the American idea, and that, if successful, would give us leisure enough for cultural freedom.[76]

For illustration, Van Doren then quoted one of the key passages (quoted previously in the chapter; see note 7) from *Democratic Vistas* in which Whitman described his vision of Higher Progress.

Other Nineteenth-Century Voices

Rhetoric making an explicit connection between shorter work hours and Higher Progress swirled about Whitman throughout his life: in the laborites' defense of the ten-hour system; the sermons of millennialists; the speeches of William Ellery Channing, Edward Everett, and Charles Dudley Warner; the bombast of

Horace Greeley; and the mouths of dear friends such as Horace Traubel.[77] Henry David Thoreau, Ralph Waldo Emerson, numerous utopian novelists, and scores of others sounded Whitman's themes—abundance, humane and moral progress, and democratic culture—grounding their hopes on steady technological advances and reductions in working hours.[78]

Daniel Rodgers called Henry David Thoreau "a conservative and a traditionalist" because he spoke for the "first American dream, before the others shoved it rudely aside . . . not of work but of leisure."[79] As a "traditionalist," Thoreau agreed that increasing leisure made humane and moral advance possible. He also offered critiques of the selfishness represented by the new industrial order and of the emergence of a new laissez-faire morality that valued work and wealth as superior ends in themselves.[80] Like William Ellery Channing, he believed that work was still valuable primarily as a means to other, better ends and that the best function of what Channing had called "the work school" was preparing its students to be free: "Those who would not know what to do with more leisure than they now enjoy, I might advise to work twice as hard as they do, work till they pay for themselves, and get their free papers."[81]

Thoreau also reiterated the possibility that Whitman and others recognized that individuals had the potential to establish free relationships with the natural world, based in leisure (Thoreau claimed that "sauntering" in the country was his primary occupation), appreciation, and enjoyment. Guarding his personal leisure against what he believed were the spurious claims of the world of commerce, Thoreau, with the Lowell mill women, saw thrift and simple living as the ways to freedom and expensive habits the way to slavery. He also pointed out that the traditional feudal culture, an aristocratic few served by others, needed to give way to democratic cultures founded locally in communities of discourse and created by the active participation (in leisure) of ordinary citizens:

> It is time that we had uncommon schools, that we did not leave off our education when we begin to be men and women. It is time that villages were universities, and their elder inhabitants the fellows of universities, with leisure . . . to pursue liberal studies the rest of their lives. Shall the world be confined to one Paris or one Oxford forever? In this country, the village should in some respects take the place of the nobleman of Europe. . . . The one hundred and twenty-five dollars annually subscribed for a Lyceum in the winter is better spent than any other equal sum raised in the town. . . . Instead of noblemen, let us have noble villages of men.[82]

Charles Dudley Warner, editor of *Harper's Magazine* and the *Hartford Courant* in the 1880s and 1890s, made one of the strongest cases against the continuation of feudal culture and for the founding of a democratic culture of participation. Warner noticed a "ground-swell" of "contempt" for literature and the fine arts. He attributed this unfortunate development to "culture" and art being produced and enjoyed by a privileged few, who were freed by wealth and increasingly by education from having to earn a living. A "great gulf" still existed between "the scholar" and the democratic majority. Retiring "into his own selfishness" to live and work in isolation, only addressing others in his caste, "the scholar is largely responsible for the isolation of his position and the want of sympathy it begets." Such "intellectual . . . greediness" could not stand in a democracy:

> One of the chief evidences of our progress in this century is the recognition of the truth that there is no selfishness so supreme—not even that in the possession of wealth—as that which retires into itself with all the accomplishments of liberal learning and rare opportunities, and looks upon the intellectual poverty of the world without a wish to relieve it.[83]

Observing that "the great movement of labor" aimed to "unsettle society and change social and political relations," Warner proposed that "the scholar" assist with the unsettling. Recognizing that "his culture is out of sympathy with the great mass that needs it," the scholar should see to it that "the possession of the few be made to leaven the world and to elevate and sweeten ordinary life."[84]

Ordinary methods of cultural uplift such as cheap printing, speeches, theaters, and museums would no longer suffice; they were mere "letters-missive from one class to another." In a democracy, culture could not be thus distributed as a form of charity, because the worker, "finding a voice at length, bitterly repels the condescensions of charity."

What was needed was "more personal contact . . . human sympathy, diffused and living." The cultured few needed to become part of a local democratic community, abandoning their privileged isolation and status, sharing their lives, and creating their art in egalitarian settings: "Nothing will bring [the classes] into this desirable mutual understanding except sympathy and personal contact."[85]

The "instincts of the mass of men" that led them to fight for freedom also led them to struggle with the questions of their humanity. Claiming the right to find meaning and purpose on their own, they were resentful of those who tried to do these things for them. The intellectual's primary responsibility in a democracy was not cultural "charity." Instead, it was to find ways to promote what Emerson called "self-culture," leading by example in communities of discourse that created and consumed their own culture, thus helping "unsettle society and change social and political relations."

Warner concluded, "The idea seems to be well-nigh universal that the millennium is to come by a great deal less work and a great deal more pay." However, these two only provided the means to the more important millennial objective: "the infusion into all society of a truer culture."[86]

Glyndon G. Van Deusen, biographer of Horace Greeley, observed that Greeley was capable of a "profoundly conservative attitude toward labor and capitalist-labor relations" and had opposed Van Buren's ten-hour initiative early in his career.[87] However, he came to be a strong advocate for labor, accepting the need to limit working hours by law.[88] He also shared laborites' vision of emancipation. In his well-known essay "The Emancipation of Labor," Greeley identified labor reform with "the regulation of working hours," explaining that while all "noted writers of Social Economy" agreed that immediate relief from long hours was imperative, "a Limitation of the Hours of Labor, once accomplished, will be valuable mainly for the Opportunity it proffers—the prospect it opens."[89] Supporting Central Park in New York City "as a recreational center for the common man," Greeley also tried to make public provisions for "the prospect" opening with shorter hours.[90]

Many continued to fear that workers would misuse their leisure. But for Greeley, increasing leisure for all was the continuation of America's experiment in liberty. Freedom must be given a try:

> Let us give Human Nature a fair trial . . . before we pronounce it a hopeless failure, to be managed only with the strait-jacket and halter. Let us give fair and full trial of a Laboring Class thoroughly educated, not overworked, fairly remunerated, with ample leisure, and adequate opportunities for Social, Moral, and Intellectual culture and enjoyment. . . . But I can not doubt that a better Social condition, enlarged opportunities of good, and atmosphere of Humanity and Hope, would insure a nobler and truer Character . . . for the improvement of Liberty and Leisure.[91]

Greeley praised the technological advances of American business and industry as the fountainheads of liberation. Writing about America's "great industries," Greeley and his colleagues described the Connecticut steel tools firm Collins and Company. Collins was "great" because it was increasing the "aggregate wealth" of the nation "by geometrical progression." But material wealth was only half the Collins story; it included the wealth of shorter working hours as well:

> The [Collins] approach of the "good time coming" is an approach of the time when men shall be more worthy of leisure, and yet less fond of idleness; when they shall have freed themselves more than now from the rapacious demands which bodily necessities make upon their time; when they shall have more fully conquered nature into working for them, and thus leaving them more opportunity for self-culture. Nothing contributes more to this end than steel, and the better the steel the more effectual the contribution. The manufactures of "Collins & Company" are better helps to speed the millennium than a hundred prize essays could be; for they do not absorb wealth—they create it.[92]

Edward Everett, Whig politician and perhaps the best-known orator of the nineteenth century, noting "the intimate connection of the useful and mechanic arts with intellectual progress," observed:

> I look upon the intellectual and moral influence of the useful arts, as the most important aspect [of the mechanical tendency of the age]. . . . The immediate result of every improvement in these arts . . . often is, and always might and should be, by making less labor and time necessary for the supply of human wants, to raise the standard of comfortable living, increase the quantity of leisure time applicable to the culture of the mind, and thus promote the intellectual and moral progress of the mass of the community. That this is the general tendency of a progress in the useful arts, no one can doubt.[93]

Wendell Phillips, one of the leading abolitionist orators before the Civil War and "labor reform's top speaker after it," helped form the Eight-Hour League in the 1860s.[94] Addressing the first Eight-Hour League convention in 1897, Phillips asked to be excused for speaking for workers because "there are many men in the ranks of what are called the working men of Massachusetts, competent to state and argue their claim. . . . The defect lies in that long lack of leisure." But speak he did, claiming only to restate in public what workers were saying to each other and would eventually articulate. Phillips reiterated what he understood were workers' claims to be fully human, as capable of intelligence, healthy social engagement, spiritual concerns, and appreciation of beauty as any other class—the only difference was their "long lack of leisure."

The opinion of the wealthy and well educated that workers would never want, or be capable of, humane and moral progress were nearly as offensive as the slave-owners' claims about the inborn inferiority of African Americans. Eight hours constituted a real advance toward the higher, finer qualities and republican virtues to which all might aspire in a democracy: "The first question of a Christian and civilized State is, 'What is the method that will make the noblest men and women?' Yards of cotton, tons of coal, ingots of metal are not the measure . . . [shorter hours] is true civilization."[95]

Literary historian Robert T. Rhode argues that during the nineteenth century mechanization's impact on farming was as important as its impact on industry. On the farm as in the city, "culture followed" labor-saving machines such as the steam plow. Rhode notes that while Henry Ward Beecher, influential churchman and reformer, was interested in labor reform in the cities, he saw advances in farm machinery as setting the pattern for progress.[96] Writing about the introduction of the steam plow in 1855, Beecher maintained that machines "promise . . . to set men free, and to make a servant of iron that will toil for him . . . with quadruple speed. . . . Then Labour shall have leisure for culture."[97]

Daniel Rodgers sees such passages as indications of Beecher's ambivalence, or confusion, about the Protestant work ethic, which Beecher also championed in his sermons and writings.[98] But Beecher, as well as other staunch defenders of both the work ethic and the reduction of work hours, was less confused and contradictory than hopeful about progress:

> Men say, "There is less necessity of work, and therefore there is more lei-
> sure." Well, blessed be God for leisure. I hate laziness, and love leisure.
> He whose feet rest, and whose hands no longer toil, may keep the golden
> wheels of the mind working all the more. The highest products of life are
> not those which are found in warehouses. Better than these are books,
> pictures, statues—the various elements which belong to intellectual life,
> and which leisure breeds. There can be no high civilization where there is
> not ample leisure. And as you go toward the spiritual world, there will be
> more leisure and less laziness.[99]

With many others in the nineteenth century, Beecher made a distinction between leisure and idleness nearly forgotten today. He also continued to believe that the work ethic was a means to more valuable ends rather than an end in itself. Hard work and machines freed humans, not for idleness but for ever more intensive effort transcending the "selfish system" and marketplace and from the prods of necessity.

Rhode argues persuasively that Abraham Lincoln shared Beecher's vision— that both "expect[ed] that the promise of civilization [represented by the steam plow] will extend not only to a poet like Whitman but also to the majority of Americans. They envision[ed] the mass of Americans leading poetic lives."[100]

4

The Eight-Hour Day

Labor from the Civil War to the 1920s

Continuing to be inspired by their vision of "the reduction of human labor to its lowest terms," American workingmen and workingwomen renewed their efforts to win the eight-hour day after the Civil War, making significant advances.[1] As Karl Marx famously observed, "The first fruit of the Civil War was the eight-hours' agitation that ran with the seven-leagued boots of the locomotive from the Atlantic to the Pacific, from New England to California."[2]

Just as it had been during the origins of the labor movement, the shorter-hours movement continued as a grassroots effort. Middle-class reformers and observers lent their support and, stirred by what workers were doing, speculated about what mechanization and the new free time might mean for America's future. Some also helped build public infrastructure to accommodate the new freedom. But the impetus continued to come from workers. They remained far ahead of middle-class reformers and moralists in imagining life in which work was put in its proper place, subordinate to the more important business of living. Daniel Rodgers observed of the late nineteenth century:

> Long in advance of the hesitant middle-class recognition of the claims of leisure, workers dreamed of a workday short enough to push labor out of the center of their lives. . . . How much of a man's life should work consume? No work related question was as important as this.[3]

Having consistently found strong, frequently "overwhelming" support for shorter hours in New England, researchers from the Massachusetts Bureau of Statistics of Labor concluded in 1889, "The predominant question of interest to manual workers is, at present, the shortening of the working day."[4] Labor leaders seized on the popularity of the eight-hour day to recruit new members and court politicians, reiterating that eight hours was only one step along the way.[5] Continuing laborites' identification of shorter hours with liberty, Samuel Gompers declared, "Freedom is synonymous with the hours for leisure," later adding, "Eight hours today, fewer tomorrow."[6] Bill Haywood, leader of the Industrial Workers of the World, echoed, "The less work the better."[7] By 1897 George Gunton was afraid laborites had overdone such rhetoric. It seemed to Gunton that the repeated claims that "if twelve hours' labor a day is better than fourteen, then six must be better than twelve, three better than six" had become "stale." He believed labor leaders ought to concentrate on practical goals; claims that work might eventually be eliminated and that "even none would be still better" were going too far.[8]

Gunton's advice to moderate the rhetoric had little effect, however, because the vision of "the progressive shortening of the hours of labor" thrived well into the twentieth century, persistently at the forefront of organized labor's efforts.[9] The issue continued to generate widespread political activity as well, sustaining the political awareness of workers as workers and remaining one of their identifying political causes through mid-twentieth century. The complicated and fascinating story of labor's efforts to organize around shorter hours and use the issue to gain political influence has been well told before and may be summarized briefly here.

Indeed, the story's complexity often gets in the way of the simple narrative, and straying too far into details obscures the story's simple contours: workers continued to want ever-shorter work hours and were successful for over a century. Historians have also spent considerable effort trying to divine workers' motives, finding another complexity of economic and cultural purposes that often veils the obvious. Through all the labor leaders' intricate justifications and elaborate theorizing about the economy, all the bourgeois moralizing and speculating, all the politicians' pontificating, worker motives shine clearly: they fought for shorter hours because they preferred their free time to the work created by laissez-faire capitalism and took back their time when they could afford to do so. What Daniel Rodgers called "the obvious relief from toil" is the best explanation for the century of shorter hours.[10]

Here also is the essence, the bedrock of workers' "radicalism" and class identity in America. As David Montgomery explained, "[Herbert] Gutman showed that the basic thrust of the 19th century workers' struggles entailed a rejection of economic man."[11] Nowhere is this "basic thrust" more in evidence or more important than in the struggle for the "progressive shortening of the hours of labor." Acting on the simple, powerful urge to escape the confines of modern jobs, workers choose free time for more than a century, often sacrificing wages, hoping for and often finding better things to do than be part of the "selfish system." Shorter hours not only represented the nonpecuniary, cultural motives that historians have found to be of vital importance for understanding American workers, but leisure provided the necessary means for their expression as well as for an escape from capitalism.[12]

Workers' struggle for shorter hours also gave substance to middle-class speculations about the coming of abundance—of a time when people would be able to afford enough material goods that they could move on to freedom beyond work and the marketplace. Over the years economists have argued that the choice to work less, "buying" time instead of more goods and services with an increase in hourly wages, marks the point of abundance determined in the marketplace by the individual—abundance is the moment that a person decides he or she can afford additional leisure relative to the need or desire for additional spending. This claim is given additional credence by historians' recent turn to interpretations of consumerist behavior: no more fundamental consumer choice exists than the choice between work/wages and leisure.[13]

Pressed by reporters, surveyors, and others to explain why they wanted shorter hours and to account for what they were doing with their new freedom, workers began to give more detailed justifications. Just as they had done during the antebellum period, they explained their choice primarily in terms of liberty and the freedom from slavery and oppression. Whereas before the Civil War they had made reference to the American Revolution, afterward they made frequent analogies between their struggle and the emancipation of slaves, still claiming that theirs was the cause of liberty—the cause that defined their nation.

In the autumn of 1880, the Massachusetts Bureau of Statistics of Labor surveyed textile and paper mills in Maine, New Hampshire, Massachusetts, Rhode Island, Connecticut, and New York. After "quite thoroughly" canvassing 246 manufacturing establishments and asking employees about the possibility of reducing work hours, the bureau analyzed 791 individual questionnaires, constructing frequency tables and recording pages of truncated quotes from the workers.

The listing of possible uses of leisure, ranging from everyday pleasures to lofty ones, creates a novel-like, stream-of-consciousness effect. In response to the question "What disposition would be made of leisure hours?" workers replied: "sit down and have a smoke"; "sit 'round the store"; "[have] more time at home"; "[take] an hour after dinner . . . [to] educate themselves, read the paper"; "work around the house, and improve its appearance"; "educate my children and increas[e] pleasures at home"; "go out riding with my friends"; "dress up and go visiting"; "play[] ball . . . [or] walk about"; "garden"; "learn to play in a band"; "[enjoy] out-door exercise and evening amusements"; "[re]store my mind"; "[seek] mental improvement."[14]

Over 85 percent of those surveyed thought that they and others would "make good use" of the additional leisure. Yet most were uncertain about specifics, saying things like "Breath[e] the pure air, and look about me to see what's going on"; "It would not be hard to find a good use for more leisure time"; "They would find use for it [leisure]"; and "Go down the street, look about me."[15] Similar to the Parisian laborers Jacques Rancière described, American workers in New England were continuing to live into their new leisure after the Civil War, experimenting with new possibilities in a kind of freedom never before available to the majority of human beings.

By all accounts, the most frequent, definite use of the new time was with family and friends. "Looking about" them "to see what's going on," workers returned to the traditional institutions that industrialization had disrupted.[16] However, because extended families had been separated and traditional communities disturbed, they often found it necessary to repair or rebuild them. Immigrants in particular faced the need to construct new communities and family arrangements. Industrialization had made the novel freedom of leisure available for workers, but it had also begun to clear away age-old patterns of living—together with social mores, customs, and constraints. Certainly, many workers returned to patriarchal families and tradition-bound neighborhoods. Still, while not facing a totally blank page, other workers found unprecedented freedom to experiment with their living arrangements and discover new ways to live together.

Arguably, such a project was unavoidable in America during the late nineteenth and early twentieth centuries. For the family and community to survive, it became necessary to reconceive and attempt to reconstruct these traditional institutions as their age-old economic functions were steadily taken over by modern capitalism, professions, and bureaucracies. As Stuart and Elizabeth Ewen observed:

> By 1900 . . . the home had ceased production; the factory had taken its place. People now purchased what they had once produced for themselves. Production and consumption had become distinct activities, a fundamental rearrangement in the way people apprehended their material world.[17]

Challenges naturally arose concerning how people might continue to relate to each other when necessary tasks and responsibilities were outsourced. To the extent that the cash nexus replaced traditional family and community relationships, family and community members faced the necessity of reconceptualizing these fundamental institutions. Gradually, as the Ewens relate, families and communities were rebuilt, in part on the new economic foundation of consumerism. However, families and communities also experimented with new ways of living together in their new leisure. They began to find new intersubjective meanings and purposes together and construct new, free identities alternative to the dominant capitalist order that mandated consumerism—leisure continued to hold open a convivial alternative (what the Lowell "mill girls" called the ten-hour system) to capitalism's "selfish system" well into the twentieth century. This alternative, and the experimentation it entailed, disturbed middle-class morality as much as any other threat.

Mikhail Bakhtin's description of the medieval carnival crowd, "organized in their own way, the way of the people . . . outside of and *contrary* to all existing forms of coercive socioeconomic and political organization" is an apt description of American workers' experimentation with their new leisure.[18] In a process that E. P. Thompson called the "struggle about time," workers began to imagine and construct a deliberately convivial, alternative social order, "contrary" to consumerism and capitalism's "selfish system."[19]

A New Work Ethic Emerges as the Spirit of Capitalism

Businessmen, moralists, and middle-class professionals understood the threat that worker leisure represented to the future of industrial capitalism as well as to middle-class status and morality. Specifically, they recognized the threat to the emerging *secular* "work ethic"—an ethic that Max Weber called "the spirit of capitalism," which was founded on the consumerist needs of the modern economy rather than on sixteenth-century Protestant theology.[20] Middle-class moralists and businesspeople, fearing that the nation was facing a "crisis of work," represented by labor's demand for the eight-hour day, sought to redefine and promote "full-time" jobs. They began trying to convince the nation of the glory of labor that was its own reward and that hard work, in and of itself, was the organizing principle of the individual's life and the defining virtue of the nation.[21] Thus began a process in which traditional religious worldviews and republican virtue were eclipsed by the ascendancy of a new, work-based view of the world: "the spirit of capitalism."

Just as they had done before the Civil War, workers continued to resist this new secular ethic. Well into the twentieth century, laborites persistently critiqued it and offered an alternative—an alternative implicit in "the progressive shortening of the hours of labor." Beginning with the ten-hour system, laborites repeatedly made their alternative explicit, arguing that work's perfection and true glory depended on its eventual subordination—on the shifting of life's balance from work and the market to free time.

Certainly, working-class leisure offended other parts of middle-class morality as well. Seeking to control the rowdy, indecorous behavior and sexual looseness they observed around them and intent on uplifting the leisure of masses to a standard of behavior they found acceptable, reformers set about building properly monitored public spaces: parks, beaches, playgrounds, resorts, community centers, and libraries. However, they were only marginally successful in Americanizing immigrants and uplifting the masses to the kinds of recreations they felt proper. More often they had to compromise and work with the public they were attempting to serve. More importantly, they were even less successful in convincing workers of the "glory of work"—the modern bourgeois ethic and worldview that would outlive middle-class "uplift" and Victorian squeamishness to become the dominant morality of the dominant classes by the late twentieth century.

Saloons, Dance Halls, Vaudeville, Movies

Typically, workers, careful with the little free time they had, were not overly interested in the kinds of wholesome recreations urban reformers were offering. More frequently, they found commercial facilities more to their liking. Entrepreneurs, recognizing the opportunity leisure represented, accommodated them with saloons, a favorite with older workingmen; dance halls, attractive to young women and men; and new places of amusement. Coney Island, vaudeville, nickelodeons, professional sports, and the movies began to compete for the workers' free time and extra cash.

However, the commercial parts of these establishments, the things that were ostensibly for sale (liquor, concessions, rides, spectacles), were not as socially important as the venues that were made available. The price of admission often included opportunities to find companionship, build friendships, tell stories and jokes (Bakhtin's "festive laughter" was a hallmark of the turn-of-the-century saloon), display the latest fashion, argue and fight, and flirt and experiment with sexual boundaries and gender roles.[22] Commercial recreation, or "commercialized leisure," was a mix of commerce and leisure—of product and services together with time and occasion, with the latter often more valued than the former.[23] Indeed, this is one of the important discoveries of recent historical scholarship—that commercial recreation and consumerism were important parts of American culture in the twentieth century precisely because of their nonpecuniary content and cultural, extraeconomic function.

Mixing leisure with commerce, new establishments such as the café, dance hall, and saloon flourished at the turn of the twentieth century by offering places where, as Bakhtin observed of the Rabelaisian festival, "the people . . . organized in their own way, the way of the people . . . outside of and *contrary* to all existing forms of coercive socioeconomic and political organization."[24] Historians such as Lizabeth Cohen, Vicki Ruiz, and George Sanchez have confirmed that commercial amusements provided the places and new consumer products the accoutrements needed to express and extend ethnic cultures as well as maintain working-class identity.[25]

Just as the Lowell "mill girls" conceived and begin to construct a convivial ten-hour system as an alternative to capitalism's "selfish system," workers in Worchester, Massachusetts, and other American cities began to build congenial infrastructures *contrary* to prevailing "market exchange mentality"[26] after the Civil War and did so, ironically, in the very midst of entrepreneurs' successful efforts to commodify their new leisure. Roy Rosenzweig concluded:

> The saloon was actually a "democracy" of sorts—an *internal* democracy where all who could safely enter received equal treatment and respect. An ethic of mutuality and reciprocity that differed from the market exchange mentality of the dominant society prevailed within the barroom. . . .

[The saloon provided] a space in which immigrants could preserve an alternative, reciprocal value system.[27]

Similarly, Kathy Peiss discovered that some turn-of-the-century New York women found a degree of personal autonomy by taking active part in commercial amusements available after work. Even though most commercial recreation continued to be divided along gender, as well as racial and ethnic, lines, in such places as dance halls and amusements parks women began to challenge "the boundaries of domesticity and female self-sacrifice," finding new ways to express themselves and relate to others. Commercial recreation also helped build communities. Entrepreneurs recruited chaperones from the neighborhoods to go on excursions and monitor dances they organized. Vaudeville and the movies attracted men and women, young and old, "decisively breaking down the segmentation of working-class recreation."[28] Agreeing with Rosenzweig, Peiss concluded that "working-class leisure . . . offered a refuge from the dominant value system of competitive individualism," adding that "among working women, leisure came to be seen as a separate sphere of life to be consciously protected."[29]

Randy McBee agreed that young immigrant women and men at the turn of the century found a degree of freedom from family supervision and community strictures in the popular dance halls of the era. Taking delight in their youth and bodies, they pushed against heterosexual boundaries and norms, beginning a vital process of reconfiguring gender roles and relations.[30] Nan Enstad concluded that, at the turn of the century,

> working women incorporated fashion, fiction, and film products into their daily lives. The meanings of the particular products emerged not simply from the objects themselves, but from those *social practices* that gave them currency and shared value among working women . . . working women embraced dime novels, fashion, and film products and used them to create distinctive and pleasurable *social practices* and to enact identities as ladies.[31]

Angela McRobbie concluded, "Mass-produced narratives and fashion can allow women to actively create leisure and personal spaces that are female-centered, and are locations for developing positive identities. . . . Women are not . . . passive consumers."[32] Together with Worchester's saloons, New York's dance halls and amusement parks became the settings and "fashion, fiction, and film" the accouterments for ordinary people to begin to practice and develop what Rosenzweig called an "ethic of mutuality and reciprocity that differed from the market exchange mentality . . . an alternative, reciprocal value system."

Public Parks: A New Relation to the Natural World

Just as they used commercial recreation establishments for their own social purposes, workers and immigrants often co-opted public leisure facilities:

parks, playgrounds, community centers, and beaches. Thwarting bourgeois attempts to uplift and Americanize them, they found congenial ways of living together *contrary* to the dominant "exchange mentality" or Victorian morality. Genteel reformers and city planners were frequently frustrated by the lack of control they were able to exert after supporting the construction of what they hoped would be healthy, sanitary public spaces.[33]

As the nation became increasingly urban, the experience and perception of the natural world begin to change. Americans found new kinds of recreational uses for nature and a new appreciation of it, building alternatives to the ancient struggle against the natural world and to what Aldo Leopold called the "Abrahamic concept" that nature had value only when made to serve human needs. Whereas the growth of modern capitalism reinforced and continued to elaborate the age-old utilitarian view, alternative recreational, moral, esthetic, and spiritual perceptions and uses of nature also advanced from the nineteenth century to the present as a countertrend, constituting a vital part of the American dream of Higher Progress.

Historians have tended to emphasize the leadership (and dominance) of upper- and middle-class men and women in the parks, preservation, and environmental movements. Certainly, prominent men and women throughout the nineteenth and twentieth centuries most often led the way, prompted by a variety of motives: self-promotion, bourgeois fears and need to control, altruism, and a vision of Higher Progress. However, working-class men and women were among the first to develop and express a new appreciation of the natural world.

The women and men who moved to New England's towns to work in the mills before the Civil War had experienced the natural world as farmers, in utilitarian terms. However, as the historian Chad Montrie notes, for industrial workers "the aesthetic and spiritual dimensions of the environment assumed a new importance." Similar to the contrast between their new work and new free time that Jacques Rancière emphasizes, the contrast between the new factory settings and the surrounding natural world was such that a new kind of discourse about both the natural world and the city was possible for the first time.[34]

One of the Lowell "mill girls," Harriet Farley, described her experience of looking out a factory window that framed "the bright loveliness of nature." Feeling "like a prisoned bird," she wished she could fly "amidst the beautiful creation around me." Other Lowell women wrote about similar contrasts provided by similar perspective changes, some fondly remembering their rural homes, others writing about their regular visits back to the farm, still others describing outings and outdoor recreations. They not only reported an "aesthetic and spiritual" appreciation of nature from their new urban perspective but, because of their occasional movement back to rural settings, saw their lives in the city and factory from a different perspective that often prompted critical reflection.[35]

For American workers, part of the definition of Higher Progress and justification for shorter hours was the opportunity to enjoy the natural world.

Laborites made critical, effective uses of the dual perspectives offered by nature and leisure vis-à-vis city and work to support shorter hours, workers' education, and numerous recreational programs and public outdoor facilities. Dianne Glave and Mark Stoll point out that even though "it is commonly assumed that people of color and working-class European Americans" were too preoccupied by work to be interested in recreation and nature, historical counterexamples abound. During the early part of the twentieth century "black Chicagoans saw recreation in nature . . . as an essential escape" and struggled to gain access to the city's recreational facilities. The struggle culminated in 1919 in the city's worst race riot, occasioned by the exclusion of African Americans from Lake Michigan's beaches.[36]

Labor's efforts to promote and workers' interest in the "aesthetic and spiritual dimensions of the environment" did not end with rhetoric: they were manifest in very real outdoor activities, public facilities, and programs organized by the unions and consistently popular with union members. Among the best examples of workers' and immigrants' use of public facilities to discover an alternative to the "selfish system," express their own "ethic of mutuality and reciprocity," and confront social domination is New York's Central Park.

Central Park

Roy Rosenzweig and Elizabeth Blackmar describe how Central Park's founding elites were originally motivated by a complex of desires: "to make money, to display the city's cultivation, to lift up the poor, to refine the rich, to advance commercial interests, to retard commercial development, to improve public health, [and] to curry political favor."[37] Their attempts to uplift and control the recreation of park users were widely ignored, however. Individuals and groups (ethnic, labor, gay men, male and female athletes) began to use the park in their own ways. Recreation in the park began to reflect the heterogeneous makeup of the city by the turn of the twentieth century. Rosenzweig and Blackmar conclude that the park provided a vital space "for preexisting communities . . . to maintain themselves as well as for people to create new user-based friendships."[38]

Seeking opportunities to revitalize traditional communities and form new social contacts, individuals and groups used the city's parks in ways that frightened middle-class reformers. German immigrants, for example, fleeing the park's numerous prohibitions and restrictions, chose instead "Jones Wood as a space where they could maintain their traditions and ties. They could picnic in family groups, dance to German music, watch gymnastic exhibitions, drink lager beer."[39]

Middle-class reformers attempted to negotiate with the groups that used the park. Instead of attempting to enforce bourgeois standards of morality, reformers during the Progressive Era began what Joseph Huthmacher called a "constructive collaboration" with the "urban lower classes."[40] Park commissioner

Charles B. Stover (appointed in 1910) believed that the city's recreational facilities could help mitigate social inequalities and distrust between ethnic groups and become a catalyst for rebuilding the city's neighborhoods. He made access to the park easier and allowed neighborhoods to promote their heritages by erecting hyphen-American statues throughout the park and organizing ethnic celebrations. He worked with community groups, offering free concerts and play festivals that appealed to a wide range of people, expecting that they would begin to interact in their leisure and build civility, a sentiment that found support within the neighborhoods he visited. Remarkably, as Rosenzweig and Blackmar conclude, African Americans, excluded and insulted in most public places at the time, "were apparently accepted as regular users of the park in the late nineteenth century. . . . Black owned newspapers occasionally reported on the concerts, [and] encouraged youngsters to get permits for baseball and picnics in the park."[41]

Middle-class reformers and park users from adjoining communities attempted to foster intergroup (ethnic, racial, and religious) contact and understanding. Such free public spaces provided opportunities to share recreational activities and build camaraderie in sports and games—opportunities for mutuality that were rare in the world of commerce and employment where competition and exploitation more frequently divided individuals and groups.[42]

Central Park is the product of an ongoing process. It was, and remains, an open-ended, contested, and negotiated social space. Nevertheless, the contestants, the many, varied, jostling groups, have joined over the years to support what Rosenzweig and Blackmar called a "democratic ideal": an "'imagined community' of ordinary people." In the midst of discrimination and prejudice, in the very downtown of American capitalism—the exemplar of competition and self-seeking—an alternative "ethic of mutuality and reciprocity" began to form, issuing from an "imagined community" and moving toward civility. The park's reality, the crime, crass commercialism, and the exclusion of others have always seemed particularly offensive there because of the convivial dream of a truly "democratic space."[43]

Elizabeth Hasanovitz

It may be presumptuous to suggest additions to Rosenzweig and Blackmar's *The Park and the People*. However, they neglected one of the best illustrations of their claim that Central Park is "the most democratic place in New York City, if not in the United States."[44] In 1918 Elizabeth Hasanovitz, who worked in the needle trades in New York during the turbulent sweatshop years and just after the Triangle Shirtwaist fire, published *One of Them: Chapters from a Passionate Autobiography*. She told of spending many of her evenings in her "favorite corner near the reservoir in Central Park."[45] She also recalled stopping in the park for a moment early one morning on her way to work. She was struck by the contrast between the park and city: "With deep, hungry breath I drank the

frozen air which was so refreshing. I watched the little frozen lake surrounded
by naked trees covered with sleet. . . . The high rocks majestically stood out of
the white snow that covered the ground." The scene brought back memories
of "bygone days," when she would "steal" time to frolic there with her friends:
"We would go off in groups, exploring the snow-clad woods and groves, enjoying the frosty but romantic moonlight." She examined the contrast between the
deserted, peaceful park woods and the "hundreds of people" hurrying "anx-
iously" to work. She recognized an even more profound contrast between her
instant of freedom and the "hurry-up, made world" where no one had "time to
look around them."[46] Knowing only work and the "world of efficiency," most of
the hurrying people were "blinded to all natural beauty."[47]

Hasanovitz was a true believer in what Rosenzweig and Blackmar described
as the "democratic possibilities" of Central Park: her life was a search for an
"'imagined community' of ordinary people."[48] She also made explicit connections between labor unions, shorter-hours reform, and her American dream.
Lying on a blanket in Central Park beside the reservoir, one of her fellow workers complained that their union (the International Ladies' Garment Workers')
was too conservative, concentrating on wages and hours rather than more radical political remedies. Hasanovitz answered:

> But Fannie, that means so much. . . . The shorter hours in the shop enable
> us to devote more time to our spiritual development, the raise in wages
> enables us to get more wholesome food and worthy recreation. With time
> and money the best things can be accomplished.[49]

Even though she resisted the appeals of socialism and communism, she
consistently described her work as a form of "slavery," concluding:

> Nothing existed for me but the pursuits to which I gave my evenings. From
> my entrance into the shop in the morning, I waited for the clock to strike
> six, when I could leave the place and all in it behind me. . . . I would hasten
> to the Dramatic Club or some other place where I found companionship.[50]

She was in at the beginning of what several writers have called the flowering of Yiddish culture during the first part of the twentieth century. Part of the
thriving Yiddish theater, her "dramatic club" on New York's Lower East Side
attempted to create "a literary folk-theatre." Composed mostly of amateurs and
serving a local audience, they tried to rebuild local community on the foundation of their Jewish heritage, in danger of being lost.[51]

In addition to her drama club and union hall, Hasanovitz found her "coveted *America*" in New York's public places: its libraries, museums, and parks.
There she "found *freedom* and *equality!*" Her "coveted *America*," the dream
she conceived originally in Russia, had failed her at work—she had to be a slave
simply to survive. But she recognized that she had begun to realize a portion of

the "better half" of her dream—free time to live.[52] As the unions strengthened
and the economy improved, she expected that both wages and hours would get
better—"beautiful possibilities" that she envisioned at the close of her book.[53]

Hasanovitz's primary aspirations were literary: "good literature" and serious theater. Her favorite authors were "Ibsen, Maeterlinck, Prshebishevsky,
Andreev, Strindberg, Gorky."[54] She had little patience with her fellow workers, "queens of imitation," who wasted their lives and money on fashion and
trivial amusements. Such commercial traps distracted them from the serious
business at hand, political action and union organization. But even worse, they
diverted attention from what she believed were essential pursuits. She felt herself "starved spiritually" by the lack of time for education and lectures, music
and the opera, the beauty of nature, and most of all, for opportunities to be
with her friends to discuss such things. She described those around her, such as
her friend Clara, as being "soul-hungry for beauty, for art, for good literature."
She also saw wisdom in thrift and simple living, urging her fellow workers to
practice these old-fashioned, republican virtues.[55] These were the virtues that
would free them from dependence on capitalism and allow them to have more
leisure—more time to renew their heritage and reestablish families and communities, satisfying their starving souls and minds and helping local Yiddish
culture flower in America.

Workers' Education: An "Ethic of Mutuality and Reciprocity"

Education and culture were also central to the middle-class plans to uplift
workers and Americanize immigrants—projects that historians often dismiss
as covers for attempts to control and exploit workers. However, workers and
their unions appeared to have shared these goals; Elizabeth Hasanovitz's autobiography is a case in point. During the century-long struggle for shorter
hours, labor leaders, labor newspapers, and union publications consistently
stressed the educational and cultural uses of free time. The survey published
in 1881 by the Massachusetts Bureau of Statistics of Labor reported that nearly
as many workers said that given extra time they would read, study, write, play
music, take classes, and go to school as said they would spend more time with
family and friends.

There is no doubt that the unions and workers used the same words as their
middle-class supporters: education, culture, uplift, self-improvement, "the classics." But it is also clear that these words had different meanings. Just as they
had found their own ways to use commercial recreation establishments and
public leisure facilities, workers and immigrants often co-opted what bourgeois
culture had "for sale": lectures, classes, fine literature, serious theater, and music. The saloon's customers valued the conviviality they found as much as the
liquor they drank, and working-class consumers of culture looked for a similar
active role. Still pursuing what Rosenzweig called an "ethic of mutuality and
reciprocity," they sought to actively engage the best of what Western civilization

had so far produced and put it to practical, convivial use, building fellowship and community.[56]

While the National Labor Union, Knights of Labor, and American Federation of Labor (AFL) had provided reading rooms and libraries for their members somewhat earlier, women workers initiated workers' education in the twentieth century. The National Women's Trade Union League began to offer free English classes for immigrant women after 1904, establishing a Training School for Women Organizers in 1914. In 1916, responding to its local affiliates' initiatives and led by Juliet Stuart Poyntz and Fannia Mary Cohn, the International Ladies' Garment Workers' Union (ILGWU) launched its workers' educational program.[57]

Following the ILGWU lead, unions across the United States began programs, creating a "boom in workers' education, which, by 1921, produced over two dozen labor schools."[58] Responding to what they understood was a clear demand, unions, socialist groups, and the Industrial Workers of the World opened schools. The University of Chicago, Bryn Mawr, Northwestern, and other colleges offered worker education programs and classes. Workers flocked to night schools and summer programs. David Roediger and Philip Foner found that

> a remarkable intellectual life, conducted in many languages, graced the left and labor movements and the classics along with cheaply available left-wing pamphlets circulated among activists. One of the most popular works, Paul Lafargue's *The Right to Be Lazy*, extolled proletarian leisure.[59]

In few places was labor radicalism more in evidence. Moreover, the connection to shorter hours was unmistakable: Roediger and Foner suggest that workers' education grew out of labor's eight-hour demand.[60] At the time, the prominent socialist Mary Marcy recognized the same connections: "It is obvious that men or women working from ten to sixteen hours a day will have little strength or leisure for study, or activity in revolutionary work. . . . The eight-hour day . . . would insure us leisure for study and recreation—for work in the Army of the Revolution."[61]

Like Mary Marcy, Juliet Poyntz, college educated (Barnard and Oxford) and middle class, came to believe that workers' education naturally served revolutionary purposes. For Fannia Cohn, born in Russia and a member of the Socialist Revolutionary Party there, "socialism was a basic creed, an article of faith."[62] Together, working with their local union to establish workers' education programs, they fashioned the ILGWU's singular trade union philosophy, what has come to be known as "Social unionism."[63] Arguably conceived by working women during the 1912 Lawrence, Massachusetts, textile strike that produced the feminist slogan "Bread and Roses,"[64] "Social unionism" extended the focus of Gompers's "pure and simple unionism" on hours and wages to include social and cultural needs.[65] Susan Stone Wong observes, "Social unions tied the building of a union to the creation of a new and better social order."[66]

In 1923 the ILGWU's educational committee summarized what it had been trying to do, offering a glimpse of the "better social order" it envisioned:

> The International Ladies' Garment Workers' Union was practically the first labor organization in America to recognize the truth that in addition to providing for the economic needs of its members, a Labor Union has other functions; among the most important of these is that of providing for their spiritual needs.[67]

The "roses" part of "Bread and Roses" and the ILGWU's "spiritual needs" were vague, open-ended terms. Nevertheless, for Cohn, Poyntz, and Pauline Newman and Rose Schneiderman (also prominent ILGWU leaders and often credited with coining the phrase "Bread and Roses"), such words represented workingwomen's very real yearnings for something better than a life of constant work and worry about making a living. Such words expressed their sisters' belief there must be an alternative to living in a capitalist world where competition, control, and self-seeking infused more and more human relationships. They also expressed the immigrant dreams of women such as Elizabeth Hasanovitz—dreams of America as the place of cultural, social, and intellectual possibilities, as well as material prosperity.

Under pressure from union leaders, Poyntz left the ILGWU shortly after its 1918 convention, becoming a Communist Party organizer. "Most militant women" in the union departed with Poyntz or soon after.[68] Cohn remained but was left with the task of negotiating between the unions' warring factions (socialist and communists) and convincing an increasingly conservative AFL to continue supporting workers' education and the new "Social unionism" she helped conceive.[69]

Fannia Cohn

While keeping her radical edge (she would not submit to union leaders' demand to exclude Communist Party members from her Education Department's activities—David Dubinsky, president of the ILGWU from 1932 to 1966, called her his "cross to bear"), Cohn nevertheless adapted to labor's conservative turn, shedding most of her socialist "creed" and "faith," maintaining that unions were the realistic hope for women to improve their daily lives, and beginning to develop a philosophy similar to what some have recently called "deliberative democracy."[70] As early as 1918 she pointed out, "Unfortunately many people wait for the social revolution." Such people had to "learn to be practical idealists in the union," fighting for "the emancipation of the workers" through the unions' "economic struggle" for wages and hours.[71] In 1926 she wrote, "I am now more certain than ever . . . that in my position as head of the Education Department, I should not be involved in politics."[72] In 1932 she reiterated, "Women . . . by studying history, will soon learn that while the driving force of the labor movement is idealistic, the approach will have to be realistic [and based on union action, organization, and negotiations]."[73]

Nevertheless, still hoping for "roses," she turned from "politics" to reductions in working hours to realize her vision of "Social unionism."[74] She continued to use the fiery language of her youth: "The existing economic system is unsatisfactory and should be improved and changed"; there should be "social reconstruction," "emancipation of the workers," and a "new social order."[75] But she came to believe that workers' education would

> furnish [workers] with the materials which will enrich the leisure hours which had been won by their organization in its struggles on the economic field. It will develop . . . an intelligent rank and file, educated, healthy, full of life, full of desire for a new world. They will be trained for self-expression. . . . Educational activities will develop in the workers a new vision of brotherhood and cooperative effort to be attained by organization in the Labor Union and the Labor Movement.[76]

Cohn and her sisters demanded more than higher wages and economic reforms—that their unions offer "something more than the economic question."[77] Having to exist in a capitalist, competitive world, they nevertheless continued to articulate an "alternative vision,"[78] finding ways to "transform relationships between women, between male and female workers, between husbands and wives" to include what the historian Annelise Orleck calls "the spirit of intimacy and solidarity."[79] Their imaginations were captured by the idea of large-scale social transformation. They also agreed that the best way to achieve such a goal was not by radical political change but by educating themselves and others for the new leisure to come.

Cohn believed that her immigrant hopes and her sisters' dreams had been shared by those who founded her adopted nation:

> The struggles of the workers . . . can be compared with the story of the Pilgrims . . . Any school boy or girl can tell you that they came to the New World to live the kind of lives they chose. . . . It was not, however, until they . . . were secure in the essentials of civilized life that the Pilgrims began to plan to satisfy their social, spiritual, cultural, and intellectual desires. . . . The workers, too, had to wage *their* battles in a ruthless, uncontrolled, exploiting industrial environment. The workers want, through organization, to be able to lead a better life, to provide for themselves and their families. . . . They want enough leisure to enjoy the best that there is in our culture.[80]

Cohn believed that "enough leisure" was a central part of "woman's eternal struggle":

More and more women want to reverse the historic position assigned to them by men. They want to be their own inspiration. . . . These women dream of a cooperative commonwealth that will embrace the entire human race . . . in which real freedom, happiness and comradeship should be the driving force.[81]

For Cohn, "real comradeship" included "the spirit of intimacy and solidarity" (what Janice Raymond called "deep community") and involved a "cooperative commonwealth" beyond the pecuniary realms of competition and capitalist control. Such a transeconomic and transpolitical commonwealth would nurture free relationships that developed and intensified, requiring acquired skills, sustained effort, and careful nurture, taught and facilitated by workers' education:[82]

The labor union . . . tends to reconstruct society. Our members have a dream of the new world where social justice is to prevail, where men and women will not sneer at friendship and love. . . . We do not need to supply our members with isms . . . our members are interested in other things besides their economic and social problems. They are human beings endowed with the irresistible desire for play, joy, and happiness. [Therefore workers' education satisfies] the desire of our members . . . for the best of literature . . . music, the joys of dancing and play, the pleasure of social gatherings and delights of nature.[83]

The reporter Arthur Gleason wrote to her in 1921, "You are a true follower of Whitman." Orleck interprets this quotation as Gleason praising Cohn's "earthiness and fierce belief in democracy and the human spirit."[84] But Gleason may also have recognized that Cohn shared Walt Whitman's belief in "adhesiveness"—free human bondings that created new, democratic opportunities for conviviality and poetry.

For Cohn, union organization and power were means to achieve, and workers' education uniquely suited to facilitate, "woman's eternal struggle." While most women yearned instinctively for "deep community," because they were born or raised in capitalism's masculine, competitive world they needed to be reminded that their hopes were not foolish and that the practical means to freedom from the competitive culture were available through the unions' battle for shorter hours.[85]

Workers' education differed from that provided by the capitalist system not only because of its lack of instruction in the importance of competition, individual success, and escape from the working class. For Cohn, most workers' education programs distinguished between "the conventional . . . bourgeois conception of 'success' and 'failure' and our conceptions of the same things."[86] Moreover, workers' education was based on active questioning and involvement rather than passive indoctrination, in preparing for and putting into practice a deliberative democracy. Since worker education's primary goal was to build solidarity, participation was essential, providing practical experience in civil discourse: "Emphasis is always placed upon discussion—and more discussion—on the part of students."[87] "Since our education exists for the sake of helping forward democracy, we try to foster self-government in workers' education. We guard against an over-centralization of educational control."[88]

Workers' education also taught students to "become increasingly aware of their common heritage . . . our people then realize the opportunities that their community offers . . . [and] begin to realize the responsibility that rests with each individual to enrich the life of the community through enlightened active participation."[89]

As Elizabeth Hasanovitz found, "the classics," the best literature and music of the past, may be enjoyed for themselves by individuals—she took genuine delight in opera and in fine literature. However, as Cohn recognized, "the classics" and the "enduring wisdom" they contained typically pointed to the importance of community and the life of the mind—one of the reasons the classics endured was that they encouraged active engagement with others in shared experiences of thought and discourse. The classics also provided connections to a variety of ethnic heritages, allowing for the preservation of ethnic cultures endangered by America's melting pot.

Workers' education taught other vital skills necessary for community life such as public speaking, music, and drama. Often involving the classics, such instruction in do-it-yourself, democratic culture differed markedly from bourgeois schools that, according to Cohn and others, were teaching students to be passive audiences and consumers of information and entertainment, in keeping with the needs of the commercial world for paying customers.

Moreover, Cohn and other leaders of workers' education believed that commercial recreation and mass entertainment distracted workers, luring them to accept the role of passive, easily manipulated audiences. Advertisers and hucksters spent millions teaching people to be passive consumers. Workers' education had to be equally aggressive and clever, advertising and luring people with entertainments, games, recreation, and travel opportunities. Cohn concluded:

> Experienced teachers . . . successfully blended educational and recreational activities. The nature of our program in these [workers' education] Centers is expressed in our slogan: "Learning-Playing-Action." We have found that a program which combines in one evening educational, social and recreational elements is the most successful formula. Therefore, the first part of the evening is spent in the classroom, the second in the gymnasium.[90]

The gymnasium was as vital as the classroom. It was the place for free play, for fun and physical exuberance for their own sakes. Recreation allowed students to learn by doing, using the "tools for conviviality" essential for civic engagement and deep community:[91]

> This recreational program is important . . . for its social dividends. . . . The play on the gym floor, group singing, the square dance, folk dance, all build up a sense of cooperative activity which is of primary importance in developing the alert and active trade unionist and citizen.[92]

Cohn thought of herself as a trade unionist rather than a feminist. Nevertheless, she displayed the characteristics of what Mildred Moore called "industrial feminism," defined as "the woman's point of view, the desire for the good of all."[93] Writing in Chicago at the time when Cohn was just beginning her work with the ILGWU, Moore found that "women notably seek organization less often for selfish power," trying instead to find an "avenue of approach to the nobler, higher traits which are essentially human." Organizations such as Woman's Trade Union League of Chicago were "working with the trend of evolution . . . [to accomplish] wonderful things": an industrial democracy in which workers found justice and the freedom to express "nobler, higher traits."[94]

For the most part, Moore left it to the future to discover the "wonderful things" that would come with democracy's natural evolution. However, as she summarized her findings, she quoted from Josephine Goldmark's *Fatigue and Efficiency*: "Democracy's demand is, that the energies of man be conserved." The context of the Goldmark quote is revealing, offering a further insight into Moore's "industrial feminism":

> We must bear in mind throughout that the essence of this [broader physiological] view is its insistence on conserving the energies of men . . . [which is the] larger, intrinsic demand of Democracy itself. [The physiologist] cannot consider man's output separate from himself. . . . The workers' time and vitality need not be all consumed in their tasks. In leisure other ranges of the spirit are unfolded: "another race hath been, and other palms are won." The limitation of working hours, therefore, which assures leisure, is not a merely negative program. . . . It frees the worker from toil . . . [for] leisure . . . [and] its potentialities.[95]

Arthur Gleason

Arthur Gleason was among Cohn's strongest middle-class supporters. In his survey of workers' education programs, Gleason reported that Cohn's dream of social reconstruction and methods of teaching had spread across the country by 1921. Gleason, an American reporter with strong socialist views before and during the war, recorded labor's conservative turn in the 1920s.[96] By 1920 he also had modified his views and, influenced by Cohn and the workers he interviewed, turned his attention from socialism to craft unionism and workers' education.[97] With Cohn, he had come to believe that

> *workers' control is a means, and not an end.* Work in the modern industrial world is unpleasant for the majority of workers. They will find their expression as human beings outside the working hours—in the use of leisure for family life, education, recreation, a hobby. Control they will use to get efficient management and machinery, with which to shorten hours to the minimum. . . . Control, they wish, to save them from the waste and insecurity and long hours of the present system. . . . A minimum of work consistent with a production which will give sufficient commodities for a good life for all workers: they will use control to obtain that. *But control will never of itself be an answer to the instincts thwarted by standardized machine industry. The answer will be found outside of working hours.*[98]

For Gleason, labor's future in the United States, as in Britain, would transcend politics—it would make little difference if workers' "expression as human beings outside the working hours" came as a result of the AFL's pure and simple unionism or guild socialism. Reduction of "work hours to the minimum" was the key to the "new social order." Gleason's radicalism, which he claimed to share with the majority of American and British workers, had come to resemble the Lowell women's 1840s ten-hour system more than socialist statism or communist revolution. Liberation would finally come "outside of working hours" and beyond the economy. The function of the state, in whatever form, was ultimately to serve that liberation.

Believing that he was following workers in their pursuit of a "dream of a better world . . . and remoulding of the scheme of things," Gleason, like Cohn, turned from politics to workers' education: "Labor education . . . is training in the science of reconstruction. It is means to the liberating of the working class, individually and collectively."[99] The process would be gradual. Humans in a natural state, or exploited and indoctrinated by laissez-faire capitalism, generally had a hard time living together freely. Thus, individuals and communities would have to grow beyond their natural or acquired selfishness, progressing toward civility and conviviality, learning the arts of freedom and the skills necessary to express them in community. This was the purpose of worker control and the substance of human progress.[100]

Reporting on programs throughout America, and quoting extensively from his original research, Gleason concluded that after taking care of business, training union leaders and organizers, worker education's primary object had emerged as "community building—[teaching people] how to live together . . . a social and civic education. . . . Education is the effort of the soul to find a true expression or interpretation of experience, and to find it, not alone, but with the help of others, fellow-students."[101]

He observed that workers' education had rejected the educational principles of the capitalist system. Its purpose "is emphatically not . . . to lift workers into the middle class."[102] He offered as evidence statements from the Workers' College of Seattle: "Education in our universities and colleges is essentially capitalistic, in that it glorifies competition. . . . Education that may properly be called labor education is essentially socialistic, in that it glorifies cooperation."[103] Gleason, like Cohn, expected that the essence of socialism, the subordination of economics to societal ends and values, would be realized through craft unionism's crusade for shorter hours and developed through its educational initiatives rather than through a change in the form of American government. For Gleason, Gompers's observation that "eight hours is the cry which can unite all forces" seemed as relevant for the 1920s as it did for the 1880s.[104]

Moreover, the differences between workers' expectations about their education and most middle-class views were obvious. The differences had already created friction in the classrooms: "The miner and railwayman, adult and having knowledge of life, would not submit to the autocracy of orthodox teachers. A 'grown man' or woman will not sit silently each week for several years while a lecturer or an orator holds the platform."[105]

Demanding an active voice in their education, "the miner and railwayman" had forced their schools to reinstate the "correct *method* of teaching . . . , [the] Socratic . . . question and answer discussion." Workers' classrooms were places of active, often boisterous learning, in marked contrast to the passivity demanded by most schools and commercial amusements. As a consequence, good teachers had proved hard to find. Most teachers who had shown up, dogmatic, "bearded professors" and patronizing young tutors, taught their subject as they always had, didactically by lecture and by set assignments and examinations. These soon left, disillusioned and discouraged. Those who persevered learned the "correct method" on the job. They learned to give a clear, simple exposition of their subject and then to "suffer heckling gladly and call out group discussion." Such teachers were successful because of temperament, certainly not by training. They exhibited a "type . . . of humble minded scholarship set in charming democratic personality." They joined with those they taught in "the effort of the soul to find a true expression or interpretation of experience, and to find it . . . with the help of others."[106] Successful teachers were willing to be taught by their students that their job was

> to walk humbly into that new world of experience, conditions and ideas, to be more concerned with discovery than exhortation, more concerned with the definition and interpretation of labor to itself than with the superimposition of his learning or his policy . . . revealing by discussion what the workers want.[107]

However, workers' education faced the serious problem of uninterested workers. Workers were attracted to "mass entertainments," spectacles, and the "commercialized show," which, like most public schools, distracted workers from their struggle with the capitalist world and their desire to leave it, encouraging passive acceptance rather than active engagement and resistance.[108] Labor educators had to learn to compete on the same level, advertising and promoting what they had to offer, providing inducements—using tricks if necessary:

> A third object of workers' education is to reach the rank and file [as yet unawakened] with education for the love of it, with semi-entertainment with a cultural slant. . . . Various devices for stirring desire for education will be used. Bribes and lures will be applied. . . . Three-quarters of the time will be used in attracting people. The other quarter will contain some bit of information. [Thus] . . . education by mass semi-entertainment will contribute to solidarity and enthusiasm.[109]

In his reporting on workers' education programs across America, Gleason found that most were offering some form of participatory "social or civic education," including courses in history, economics, and literature. Most programs also recognized the connection between the need for workers' education and shorter work hours. Typically, the preamble to the constitution of the Trade Union College of Washington, D.C., stated that the goal of the trade union movement was to provide members "with sufficient leisure in which to develop their social, moral and intellectual faculties as well as the advantages, benefits and pleasures of mutual association," and it concluded that the college's primary responsibilities were to assist that development and provide for that association.[110]

Other programs articulated the vision of a "new social order" even while disavowing labor's radicalism. In its promotional literature, Brookwood Resident Workers' College in Katonah, New York, stressed that it did not intend "to educate workers out of their class," but it also stated:

> Save for the fact that it stands for a new and *better order, motivated by social values rather than pecuniary ones,* Brookwood is not a propagandist institution . . . activities are also organized so as to help to a full appreciation of the fine things in music, art, and letters, especially the drama. One of the significant features at Brookwood, is the community [teachers and students] living together which itself presents and offers opportunity to work out the problems of democracy as they arise from day to day.[111]

The "cultural side of life" was featured prominently at Brookwood. In addition to the above list, courses in English and literature were popular because they "taught the art of self expression," building skills necessary for the "community living" that was central to its mission. Gleason concluded in 1921 that approximately ten thousand workers were "studying with some regularity" in workers' education classes around the nation.[112]

Workers' Education Bureau

In 1921 an impressive gathering of laborites and their supporters, including Fannia Cohn, Arthur Gleason, Charles and Mary Beard, Joseph Schlossberg, and Broadus Mitchell, created the Workers' Education Bureau (WEB), a national "clearing-house for workers' education enterprises."[113] As it developed through the 1920s, WEB followed Gleason's movement away from socialism. A condition of AFL's support ($50,000 by 1925) of the bureau was that it publicly disavow connections with radical causes.[114] To mollify the AFL and Samuel Gompers, Spencer Miller, WEB secretary, issued a statement that "the bureau has no relation, support, or affiliation with the Socialist Party of America" and would not support any "form of propaganda": "[WEB] is not interested in teaching people what to think, but how to think."[115] The AFL also pressured the bureau to withdraw support from left-wing and progressive labor colleges. In 1925 the *New York Times* reported that during its convention WEB "went out of its way to prove it would have nothing to do with radicalism."[116] The same year, the paper reported that nearly all WEB officers "hold positions under the AFL, the prevailing policy of which is avowedly capitalistic." Hence, "the movement is sincerely educational."[117]

Nevertheless, in somewhat cryptic fashion, the *Times* reporter concluded that labor and WEB were engaging "in class struggle as intense as that proposed by the theoretical and utopian socialist" and that "it is possible that education may lead . . . to a more severe class struggle."[118]

Soon after it formed, WEB began publication of a set of books, the Workers' Bookshelf. Designed to be used by workers' education classes as "an outline" that would be continually revised as students provided feedback and criticism, the books provide a clue to understanding the kind of nonradical, "severe class struggle" the *New York Times* detected. The editors of the books pledged that the set would not follow the capitalist educational model, containing neither "vocational guidance" nor "short cuts to material success."[119] The first book in the series was written by Alfred Sheffield, professor of rhetoric at Wellesley College and instructor at the Boston Trade Union College. Published in 1922, *Joining in Public Discussion* was designed to be a manual for conducting classes in the kinds of democratic education that Cohn and Gleason envisioned but remains today as a practical guidebook to deliberative democracy.

Sheffield insisted that the "first move" for both teacher and student

> is to turn one's thought outward from one's self to the group of people among whom one is to speak. This takes an effort of will. He must begin by mastering the technique of *discussion*—by which the whole group is maneuvered into co-operative thinking and speaking. *The real technicians of modern democracy are those who win insight into the forces of thought and feeling that can be touched into activity when people sit down together.* The student of discussion, therefore, should picture a deliberative

meeting as a sort of field of magnetic forces wherein his mind can con-
spire with other minds to organize socially advantageous currents. His
speaking is ideally influential when it precipitates a general mood to create an understanding.[120]

Some educational professionals had criticized this Socratic, participatory
method of teaching, claiming that "experts . . . the ablest minds" had to be involved in the classroom. But Sheffield insisted:

> Any solution of a controversy which is really to prevail in a practical
> sense must get from the group something more than a majority assent.
> It must take up into itself most of the emotional forces that have centered
> in the differing ideas represented in the group. Otherwise the solution
> will embody ideas that are charged with the *action-tendencies* only of the
> experts—not of the whole group that is to carry it out. Group thinking
> pools the ideas of all for the inspiration of each.[121]

A new breed of experts, "real technicians of modern democracy," was
needed to teach the importance of "group thinking," as well as the skills of
conversation and discourse essential for such intersubjectivity. A "student of
discussion" was important in the construction of authentic working-class communities.[122] Sheffield explained that the "more severe class struggle," which the
New York Times reporter would detect in 1925, would issue from a democratic
culture in which cultural "experts" and "professionals" lost their class dominance and, with Gleason's instructors, "walk[ed] humbly into that new world of
experience . . . as servants of the working classes."[123]

Ira Steward and the Advent of the New Needs, "Wisdom and Love"

Historians have long recognized Ira Steward as one of the most important the-
oreticians of the labor movement. He is frequently credited with being among
the first to notice that, as people became better off and were able to meet their
most pressing material needs, with more money and increased leisure they
naturally develop new needs and desires. Shorter hours and higher wages thus
facilitate the entrepreneur's job of providing the new goods and services necessary for continual economic growth. In short, additional leisure helps increase
consumption and raise wages. Thus, the old fear of, or hope for, abundance
(economic maturity) was unfounded.

However, read carefully, Steward's texts reveal that he anticipated Cohn,
Gleason, and Sheffield's deliberative democracy more than he helped found the
modern faith in perpetual work and everlasting economic growth. At the beginning of his famous 1865 tract, Steward argued that workers with additional

leisure would "have time to cultivate tastes and create wants *in addition to mere physical comforts.*"[124] Immediately following, he enumerated the "wants" that were being repressed by long hours: reading newspapers and books, visiting and entertaining at home, writing letters, voting, cultivating flowers, walking with the family, taking baths, going to meetings, and enjoying "works of art." His first list of new "needs" were *social*, "time-intensive" activities—things done freely in leisure with a minimum of expense.

Such new social experiences then acted as spurs, prodding people to want better clothes and houses and in general to want the economic goods others enjoyed: "Give the masses time to come together and they cannot be kept apart; for man is a social being; and when they come together expenses multiply, because the inferior will struggle to imitate the superior in many things which cost. To see is to desire."[125] However, imitation was not limited to "things which cost." Additional leisure also allowed workers "to attend an evening concert, which adds a little to the expense, but much to the enjoyment of the family. The Smiths' and Jones' 'and everybody' are going, 'and who wants to be different from everybody else.'"[126]

That most people would eventually be able to afford the luxuries then reserved to the rich seemed improbable at the time—as unlikely as the hope that humans would learn to live together cordially, taking increasingly active parts in the construction of their cultures. Nevertheless, Steward argued, "humane and moral progress,"[127] like economic progress, would be driven by pride and the "inexorable law of self-interest":[128]

> Men who are governed only by their pride, are low indeed; but those who have no pride at all, are very much lower. We must take human nature as we find it; hoping and believing that the era of *personal* display will be succeeded by one of mental and moral accomplishments.[129]

Initially, desires for "things that cost" and "mental and moral accomplishments" would grow together—progress was not confined to the one or the other. Eventually, though, an era of "mental and moral accomplishments" and "progress in the Arts and Sciences" would emerge from the chrysalis of "personal display," "self-interest," and "pride": "Leisure is *still more* necessary, to supply some ... motives [for material goods] which [workers] can appreciate and *will struggle for*, until educated up to an interest in matters of real importance."[130]

Writing for Steward, George Gunton concluded:

> The progress of mental and moral development and of social, religious, and political freedom are the consequence of, and therefore commensurate with, the permanent increase in the consumption of wealth per capita of the laboring population—we have a right to expect, with such a permanent rise in the general rate of real wages, to find a higher standard of intelligence and general culture, and a greater degree of political power

among the masses. . . . Leisure, therefore, may be defined as unemployed time capable of being devoted to industrial and social, and, therefore, intellectual and moral, improvement.[131]

Steward ended his tract on "the meaning of the eight hour movement" with a prediction that the six-hour day would follow the eight-hour day "within ten years," declaring in Whitmanesque fashion that, as a result, "the Nation will engage in the peaceful discussion of its moral and material problems. The great people, no longer in vassalage to the 'Money-power' of our Age, will move on and on, higher and still higher, illuminating the whole earth, with their Wisdom and Love."[132]

5

Infrastructures of Freedom

> And thou America . . .
> Whatever else withheld withhold not from us
> Belief in plan of Thee enclosed in Time and Space
> —WALT WHITMAN, quoted in Frank Lloyd Wright,
> *When Democracy Builds*[1]

More than thirty years after its publication, Daniel Rodgers's book *The Work Ethic in Industrial America, 1850–1920* remains one of the best accounts of work attitudes in the United States. He, and James Gilbert in *Work without Salvation*, described a crisis that occurred during the last decades of the nineteenth century: a period of dissolution in which the "work ethic," a traditional amalgam of cultural values and republican virtues (independence, self-reliance, control, creativity, self-expression, and social mobility) rapidly eroded in the onrush of technology. Whereas the "industrial economy was in large part a creature of the intense regional faith in the worth of labor," the advent of the assembly line and new, more efficient machines created jobs that were deskilled, monotonous, and far from ideal, sparking debate about how best to reform modern work—the Arts and Crafts movement being one of the more noteworthy responses.[2] However, Rodgers observed that, rather than trying to save work by somehow restoring work's lost virtues,

> most critics of industrial monotony came to a far simpler answer: if modern industrial work was soulless, then men should do less of it. . . . [By the early twentieth century] a sizable number of Northern Protestant moralists had begun to argue that it was not in self-discipline that a man's spiritual essence was revealed but in the free, spontaneous activity of play.[3]

Observing further that "the critics of routinized work turned at last toward leisure," Rodgers provided accounts of such critics as Henry Ward Beecher, Albert Bushnell, Joseph Lee, and Simon Patten who, beginning to doubt the traditional faith in work, mounted a modern defense of leisure.[4] He also included individuals and groups, such as Harvard's Charles Eliot and some within the

Arts and Crafts movement, that tried to mitigate the crisis at fin de siècle by affirming work as life's center and rejecting the leisure alternative. However, Rodgers concluded, "In the end, the most significant shift of the industrial age was . . . the increasing frequency with which the moralists demoted work from an essential to an instrumental virtue."[5]

Some would argue (see Chapter 2) that the work ethic had been difficult to support even during its formative period (before 1850) and that it was only the promise of continuing work reductions that made its widespread acceptance possible. Throughout the nineteenth century, work's perfection was most often seen, particularly among workers, in its eventual subordination to the rest of life—when those things necessary to live were fully supplied by industrial progress.[6] Long before the waxing of factory and machine production in the United States in the second half of the nineteenth century, what Sean Wilentz called the "bastard system" of production largely replaced the virtuous artisanal workshop, forcing workers to look to their free time to find virtue and express values such as craftsmanship and community.[7]

One may also argue that the peculiar twentieth-century, *secular* "work ethic," devoid of the promise of gradual liberation from the marketplace, standing alone outside traditional religious contexts and beyond republican virtue, was an invention of middle-class businessmen and professionals responding to crises that work and the work ethic experienced during the late nineteenth and twentieth centuries. From the beginning of the industrial age, the belief that work in its modern incarnations should be the center of human existence has been difficult to promote and sustain.[8]

While one may take issue with Rodgers about the timing of the "turn[] . . . toward leisure," his seminal book may also be read as an invitation to continue his investigations. During the early decades of the twentieth century, individuals and groups began not only to talk and write about the promise of leisure; they began to build infrastructures of freedom: free, public places for the newly freed time, such as parks, community centers, community theaters, playgrounds, libraries, museums, and sports fields and arenas. Frank Lloyd Wright was one of the most influential individuals who, fitting Rodgers's pattern perfectly, "turned . . . toward leisure" at the beginning of the twentieth century and devoted his life to building for that new freedom.

Frank Lloyd Wright: "Belief in Plan of Thee Enclosed in Time and Space"

"The Art and Craft of the Machine" was Frank Lloyd Wright's first attempt to make his vision a coherent and, as he would have called it, an "organic" whole.[9] It was an essay that he would return to time and again, revising parts but keeping the central message intact.[10] His uncle, Jenkin Lloyd Jones, a Unitarian minister and a leader of the welfare work being done in Chicago at the time, introduced Wright to Jane Addams and Hull House.[11] Wright became active in that center of reform and was asked to speak there to the Chicago Arts and Crafts Society on March 6, 1901.

Wright used the opportunity to respond to the Arts and Crafts movement, which was making considerable headway in the United States at the time. Conceived in England by John Ruskin and William Morris among others and championed in the United States by Gustav Stickley and the Chicago group, the movement had been designed primarily to reform British society and improve working conditions.[12] However, in the United States the movement's leaders were concerned that a democratic base be established and a democratic purpose served. One issue that troubled Americans was that the products of the arts and crafts shops in England were expensive. Craftsmen were able once again to be creative and take delight in their work but found themselves working once again for the rich—a troubling regression to servant classes and feudal practices.[13] Americans were also wary of the British lack of appreciation for what the entrepreneur, machines, and factories could do: produce satisfactory if not excellent things cheaply for those who were not rich. Moreover, the socialist agenda of people such as William Morris concerned many leaders in the United States, among them Frank Lloyd Wright.

Wright began his essay by invoking his version of the American dream: "As we work along our various ways, there takes shape within us, in some sort, an ideal—something we are to become. . . . This, I think, is denied to very few, and we begin really to live only when the thrill of this ideality moves us in what we will to accomplish!"[14]

His experience as a youth on the Lloyd Jones farm in Wisconsin and as an architect in Chicago had taught him that the "the Machine" was not the threat to the craftsmen and artists that some in the Arts and Crafts movement feared. Rather, he held "a gradually deepening conviction that in the Machine lies the only future of art and craft—as I believe, a glorious future . . . higher than the world has yet seen!" William Morris and his "disciples . . . cling to an opposite view." They had rightly protested "the Machine" in Britain because selfishness and greed had "usurped it and made of it a terrible engine of enslavement." But they had not yet recognized its potential. In America technological progress had advanced to the point that the Machine, taken firmly in hand, would be able to "undo the mischief it has made" and become the "great forerunner of democracy."[15]

Certainly the outlook for artist and craftsman looked bleak. They seemed to be caught in the dilemma of either "catering to the leisure class of old England or [being] ground beneath the heel of commercial abuse here in the great West." Many were beginning to retreat to Paris and to cynicism, removing themselves from the realities of the modern world and the lives of ordinary people. In their self-absorbed nihilism they sought to "combat the hell-smoke of the factories they scorn to understand," with little success.[16]

The disaffected artist needed to appreciate that the Machine had the potential to free as well as enslave. Throughout history, humans had managed to use what "tools and contrivances" they created to save "the most precious thing in the world—human effort." Through the ages, the time that tools had freed had been used to build civilization and create culture and art. During the Classical Age, the Greeks had used women and slaves this way—as an "essential tool of . . . art and civilization."[17]

But humans were not tools. Their function was not to serve as a means to other ends. They were ends in themselves. Fortunately, science and modern technology had the potential to free every man and woman to live in a true democracy in which all could claim the right to create beauty and practice their culture. The modern artist and craftsman had to recognize that

> the Machine is Intellect mastering the drudgery of earth that the plastic art may live; that the margin of leisure and strength by which man's life upon the earth can be made beautiful, may immeasurably widen; its function ultimately to emancipate human expression![18]

The "poor . . . side-tracked" American artist needed to return from self-imposed exile and enter the fray. Artists, more than any other group, had the potential to lead the nation with imagination and vision, if only they would realize that the Machine could become "a universal educator, surely raising the level of human intelligence, so carrying within itself the power to destroy, by its own momentum, the greed which in Morris's time and still in our own time turns it to a deadly engine of enslavement."[19]

The Machine marked a great divide between "the Art of old and the Art to come." Because it "frees human labor, lengthens and broadens the life of the simplest man," the Machine had established the foundation for "the Democracy upon which we insist."[20] Arts and crafts by and for the people were sure to eclipse the "art of feudalism." The artists of Wright's generation had the rare and precious opportunity to lead the way to "a new aesthetic . . . a new idea of what constitutes 'profit'; a new idea of what constitutes Success; a new idea of what constitutes luxury."[21]

Wright pledged to use such an opportunity to harness the Machine to architecture, using industry's new building tools and modern plastic materials to represent the process by which technology was freeing humans, his buildings then standing as metaphors of a historical process he thought perfectly obvious. Humans were gaining mastery over the natural world with their tools. They now had the opportunity to free themselves in the time and spaces in which they lived and moved. Buildings that freed more than they confined would stand as signs and emblems for the loosening of the chains of necessity that the Machine was making possible—a release that was taking the very real form of expanding leisure for all to do whatsoever the human spirit fancied.

Wright's buildings came to embody in their free spaces his "ideal": the "Art of Democracy," the "plan of Thee enclosed in Time and Space," the original American dream:

The new [architecture] will weave for the necessities of mankind, which his Machine will have mastered, a robe of ideality no less truthful, but more poetical, with a rational freedom made possible by the machine, beside which the art of old will be as the sweet, plaintive wail of the pipe to the outpouring of full orchestra. It will clothe Necessity with the living flesh of virile imagination, as the living flesh lends living grace to the hard and bony human skeleton. The new will pass from the possession of kings and classes to the every-day lives of all.[22]

But men and women would have to make the choice. The immediate danger was that in their ignorance they were rejecting freedom, voluntarily returning (or being lured) to slavery in the cities and to the artistic forms of the feudal past. Contrasted with Wright's architecture of freedom, the modern city and skyscraper represented the new slavery. Like cages, the city and skyscraper confined and crowded people, making movement difficult. Those who owned the buildings exploited the "wage slaves," charging rent on land, money, and the means of production. More interested in continuing to enslave their fellows than freeing them, they lived as parasites on those who actually produced wealth, depending on the "unearned increments" of land values, speculation, and deceitful trading to maintain their power.[23]

Wright concluded "The Art and Craft of the Machine" with a challenge to artists and craftsmen to lead the way to the American dream by finding practical ways

to alleviate the insensate numbness of the poor fellow out in the cold, hard shops . . . [by helping him adjust] to a true sense of his importance as a factor in society, though he does tend a machine. Teach him that the machine is his best friend—will have widened the margin of his leisure until enlightenment shall bring him a further sense of the *magnificent ground plan of progress* in which he too justly plays his significant part. If the art of the Greek, produced at such cost of human life, was so noble and enduring, what limit dare we now imagine to an Art based upon an adequate life for the individual? The machine is his! In due time it will come to him![24]

One of the most important of Wright's elaborations of the "American Ideal," and his most controversial contribution to city planning, was Broadacre City.[25] Wright introduced the concept in *The Disappearing City*, a book published in 1932 and twice revised, as *When Democracy Builds* in 1945 and as *The Living City* in 1958.[26]

Bruce Brooks Pfeiffer called two of the Kahn Lectures that Wright delivered at Princeton University in 1930 "prophetic of his vision for city planning . . . that would materialize . . . as Broadacre City."[27] In the last of the Kahn Lectures, "The City," Wright reiterated that the machine was poised to assume all the burdens of "living on this earth. The margin of leisure even now widens as the machine succeeds. . . . The margin should be expanded and devoted to making beautiful the environment in which human beings are born to live, into which one brings the children."[28]

For Wright, the only proper place to live out leisure's new freedom would be in the country. It would be increasingly possible for all to experience "the sense of freedom in space" as automobiles allowed populations to disperse, following the "horizontal line . . . of domesticity, the earthline of human life" and allowing the freedom the city had taken away with its verticality. The "realm of freedom" and the realm of the "simply utilitarian" would naturally divide, following the clear division of leisure from work, the countryside from capitalist city and market. The city would be "invaded at ten o'clock, abandoned at four, for three days of the week. The other four days . . . will be devoted to the more or less joyful matter of living elsewhere under conditions natural to man."[29] Work in the city would be a kind of time tax that would pay for all the necessities of life, allowing progressively more of human existence to become "a festival of life."[30]

Broadacre City was as much metaphor as it was a utopian dream. Like his houses, Broadacre City represented in three-dimensional space the opening "realm of freedom" that Wright envisioned for his nation. Wright conceded that Broadacre City was a remote possibility. But for him, like Whitman, the important question was commitment and vision:

> The question that is important however, is: do we have it in our own hearts as it is written in our constitutional charter to be free? Is it sincerely and passionately our ideal to be free? Notwithstanding so much cowardly advice to the contrary, I say it is our ideal. Those highest in the realm of freedom should build suitable buildings . . . for that spirit first, and for America to ponder.[31]

Organic Architecture: A New Relation to the Natural World

Wright is probably best known for Fallingwater in rural southwestern Pennsylvania and other such buildings that seem to grow out of their natural settings. He learned the guiding principle of organic architecture from Louis Sullivan, a principle that is still remembered by schoolchildren: "form follows function." After leaving Chicago's skyscrapers and Sullivan's shop, Wright determined to build on a smaller scale, proportionate to the individual. So he turned to consider human function.[32]

"Function" served much the same purpose for Wright that Aristotle's questions about causality (means and ends) did for Robert Maynard Hutchins: it led him to consider the purpose of his profession and then to the possibility of a self-contained, intrinsically satisfying condition or activity—a final cause. Obviously, unlike machines and other animals, humans claimed a higher function than obedience or simply filling their bellies. Humans were not robots. In fact, it was their function to determine function. They decided where to go and what to do when they got there—they defined progress. The human function was freedom.

Such a function entailed thought and imagination about what might be— even about what should be. Such a function entailed purpose: a dream or ideal. Therefore, architecture that obeyed the laws of simplicity and organic construction on a human scale would create forms that followed: buildings that served and expressed human freedom, opening options and facilitating creativity for those who lived there.[33] Wright concluded, "Organic Architecture does reinterpret and can construct an eternal Idea of human Freedom."[34]

Wright offered the example of working with wood to illustrate the principle of organic architecture. Craftsmen had been using new technologies to work against the nature of wood, creating "meaningless elaborations"—carvings and decorations that obscured wood's natural colors, grains, and forms. Rightly employed, the Machine "by its wonderful cutting, shaping, smoothing, and repetitive capacity, has made it possible . . . [to] bring out the beauty of wood . . . to so use it . . . that the poor as well as the rich may enjoy to-day beautiful surface treatments of clean, strong forms that the branch veneers of Sheraton and Chippendale only hinted at."[35]

Just as the Machine had made it possible to "wipe out the mass of meaningless torture to which wood has been subjected . . . [emancipating the] beauties of nature in wood," so it might also "wipe out the mass of meaningless torture to which mankind . . . has been more or less subjected since time began." Architecture could "bring out the beauty" of humans by accentuating the grain of human nature: the freedom to move, imagine, create, and find community.

Wright's organic architecture also suggested a new relation with the natural world based on conservation and appreciation rather than the perpetual struggle to control, dominate, and exploit.[36] His Broadacre City metaphor offered such a possibility:

> Great woods, fields, streams, mountains, ranges of hills, the wind-blown sweep of plains, all brought into the service of Man without doing violence to them, Man reconciled to their service, proud of preserving their Beauty. Citizens now, who understand, revere, and conserve all natural resources whether of Materials or Men. This—to me—is Organic Architecture![37]

In Wright's American dream, "man is now to be less separated from nature."[38] Living in harmony, sympathy, and accord with the natural world, individuals would experience a homecoming, a return to the Garden as nature's husband. Returning again to the land after having tamed nature in the city with machines, humans could reenter the natural world to enjoy it:

> Freedom? Yes. . . . The machine thus comprehended and controlled would succeed for the man himself and widen the margin of leisure increasingly

to be spent in a field, on the streams . . . or in the wood: (the wild) so easily reached. . . . [Humans would have access] to a greater natural beauty and enjoy the freer life we could honestly call Democratic. True culture must grow up with the ground [in places where] Man is *with* his own ground and not merely a parasite either upon it or away from it—only then will indigenous culture come to us as a Nation.[39]

One of the ways to "grow up with the ground" and one of the most rewarding leisure activities would be building one's own home, in tune with the natural world—a simple and direct expression of the organic, democratic culture Wright envisioned. Writing during the last years of his life and using a new term for his American dream, the "Usonian Vision," Wright described the home of everyman and everywoman as more than just a necessity. Certainly shelter was essential; indeed shelter was a "primeval instinct."[40] However, humans could use their new freedom to transfigure a house into a home: "More than a convenience . . . I see it as a modern sanctuary." Moreover, "by devotion to machinery a few hours a day he should get his house where he wants it."[41]

Earlier he had explained that the assembly line could do for homes what it had done for automobiles—make them affordable for most people. Prefabricated components, "units," could be manufactured in factories cheaply and delivered piecemeal to an inexpensive home site in the country. If "the Machine is really allowed to work for the Poor and not kept working to keep the Poor poor," they would not have to mortgage decades of their lives to own their homes or pay rent their whole lives. Instead, they could turn to the more intrinsically rewarding leisure activity of constructing their own dwellings. If the Machine were put to work for the individual, "his rent for three months in city bondage [at his job] buys him the first units of his home." From then on he could live on his new, small estate, saving the "rents" he would have paid to mortgages or landlords. In "a year or two . . . 'the poor' might own a house at least comfortably home-worthy, fairly staunch, and pretty complete."[42] Such homes might then grow in their natural setting. Owners might continue to build in tune with the nature, using natural materials available on their land and consulting designs made freely available by the best architects in the country, architects who, like Wright, were eager to serve the promise of building in and for freedom.

New, Free Human Relations

Like Walt Whitman, Wright believed that humans were by nature social creatures. Given the right circumstances, a democratic constitutional government, and a reasonable livelihood, humans would naturally find outlets for the "get-together-instinct." Being free in leisure, individuals would naturally congregate. Just as humans might find new, free ways of relating to nature, they would learn convivial ways of being together outside the competitive worlds of work and the marketplace. The home would be the starting place where free activities joined individuals together in ways that "the city" could only imitate. Moving beyond the home, humans would naturally "gratify . . . the get-together-instinct of the community," enjoying outdoor recreation together in "mountains, seasides, prairies, forests." Government might help by providing leisure services and public "recreation grounds": a "planetarium, the race track . . . concert hall . . . theatre, museums, and art galleries."[43]

Moreover, creative activities and artistic "work" would be available to more and more people. The Machine was out of control in the modern city. While it was freeing humans from toil into leisure, it was also preventing them from enjoying intrinsically rewarding kinds of expression in a process some have called "commoditization":

> The resources of the human spirit become purchasable and . . . life itself becomes purchasable. The people have sought a replica [for art and creativity]. They found that they have bought a substitute. The merchant has become the ruler for the time being of man's singing, dancing, dwelling and breeding.[44]

Moreover, modern work had "gone terribly wrong . . . because it has been made a speculative commodity." Only free productive effort, such as the construction of one's own home, done outside the city—outside the capitalist arena of complete utility—might combine intrinsic joy with extrinsic purpose; only in the "realm of freedom," when people were liberated from jobs and paychecks, would the divisions of work and leisure disappear and democratic, expressive culture appear.[45] Sharing leisure activities and artistic "work," communities that were dissolving in the city would be reconstituted in the country in the spaces and times liberated from exploitation.[46]

Government

Government needed to exert only minimal control over the "realm of freedom," providing a modicum of police protection.[47] Wright suggested that most crime was a function of irrationality and greed—of humans piled on top of each other in cities, exploited and re-enslaved by technology.[48] Critics have often characterized such views as "shallow" and anarchistic.[49] Paul E. Corcoran objected to Wright's views about limited government, concluding that his

> shallow defenses of individual liberty . . . meant leisure time, a commodious private dwelling, recreation, and material abundance. . . . Wright's anarchist conception of freedom is implied in his view that proper planning would make government both remote and irrelevant.[50]

However, Wright's political views are best described as those of a "Jeffersonian-type laissez-fare democrat" mixed with those of a prairie Populist, rather than those of an anarchist or twentieth-first-century conservative.[51] Moreover, his hope for a renewed contact with the natural world was grounded by the reality of modern machines that made abundant leisure possible, not in a "shallow" desire to return to a preindustrial, agrarian America.

Wright believed that fascist Italy, Germany, and communist Russia, together with the capitalist countries, had dramatically increased "social organization" during the depression and the world wars. Corporations and governments around the world were busy regimenting people. The individual personality was being defeated and with it the possibilities of democratic culture and reconstituted communities.[52] Centralization and government control made sense for some parts of the economy: "In some fields in industry, transportation, and public utilities, government ownership and controls are probably the most feasible method of correction of those evils [of] . . . industry's anti-social tendencies."[53] But otherwise,

> highly organized society . . . is a disintegrating influence on persons . . . [moving all] towards impersonal ends. It gains in power and fluidity at the person's expense. . . . The socialist assumption that centralization in all fields is itself the natural and best pattern of economic and social life is by no means justified.[54]

Wright's view that government should become increasingly "remote and irrelevant" was the logical outcome of his hope that the "realm of freedom" would continue to expand. As the Machine provided humans with basic necessities, they might simply choose to leave the economy, abandoning the city after eighteen hours of necessary work each week to live on their own, beyond the reach of "White-collarites"—including government bureaucrats, politicians, "professionals," admen, and the "big boys" of finance and industry: "We may now dream of a time when there will be less government, yet more ordered freedom. . . . The Machine will then have become the Liberator of Human Life. And our Architecture will reflect this."[55]

The power of the state and corporations would be increasingly irrelevant as more people chose to spend more of their lives elsewhere. Wright reasoned that individuals would have to "build a new world" on their own, largely independent of the state. The key to reform would be a "reawakening of popular consciousness brought about by the development of an organic culture."[56]

Certainly, government had responsibilities other than assuring everyone the basic, constitutionally guaranteed freedoms. One of the state's main functions, like the architect's, would be to support the emerging realm of freedom. Provision of public spaces and programs serving the new freedom would continue to be important as the American ideal emerged. One of the best ways that government might be of service was to guarantee everyone at least an acre of land as their inalienable birthright. Free in their own space, individuals might live independent of marketplace as well as government and so reconstruct their lives in families and communities in close contact with nature:

> The man of our country will thus make his own way, and *grow* to the natural place thus due him, promised—yes, promised by our charter, the Declaration of Independence. But this place of his is not to be made over to fit him by reform . . . [but] will become his by his own use of the means at hand. He must himself build a new world. The day of the individual is not over—instead, it is just about to begin. The machine does not write the doom of liberty, but is waiting at man's hand as a peerless tool, for him to use to put foundations beneath a genuine democracy. Then the machine may conquer human drudgery to some purpose, taking it upon itself to broaden, lengthen, strengthen, and deepen the life of the simplest man.[57]

In 1951, eight years before he died, Wright was shown around an exhibit of his works at Gimbels department store in Philadelphia. The retrospective, "Sixty Years of Living Architecture," featured a scale model of Broadacre City, Wright's lifelong vision rendered in plaster of paris and balsa wood. Afterward, Oskar Stonorov, a Philadelphia architect and coordinator of the exhibition, interviewed Wright, who restated the fundamentals of his vision:

> Waste of time and life is here, in Broadacre City, ended in favor of a better use of life to understand ourselves and to cultivate leisure in the enjoyment of our own nature. That is the modern opportunity given to us by the machine and must be the aim of culture in our democracy if we ever reach that state as organic.[58]

Wright often remarked about the continuity of the vision that he realized he shared with Whitman and others.[59] He did so again, a year before he died, in the concluding pages of *The Living City*.[60] Asking, "Does 'The Art and Craft of the Machine,' the paper first read at Hull House . . . seem to suffer contradiction here?" He answered, "No. I then dreaded the machine unless well in the hand of the creative artist."[61] In what was to be the final year of his life, Wright described the hope that inspired him when he was starting out—that modern technology would free humans to express and develop the "Higher human faculties," bringing to fruition the original American dream—his "Usonian Vision."[62]

However, at the end, Wright's hope, like Whitman's, had become desperate. More than ever, he feared that the dream was being neglected and forgotten. The power of the machine and the machinations of powerful, selfish people in corporations, professions, and government were choking the growth of freedom and might finally destroy the promise of democracy. Observing, "We are imprisoned. . . . [N]ovelty is mistaken for progress," he asked, "What of Real Sun, Real Air, Real Leisure?" finally lamenting, "The Machine is running away."[63]

Infrastructures of Freedom: Community Theaters

Wright's contemporary Percy MacKaye devoted his life to building the theater to serve America's growing free time. MacKaye, with Wright, attempted to make it possible for all to find community beyond the marketplace and its "instrumental rationality" by constructing an alternative arena of "rational action," for what Jürgen Habermas called "dramaturgical action."[64] Son of the actor, impresario, and playwright Steele MacKaye, one of the best-known figures of late nineteenth-century American theater, Percy MacKaye published *The Civic Theatre in Relation to the Redemption of Leisure* in 1912.[65] Following his "reforming crusader" father, whom he called a "new type of educator in the field of democratic culture," MacKaye set out to promote Higher Progress in "indigenous" American theater.[66]

Like Frank Lloyd Wright, MacKaye argued that in "the vocations of modern industry the divorce between joy and labor has become too absolute to reconcile."[67] He also recognized with Wright that "the machine will become [democracy's] ultimate salvation . . . by reducing to its minimum the time expended in all joyless labor, and by increasing to its maximum the time devotable to the imaginative labor of leisure." American workers had rightly raised a "cry and protest for shorter hours of industrial labor," so that in the "recreative labor of leisure . . . labor is again reconciled with joy."[68] The "recreative labor of leisure" was "the real goal of all the vast striving of our momentous age" and the definition of American progress. Millions had battled "desperately . . . to emancipate themselves" from joyless work and capitalism to liberate "the deepest instinct of humanity—the need for happiness": "No issue, political or industrial, before the people to-day exceeds in immediate importance, or prophetic meaning, the problem of public recreation."[69]

The Civic Theater and the Self-Government of Leisure

Alarmed by the continuation of what Whitman and Wright called "feudal culture"[70] and by the "amusement business'" exploitation of workers' leisure, MacKaye proposed that the civic theater, a new *public* and distinctly American institution just beginning to form, be nurtured and developed:

> The Civic Theatre idea, as a distinctive issue, implies the conscious awakening of a people to self-government in the activities of its leisure. To this end, organization of the arts of the theatre, participation by the people in these arts (not mere spectatorship) . . . [will open] a new and nobler scope for the art of the theatre itself. Involving, then, a new expression of democracy. . . . The Drama of Democracy . . . [involves] the vital principles of participation and self expression.[71]

Following his father's impresario lead, he set about drawing up blueprints for local civic theaters.[72] He envisioned a local umbrella organization, gathering all the "recreative arts of the community" together in one publicly supported facility. He proposed that the federal government create a "Bureau in Washington," similar to the recently organized U.S. Forest Service (his brother, Benton, was a pioneer in the Forest Service), to promote community building in the city based on active forms of recreation and "self-government" in leisure and to coordinate the public leisure infrastructure already forming: parks, forests, playgrounds, public libraries, museums, community centers, and the theater.[73]

In addition to the "amusement business," other threats remained. Leisure had become "the test of civilization." The nation could fail the test by sinking to commercial, passive, meaningless, and solitary amusements. It might also turn from leisure to embrace work as "an end instead of a means to life," as Wright also feared.[74] But MacKaye remained optimistic, seeing about him the "regeneration of leisure"—the flowering of amateurism in the "astonishing response" to "public music," pageantry, storytelling and local folk lore, arts and crafts, and outdoor recreation and theaters.[75]

MacKaye wrote, "Here, then, is a vista of the American theatre."[76] With Walt Whitman he insisted that all are born poets—all children take joy in their world and words.[77] Soon, however, the "serious" world of business intrudes, killing off nature's poets with demands to conform and consume and with unimaginative, joyless work: "Next, the killing out. The great mass, with no choice except between death and life, ply the vast loom of songless labor and unimaginative hope."[78]

The masses were left unfulfilled, their wonder, imagination, and exuberance withering, with no voice left and nowhere to turn. Surrounded by pretenders and self-promoters, a swarm of "parasites of true poetry: the dilettantes and the aesthetes," workers lost sight of freedom and found it increasingly difficult to imagine an alternative.[79]

But the true poet, like Whitman, recognized a great responsibility: "The poet is, perhaps, the most laborious of toilers," for he or she sees the necessity of building a democratic culture of participation, a civic theater, to provide everyone with opportunities to express the "greater joy, beauty, understanding" too long denied.[80] Reviewing MacKaye's book, Walter Lippmann, who shared MacKaye's views about the future of leisure and American progress for a brief while, wrote that "leisure will really find its redemption" only when "the chasm between the audience and the art" is bridged by "participation of the people instead of mere spectatorship."[81]

Community, University, and Outdoor Theaters

Percy MacKaye has long been acknowledged as one of the community theater movement's original inspirations. In the dedication of *Curtains Going Up*, Carl Glick (with MacKaye, a founder of the community theater movement) and A. McCleery called MacKaye "the Pioneer who pointed the way [to] a democratic theatre."[82] In several respects, the community theater movement parallels the parks and recreation movement; the MacKaye brothers, Benton the advocate of wilderness and Percy the founder of civic theater, represent the similarities. Both movements were spawned in part by the widespread expectation of the coming age of mass leisure. Both were developed as responses to the perceived need to build new public infrastructures for the new freedom. Both were founded on egalitarian concerns to democratize access to cultural and recreational resources. Both criticized commercial amusement for encouraging passive watching and effortless consumption and deliberately offered active forms of culture-making, civic engagement, and outdoor recreation.[83]

Following the publication of MacKaye's books, "little theatres" sprang up in North Dakota, Illinois, Wisconsin, and Iowa and then spread nationwide to California, North Carolina, and New York. In North Dakota, Alfred Arvold and Frederick Koch started what may have been the first community theaters in the country, attempting to dramatize the lives of living pioneers and develop an amateur, local basis for "indigenous" drama.[84] E. C. Mabie attempted a similar feat at the University of Iowa, supported in the state by people such as Carl Glick, who had established one of the first community theaters in the nation in Waterloo, Iowa, in 1916.[85] Robert Edward Gard founded the Wisconsin Rural Writers Association.[86] Paul Green exported the movement to North Carolina, where he wrote:

> For here to our hand, with the possible leisure which ever more and more perfect servant machines are providing for us, is the chance to create a culture, a joyous way of living, a vibrant idealism, the like of which has occurred perhaps only a few times in the history of the world. For it is mainly by the glory of its thoughts, its ideals, its imagination that a nation or an age is finally great.[87]

Otto H. Kahn, chairman of the Metropolitan Opera Company in the 1930s, explained why he was working with the Winchester County, New York, Recreation Commission and the community theater to create a regular opera season for the Met in White Plains: "I believe in decentralization in everything, in government, in business, and in art . . . in line with the community theatre." He noted, "It is from these [local] places that our real art will spring because people have . . . more time for contemplation, more leisure, more creative effort." Kahn proposed to "stimulate . . . local talent," observing that America is rich in talent: "It is latent everywhere, and we have but to encourage it."[88]

6

Labor and Franklin Delano Roosevelt's New Dream

Up until the beginning of World War II, organized labor and America's workingmen and workingwomen struggled to reduce their working hours. Even after the war and through the 1960s, labor pressed for the reform, continuing to fuel widespread expectations that an age of leisure would soon be a reality. Workers held fast to their traditional understanding that industrial progress meant higher wages and shorter hours. The Great Depression intensified speculation that the age of leisure was fast approaching.

The reasons given for shorter hours remained constant, with minor variations. In the place of British tyranny or Southern slavery, the image of the industrial robot came to symbolize the workers' plight. Even though progress had been made in reducing work time, the remaining hours were seen to be increasingly stressful. Modern machines and management continued to purge jobs of their nonproductive elements. Stress mingled with boredom in jobs that were so closely supervised that simple conversation was difficult; labor leaders and their supporters continued to complain of devitalized jobs.

Certainly, workers shared the widespread interest in improving jobs and making the workplace as pleasant as possible. Nevertheless, through mid-century, workers and labor leaders continued to see work's perfection in the "progressive shortening of the hours of labor," still resisting what Hannah Arendt called the "modern glorification of labor."[1] When work was decentered, made subordinate to the more important business of living, then would be the time to discuss whether work might become "glorious" and valuable in and for itself—worth "running to . . . as to a festival" as the utopian socialist Charles Fourier had predicted.[2]

Labor's vision of Higher Progress also persisted through mid-twentieth century. During the 1920s and 1930s, labor leaders reiterated and elaborated the century-long dream of liberation from capitalism's "selfish system." William Green, president of the American Federation of Labor during the second quarter of the twentieth century, summed up labor's position. Arguing that the "general mechanizing process" of industry threatened to overwhelm "our social and human values" and merge "the lives of workers . . . with the machine until they, too, become mechanical," Green maintained that "there must be a progressive shortening of the hours of labor . . . to safeguard our human nature . . . and thereby [lay] the foundation . . . for the higher development of spiritual and intellectual powers."[3]

With the Lowell mill women, Fannia Cohn, and generations of labor leaders who preceded him, Green predicted the "the dawn of a new era—leisure for all," a "revolution of living." "The leisured proletariat" was gaining access to "good music, the fine arts, literature, travel, and beauty in all guises." In such "cultural use of leisure . . . workers find themselves . . . sharing in the common life of the community" and becoming "heirs of knowledge and culture of past generations." The opportunities that work used to offer, such as craftsmanship, creativity, and purpose and meaning, were being recovered in freely chosen leisure activities; the family and community were being restored and reinvigorated.[4]

Green's agenda was in keeping with the resolution passed in 1926 by the Forty-Sixth Annual Meeting of the AFL:

> Whereas under present methods of modern machine industry the workers are continually subject to the strain of mechanized processes which sap their vitality, and;
> Whereas if compelled to work for long hours under modern processes of production, the vitality, health, and very life of workers are put in serious jeopardy;
> *Resolved*, that this convention place itself on record as favoring a progressive shortening of the hours of labor and the days per week and that the Executive Council be requested to inaugurate a campaign of education and organization to that end.[5]

A New Theory of Shorter Hours

Summing up what he understood to be the aspirations of union members, William Green concluded, "The human values of leisure are even greater than its economic significance."[6] This statement represented the beginning of a change in organized labor's eight-hour philosophy. Whereas up until the turn of the century labor leaders had maintained that shortening the hours of labor would, by constricting the labor supply, dry up labor surpluses (unemployment), drive up wages, and redistribute wealth, after World War I labor began to turn to a more conventional view of the economy. Samuel Gompers started to talk more about bigger pies and less about getting a bigger piece for labor. For whatever reason, perhaps labor's declining fortunes, in their conservative turn unions began to move toward labor-management cooperation in service to the larger goal of increased productivity.[7]

In 1926 the *New York Times* reported:

> Labor is making this latest demand [for wages and hours] on entirely new grounds. . . . The new labor theories . . . are an elaboration of the stand taken a year ago when, for the first time, the AF of L accepted joint responsibility for production and officially announced it was willing to cooperate with employers for greater output in return for a share of the accrued profits . . . the federation has made a definite concession in its philosophy. . . . There has been [since 1925] a definite acceptance of the fact that a shorter work week with the same wages can now come only by increasing the output per worker.[8]

In 1935 the prominent labor economist Harry A. Millis pointed out that labor had officially adopted the productivity theory of wages in 1925—a theory that, as the *New York Times* reported, included a productivity theory of shorter hours as an integral part.[9] Green and other labor leaders began to promote increased productivity as the essential wealth-producing engine of the economy. Mechanization and better design, improved planning and management, and hardworking men and women produced more per hour. Two kinds of potential wealth were thus generated: more could be produced in the same time at work or just as much produced with less work. Higher wages and shorter hours were the two forms that productivity's new wealth could take.

Instead of resisting technological innovation and demanding that workers take more, "their fair share," of the nation's wealth, labor leaders came to insist that companies and owners distribute gains in productivity fairly. Instead of arguing that shorter hours would drive up wages, labor maintained that industrial efficiency made both shorter hours and higher wages possible. By so doing, labor leaders outlined a choice between the two and set about negotiating with management in terms of that choice. Workers could still take higher wages and shorter hours. But how they then spent their share of industry's increased productivity was up to them; the more they enjoyed of one, the less they could take of the other.

Abundance, an Exact Science

Before the twentieth century, hopes for abundance were based largely on an essentialist view of human needs as more or less constant or on the commonsense understanding that since human needs were not infinite, a growing economy would eventually reach the point where everyone would have enough. Whereas one may argue abstractly that during the nineteenth and early twentieth centuries workers' choices to work shorter hours were the implicit historical expression of abundance, labor's new productivity theory of wages and hours made abundance historically explicit, as did the decades of labor's negotiations with management during the twentieth century.

Millis recognized that economists, politicians, and businesspeople, in addition to labor leaders, had begun to understand abundance in the new, relative terms of increased productivity.[10] Economists may be said to have made the rhetoric of "abundance" theoretically precise. Today, introductory economics textbooks continue to define utility using the two-goods model and present as paradigmatic the fundamental consumer choice between leisure and income: utility maximized (at the point of optimal choice) with the division of the two along precisely drawn indifference curves, bristling with arcane equations.

Following the economists' lead, the historian may define "abundance," if not at the instant of individual choice, then as the general trend to reduce working hours when the alternative to make more wages existed, offering specific examples such as trading wages for hours in labor negotiations, choosing retirement, and taking a second job, and thereby extend the recent turn to consumerist history in a new direction.

Indeed, economists anticipated this possibility some time ago, beginning to quantify abundance historically in these very terms. Paul H. Douglas, the influential economist and later senator from Illinois, observed that "workers in the United States tend to divide an increase in hourly wages into two parts. The first is a higher material standard of living while the second is increased leisure." On the basis of statistical evidence from the first part of the twentieth century, he concluded that, as a general rule, "approximately two-thirds of the gain is devoted to the first and approximately one-third to one-quarter to the second."[11]

However, Clark Kerr estimated that between 1850 and 1920 workers took "half their share of productivity improvements in the form of income and the other half in the form of leisure" but that between 1920 and 1950 leisure had decreased to 40 percent of productivity's wealth.[12] Peter Henle of the U.S. Department of Labor refined Kerr's calculations, finding that between 1940 and 1960, leisure as a percentage of productivity gains had dropped still further to 11 percent.[13] After the 1940s, union-employed economists regularly argued the point. American Federation of Labor–Congress of Industrial Organizations (AFL-CIO) economist Nat Goldfinger concluded that since the workforce in 1955 produced over two and a half times more per hour than in 1910, total production would have been far greater had working hours not been shortened.[14]

Integral to labor's productivity theory of wages and hours were commonsense claims about the relationship between technological advances and wages and hours. Along with prominent businessmen such as Henry Ford, labor insisted through the twentieth century that wages be increased enough so that workers could buy the things they were producing. If wages lagged too far behind mechanization, the inevitable results would be sluggish demand and eventually glutted markets and disruptions of the economy (technological unemployment). Sustained growth required adequate demand, which required adequate wages.

Until the last decades of the twentieth century, labor leaders also reasoned that sustainable economic growth required increasingly shorter hours. Just as higher wages were essential to provide consumers the wherewithal to purchase new goods and services, increasingly shorter hours were necessary to provide adequate opportunities to use them and, just as importantly, develop desires for new consumer goods. The idea that increased leisure was essential for the cultivation of new needs for industry's new products had been a part of Ira Steward's eight-hour philosophy.[15] In *Wealth and Progress*, George Gunton pointed out, "Man is essentially a conservative as well as a social being, and only yields to changes when opposition becomes more painful than acquiescence. It is for this reason that his wants and character change slowly, and progress is by slow degrees."[16] In a growing economy, productivity and innovation usually run ahead of demand—human desire naturally lagged behind the pace of industry, making advertising, marketing, venture capital, and increasing leisure necessary.

During the 1920s and 1930s, politicians and business people began to agree with Steward and other union officials that increased leisure was an essential part of sustainable economic growth. The Committee on Recent Economic Changes, chaired by Herbert Hoover, in its influential report concluded that during the 1920s American business had discovered that the "leisure which results from an increasing man-hour productivity helps to create new needs and new and broader markets."[17] The committee pointed out that it was fortunate that in recent years reductions in working hours had accompanied rapid technological advances, because leisure provided advertisers and entrepreneurs the needed opportunities to cultivate new markets. Thus the economy had escaped high levels of "technological unemployment":

> As a people we have become steadily less concerned about the primary needs—food, clothing and shelter. . . . [W]e now demand a broad list of goods and services which come under the category of "optional purchases" [and] . . . the survey has proved conclusively what has long been held theoretically to be true, that wants are almost insatiable; that one want satisfied makes way for another. The conclusion is that economically we have a boundless field before us; that there are new wants which will make way endlessly for newer wants, as fast as they are satisfied . . . it would seem that we can go on with increasing activity. . . . Our situation is fortunate, our momentum is remarkable.[18]

Hoover's committee concluded that during the decade "the conception of leisure as 'consumable' began to be realized upon in business in a practical way and on a broad scale."[19] During his presidency, Hoover based policy initiatives

on the idea that shorter hours was a necessary part of increased consumption—
a way to combat unemployment, create jobs, stabilize the economy, and promote sustainable growth.[20]

Explaining why he put the five-day week in place in his automobile plants,
Henry Ford told an interviewer:

> But it is the influence of leisure on consumption which makes the short
> day and the short week so necessary.... Business is the exchange of goods.
> Goods are bought only as they meet needs. Needs are filled only as they
> are felt. They make themselves felt largely in leisure hours.... The five-day
> week is not the ultimate, and neither is the eight-hour day.... But prob-
> ably the next move will be in the direction of shortening the day rather
> than the week.[21]

The New Economic Gospel of Consumption

Even though there was business support for the five-day week and even the
six-hour day during and after the 1920s, suspicion remained. Even after Fred-
rick Taylor used the tools of Scientific Management to prove that eight hours
were more productive per hour than a longer day, businesspeople such as Elbert
Henry Gary, a founder of U.S. Steel, and National Association of Manufactures
president John Edgerton still objected. Businesspeople continued to argue that
the mass of human beings would never make good use of free time and that
they would always have to endure the discipline of full-time work or decline
to a subhuman existence. Most of the opposition to shorter hours remained on
this level—work hours could not get shorter simply because leisure was silly
(meaningless) and dangerous. However, in addition to these long-standing objections, a few in the business world began to fear that, apart from the threat
to morals, progressively shorter hours represented a real threat to the future of
the economy.[22]

Even while recognizing the economic necessity of shorter working hours,
Henry Ford cautioned against following labor's vision of Higher Progress too
far: "Of course, there is a humanitarian side of the shorter day and the shorter
week, but dwelling on that subject is likely to get one in trouble, for then leisure
may be put before work rather than after work—where it belongs."[23] Thomas
Nixon Carver, the noted Harvard economist, argued that at some point Higher
Progress threatened to dethrone work and the economy as the centers of human existence:

> There is no reason for believing that more leisure would ever increase the
> desire for goods. It is quite possible that the leisure would be spent in the
> cultivation of the arts and graces of life; in visiting museums, libraries,
> and art galleries, or hikes, games and inexpensive amusements. If the cult
> of leisure should result in the cultivation of Gandhiism, humanism, or any

of the highbrowisms, it would decrease the desire for material goods. If it should result in more gardening, more work about the home in making or repairing furniture, painting and repairing the house and other useful avocations, it would cut down the demand for the products of our wage-paying industries. . . . The question in the broadest aspect is simply this: "do we prefer to take our increasing prosperity in the form of more goods or more leisure?"[24]

Time was short. But the economy's need to grow was long. At some point, the time hemorrhaging from the marketplace had to stop. Ford and Carver spoke for those who identified workers' fundamental radicalism in the desire, implicit in progressively shortening of the hours of labor, to leave capitalism for longer and longer periods of time, a process that would eventually shift life's center.

In response to this "threat of leisure," optimistic business spokespersons and economists began preaching a "new economic gospel of consumption": a new, alternative vision of the future in which working hours stabilized and Americans turned their time and attention to ever more products and services, forgetting about Carver's "Gandhiism, humanism . . . gardening . . . making and repairing furniture."[25]

While admitting that continuing work reductions were possible, the economist Constance Southworth reasoned that because "the average United States citizen" would never "admit to himself that he has all he wants of everything," eventually the desire for new goods and services would naturally overcome the desire for more leisure.[26] Henry Dennison, director of the Central Bureau of Planning and Statistics in Washington, D.C., agreed with labor that productivity offered two kinds of wealth: leisure or luxuries. But in a free market, consumer choice would determine which would be preferred. Indeed, luxury or leisure was the most fundamental and important of all consumer choices. The entrepreneur, advertiser, and salesperson needed to compete with workers' desire to consume more leisure by convincing them to consume more goods and services instead, in the free time already available.[27]

The modern challenge facing industry was to find a way to expand consumption in a leisure space that remained stable, filling it with ever more goods and services, breaking industry's reliance on expanding leisure. Because time was short (the limiting factor in the economic equation), something had to stop growing eventually: the economy or leisure hours. The stationary state of leisure was much more to be desired than the marketplace's shrinking to become an anemic, secondary part of American life.

The Great Depression

The coming of the Great Depression seemed to confirm labor's claim that both higher wages and shorter hours were vital to the health of the economy.

To labor spokespersons it was obvious that markets were glutted because wages had not kept up with productivity and hours had not reduced fast enough to stimulate adequate demand. Overproduction and massive unemployment were the results. Henry Ford agreed with leaders of the AFL that the Depression proved that fewer working hours, in one form or another, were an inevitable part of economic growth—free time was bound to come; the only choice was unemployment or leisure.[28]

Labor proposed that the most practical and effective recovery measure the nation could take would be to shorten the hours of labor immediately. This would "take up some of the slack," drawing down the labor supply, which was obviously far in excess of immediate demand. Once the labor supply had equalized with existing demand, workers would became more confident that their jobs were secure. Finding more leisure at their disposal as well, they would begin to spend more. As economic activity quickened, workers could then demand better wages, thus stimulating the economy and leading the nation out of the Depression.

Shorter hours acted as a governor on the economy, discouraging runaway speculation and stimulating demand, thus counterbalancing the tendency of technology to replace workers with machines faster than it created new jobs. According to labor, during the 1920s speculation went unchecked—unsustainable economic growth was not slowed by sufficient reductions in working hours. Massive unemployment, as high as 25 percent, was the result. Free time, ordinarily trickling out of the economy in the form of shorter hours, had then burst forth in the tragic form of unemployment when demand slackened and inventories built.[29] To reestablish full employment, existing work needed to be redistributed. Sustainable economic growth could then resume and the historical equilibrium of progressively higher wages and shorter hours reestablished. The first response to the unemployment that defined the Great Depression was labor's call for sharing the work.[30]

Hoover's administration was quick to take up labor's call, using a conservative approach based on Hooverian voluntarism. The business version of work sharing began spontaneously around the country when private firms voluntarily cut hours as an alternative to laying people off. In Battle Creek, Michigan, Kellogg's went from three shifts per day of eight hours each to four shifts of six hours each, adding substantial numbers to their payroll. Goodyear in Akron, Ohio, instituted a similar schedule. Employees at Kellogg's were overwhelmingly in favor of the move because, in exchange for the lost wages, they received additional leisure (always before seen as a good thing), the satisfaction of knowing that they were helping their community, and the hope for better salaries when the economy recovered. A large majority of employees were willing to give the plan a try. Kellogg's and Goodyear's work-sharing strategy was widely heralded in business and management publications as the key to recovery—the wave of the future that managers across the nation needed to understand and begin to implement.[31]

Hoover's administration, led by Secretary of Labor William Doak, agreed that such business voluntarism was the way out of the depression and pointed with pride to its successes—in 1933, the U.S. Department of Labor calculated that 25 percent of the nation's workforce "are employed today by reason of . . . work-sharing."[32] The National Conference of Business and Industrial Committees, with Hoover's blessing, created the Teagle Commission to promote work sharing at the level of the individual firm. Public support of the plan and business cooperation were substantial. The commission claimed that three to five million jobs had been created.[33] Prominent Republicans such as New Hampshire governor John Gilbert Winant and Democrats such as Albert L. Deane and Arthur Dahlberg presented sophisticated economic analyses showing how shorter hours stabilized the economy and promoted economic recovery.[34] As governor of New York, Franklin Delano Roosevelt supported the initiative. Hoover found strong bipartisan support from other prominent individuals, including Fiorello H. LaGuardia, Frances Perkins, Henry Ford, Senators Robert F. Wagner and David Walsh, E. A. Filene, John A. Ryan, Gifford Pinchot, and Vincent Astor. On October 5, 1932, Wagner urged the permanent adoption of work sharing. During their conventions in 1932, both parties incorporated work-sharing planks in their platforms and then actively campaigned on the issue, Hoover and Roosevelt each claiming to be the original and stronger advocate of the measure.[35]

Because of the national work-sharing movement, the expectation that leisure would continue to increase grew during the early years of the Depression. The expectation was further strengthened when the AFL's Executive Council drafted a bill to limit working hours to thirty a week (with severe overtime penalties attached). The bill was introduced to Congress by Senator Hugo Black of Alabama and Representative William P. Connery Jr. of Massachusetts. Initially, Roosevelt appeared to support both this legislative approach and Hoover's initiatives.[36]

In the early days of 1933 when Roosevelt was preparing to take office and the Black-Connery bill was gaining support in Congress, he and some of his advisors met with a group of prominent businessmen and industrialists in the nation's capital. Roosevelt offered to relax some antitrust regulations in exchange for their agreeing to a national six-hour-day, five-day workweek put into operation through the trade associations—thus giving Hoover's "voluntaristic system" more time to work.[37] The trust busters in the Senate, such as George Norris from Nebraska, were reportedly willing to go along with the deal.[38]

However, Roosevelt also supported labor's bill, agreeing that a mandatory thirty-hour week would provide new jobs and stabilize the economy. Roosevelt, Secretary of Labor Frances Perkins, and Democrats in Congress began to see their efforts as an improved version of Hoover's voluntaristic system, maintaining that nationwide regulation of working hours would be more effective and reliable. Moreover, legislated work sharing topped labor's political agenda, and Democrats were interested in securing their political base.[39]

A month after Roosevelt took office, the Senate passed the Black-Connery bill, prompting Secretary of Labor Frances Perkins to go before the House Labor Committee to add the administration's imprimatur to the thirty-hour legislation. After her appearance she told reporters that the committee and administration were in substantial agreement and that the legislators were ready to "clear the way for passage" of Black-Connery. Following Perkins's appearance on April 13, newspapers throughout the nation, quoting William Green as well as Perkins, reported that the House of Representatives would pass the bill and the president would sign it before the end of April. The first nationally circulated issue of *Newsweek*, dated April 15, 1933, had for its front cover, in bold headlines, the news that the thirty-hour workweek would soon be the law of the land.[40]

These developments elicited a flurry of speculation about a future in which the nation would have to deal with an abundance of leisure. Few other historical trends were as clear in 1933. Seemingly ironic today, similar to the burning of crops and destroying of livestock throughout the Midwest that accompanied the Great Depression, concern about leisure and interest in Higher Progress were most intense at this time. Rare were those prescient enough to foresee that the century-long shorter-hours movement had come to an end and that 1933 would prove to be its political high-water mark.

Roosevelt Responds

Around the time of Perkins's meeting with the House Labor Committee, some of Roosevelt's advisors began to actively oppose work sharing—both those who favored the Republican voluntary variety and those who favored the Democratic legislative approach. Led by Rexford Tugwell and Harry Hopkins, head of the Federal Emergency Relief Administration, Roosevelt's closest advisors convinced him to mount a holding action—delaying Black-Connery, offering to give labor everything else it wanted legislatively in exchange for the holdup, buying time to come up with an alternative unemployment strategy. Subsequently and through the early days of 1935, Roosevelt's First New Deal was defined, so far as unemployment was concerned, by his trying to placate labor for his delaying passage of Black-Connery.[41]

It is far from clear what motivated Roosevelt's advisors. Certainly, business leaders were putting pressure on Roosevelt to hold Black-Connery at bay and give their voluntary efforts time to work. Hugh S. Johnson reported that business "would turn back-hand somersaults against the thirty hour week."[42] One may speculate, however, that like Henry Ford and Thomas Carver, influential businessmen and Roosevelt's advisors recognized the fundamental threat shorter hours represented to not only capitalism but also the tax base necessary for government growth.

Even though there was some talk of countercyclical government spending to stimulate the economy circulating through Roosevelt's White House from the beginning, no specific unemployment strategy or guiding economic theory emerged as a clear winner and alternative to Black-Connery before 1935. Certainly, no stimulus-spending proposal had firm political support—work sharing was the only politically viable game in town. As the administration floundered, supporting the Wagner bill (known as the National Labor Relations Act when passed)[43] to appease labor and launching the National Recovery Administration (NRA) to regulate and stabilize industry, organized labor's militancy in support of Black-Connery mounted. Just before the congressional elections of 1934, the AFL, adopting a strategy being used by the Comintern Popular Front in Europe, threatened to call a national strike if the bill was not passed. As 1935 began, political support for the bill seemed insurmountable.[44]

"Salvation by Work": Roosevelt's New American Dream of Full-Time, Full Employment

In 1935 Roosevelt helped change the direction of American history. He and his administration committed the federal government to the emerging belief that progress was perpetual economic growth and Full-Time, Full Employment— the basic tenets of the new economic gospel of consumption.[45] According to the new vision, progress would no longer be understood as higher wages and shorter hours but as a constantly improving material standard of living with "full-time" (newly defined as a forty-hour week) jobs for all, supported by new government programs and policies. Roosevelt committed government to do whatever it would take to create enough new work in the public and private sectors of the economy to replace the work taken by new technology. Government would also bridge the gap created by the tendency for economic demand to lag behind increases in productivity by developing countercyclical as well as long-term spending strategies. Labor's view that shorter work hours stimulated demand and helped stabilize the economy, allowing for sustainable growth, was discarded.[46]

The federal government began to underwrite the new vision with stimulus spending, budget deficits, and liberal treasury policies. Whenever the private sector failed to generate enough work for everyone to have a "full-time" job, something it had proved repeatedly prone to, the government would step in as the employer of last resort. Identifying new social "needs," "agendas," and "crises" and inspiring national projects, or "investments in the future" (such the Tennessee Valley Authority, Hoover Dam, National Aeronautics and Space Administration, and what would become perpetual military mobilization), the federal government set about creating and funding new jobs to meet new, politically defined purposes and necessities.[47]

From 1935 until the beginning of World War II, Roosevelt put his and the business world's new dream into operation. Leon Keyserling remembered that Roosevelt began his administration with no economic strategy in mind.

Consequently, the programs and policies of the "first New Deal" were "highly experimental, improvised and inconsistent." Keyserling wrote that it was the "desire to get rid of the Black bill" that prompted the administration to introduce such things as the Public Works Administration and National Recovery Administration (NRA), "to put in something to satisfy labor."[48] This same point was made by other notables in Roosevelt's administration, among them Raymond Moley and Rexford Tugwell, who concluded, "One of the reasons why NRA was sponsored by Roosevelt, and why the act was passed . . . was the threat of a thirty-hour law being pushed by Senator Hugo Black. It was organized labor's conception of the way to relieve unemployment."[49]

In the share-the-work issue and Black-Connery, Roosevelt and his advisors found a foil, a contrasting and coherent background of opposition that set his inchoate views in bright relief and helped disclose specific policy alternatives, which taken together revealed a guiding philosophy, what Robert Hutchins, president of the University of Chicago, would later identify as "Salvation by Work."[50] Roosevelt's new vision was simply the opposite of the old American dream—perpetual economic growth and more work instead of abundance and the opening of Higher Progress.[51] Instead of opting for expanding the realm of freedom and facing the autotelic challenge that generations of Americans, beginning with Jonathan Edwards, had struggled with, Roosevelt, and then the nation, chose the perpetual creation of needs and eternal expansion of necessity, accepting the new, daunting challenge to create sufficient work for all to have "full-time" jobs, forevermore.

One of the administration's most successful rhetorical strategies was to redefine work sharing as "sharing the poverty" or "wasting the nation's wealth." Hugh Johnson, struggling with wage and price controls, insisted that hourly wages were "the multiplier" and hours "the multiplicand" and reasoned that hours could not be reduced without impoverishing the nation.[52] With such rhetoric and new work-creating policies and programs, Roosevelt helped establish the forty-hour workweek as the enduring standard for full employment that has become "almost sacrosanct."[53] Before 1935 full employment was a sliding scale calibrated in terms of a workweek that declined from year to year. Since Roosevelt's administration, workweeks of less than forty hours have been widely understood as the loss of potential wealth and are still counted by the Conference Board as one of the nation's negative leading economic indicators.

In 1934 the Department of Commerce published its first estimates of the nation's economic health for 1929–1932. Ignoring Paul Douglas's and other economists' observations that the wealth represented by increased productivity could be spent either as shorter hours or higher wages, the department focused exclusively on what Douglas called "higher material standard of living," effectively redefining increases in leisure as lost wealth in subsequent measurements of gross national product and then gross domestic product.[54]

A similar rhetorical ploy was used in the Treasury Department by the Federal Reserve Board. Led by Marriner S. Eccles and his personal assistant,

Lauchlin Bernard Currie, the Federal Reserve Board justified the taking on of substantial government debt and lowering of interest rates by arguing that these measures would help "reemploy the idleness." Instead of simply inflating the currency (the conventional view), in a period of unemployment new debt loads and low interest rates would help create new jobs. New products and services would be produced by the new work, backing the banks' paper promises. When unemployment improved, inflation threatened, and speculation escalated, then interest rates could be increased to act as a governor on unsustainable growth—hence the shorter-hour governor could be safely discarded.[55]

The events of the Second New Deal that logically followed Roosevelt's new vision are now commonplace in standard textbooks: new Treasury policies, public works, Social Security, and preparations for the coming of the war. In 1938 Roosevelt was finally able to defeat work sharing, co-opting Black-Connery with his own bill, the Fair Labor Standards Act (FLSA). Labor held out for work sharing as long as possible but at last, outmaneuvered politically by Roosevelt, fell reluctantly in line to support FLSA. Labor also adopted FDR's new American dream for the duration because the clear national purpose, winning the war, became the national priority in the closing years of the decade, far outweighing labor's claims.[56]

7

Challenges to Full-Time, Full Employment

Criticism of Roosevelt's new vision of Full-Time, Full Employment was widespread during the Depression and began again after the war. Examples abound. Two of the best are Frank Lloyd Wright's and Robert Hutchins's.

After the Great Depression, Frank Lloyd Wright reiterated his original claim that free time was bound to increase, strengthening his argument by pointing out that the machine was obviously capable of creating enough of the basics of life for everyone.[1] The forces that humans had harnessed "in this Machine Age are the forces of Nature. They have so increased production as to have made poverty an anachronism in fact. The income of rich and poor added together cannot begin to buy the goods at anything like the rate at which they can be produced."[2]

The Depression was an irrational development—a case of "starvation in the midst of plenty."[3] Malformed and "overbuilt," modern economies "such as ours must end in periodic national catastrophe . . . [d]epressions [or] . . . war."[4] Economic collapse had been caused by poor design—by poor distribution of the abundance that all should share but that a few had mismanaged. Consistently critical of Roosevelt's work-creation programs, Wright pointed out that it was far better to accept the free time that the machine made possible than to struggle to maintain full employment.[5] Roosevelt was reenslaving men and women in new kinds of work that government was inventing as surely as corporations had enslaved them by controlling the means of production:

> It is absurd to desire to compete against the fertility of mind and resource
> in devising labor-saving schemes and appliances. The important thing is
> to digest these energies so that men are set free by them for . . . enjoyments

no longer directly concerned in "making a living." No man should be Time-bound. Nor should any man be slave for a living. He should do, in the main, what he really wants to do. That really is the legacy we have received from the Past that is valid. Only under Democracy can he collect his legacy.[6]

Wright was consistently critical of Roosevelt's policies that were designed to provide the "full-time employment . . . that we continually hear about."[7] He insisted:

> "Employment" is not enough . . . dangling employment before a man now may be, after all, only the means of keeping him tied to a form of slavery— now [to] some money-getting or money-distributing [government] system that amounts to some form of conscription. . . . "Full employment" as we continually hear about it is not enough for the democratic citizen if this country still means what it declared in 1776. No. "Full employment" is not enough because it may be and often is only a more subtle form of rent or conscription. . . . It is the baited hook to keep the worker dangling. . . . The modern crime of crimes against Democracy is conscription in any form, because conscription is inevitably a form of confiscation. Conscription is . . . most hateful to democracy because it soonest destroys freedom at its very source.[8]

The growth of government and bureaucracies that required armies of "white-collarites" (lawyers and other professionals) had to be paid for. Governments defended public debt and taxation, what Wright called new forms "of rent bred by government," by promising to ensure the nation "full-time employment." In pursuit of "full employment" government was adding to the "rents" on money, land, and machines that modern corporations had long assessed, creating new forms of wage slavery for average citizens. Governments had become complicit in this return to serfdom and the abandonment of the American "ideal of Freedom."[9]

> Once upon a time the Jeffersonian democratic ideal of these United States was, "that government best [governs] that governs least." But [now] . . . the complicated forms of super-money . . . making and holding are legitimatized by government. Government too, thus becomes [a] monstrosity . . . enormous armies of white-collarites arise . . . [creating] more bureaucracy . . . collecting "legal" extractions from the citizenry if for no other reason than to maintain such phenomenal bureaucracy. . . . Multifarious . . . laws [are] enacted by our promise-merchants, the politicians.[10]

"Overgrown government" had conspired with the Machine to make "man . . . a parasite," promising "him 'employment' but on the terms of a wage-slave."[11]

Just when the machine seemed to be liberating humans into leisure, government, joining the corporations, began to reenslave them by concocting fantastic job-creation schemes and by underwriting the perpetual growth of an already "overbuilt" economy. Instead of promoting freedom, governments had begun to support the "heartless sterilizing cinder-strip of enormous 'industrialization' . . . [and] senselessly increasing production only for the sake of more production."[12]

Wright's solution to the growing corporate and government power (what he called "centralization") was consistent through his life:

> Widening margins of leisure everywhere the machine now insures: a margin that does not mean more or less unemployment for anyone but more time to spend as the independent workman may like to spend time. . . . Once . . . free on his own, by his own character, skill and voluntary labor [or intrinsic effort beyond the reach of corporations and government,] he is bound to succeed in "the pursuit of happiness."[13]

Robert Maynard Hutchins

In 1953, two years after leaving the University of Chicago as its most celebrated president, Robert Maynard Hutchins published *The University of Utopia*, reiterating his vision of what American progress might achieve and the role educational institutions might play in realizing the American dream.[14] His vision had remained remarkably consistent throughout his career at Chicago. From the late 1920s through the early 1950s, he had defended what he understood to be the core values of American education, opposing modern trends that he feared would destroy the liberal arts and the freedoms they stood for.

He began *The University of Utopia* by quoting a John Maynard Keynes's prediction, made in 1930, that had informed Hutchins's ideas about educational reform for over twenty years. Keynes, and Hutchins, believed the industrial nations had reached and passed a historic milestone. Modern nations were now capable of producing more than enough of the basic necessities for all their peoples. As a result, modern economies had shifted "from scarcity to abundance."[15] The transition to abundance had presented human beings with the near certainty of rapidly growing freedom from work. The consummation of material progress that humans had longed for and dreamed about for ages was at hand; all that remained was to decide what to do with the new freedom.

Whereas Keynes had predicted that the "shift . . . from 'full employment' to full unemployment" would take a hundred years, Hutchins pointed out that rapid technological advances had moved "the Keynesian utopia" much closer. By 1953 the country was less than fifty years from a "wantless, workless world [in which] the machines will do the work."[16]

The United States was doing its best to postpone that day of reckoning "to which Lord Keynes looked forward," trying hard to find alternative uses for its increasing productive capacity. Governments had already embarked on an "enormous development of the public sector, building and staffing hospitals, libraries, museums, theaters, schools, colleges, universities and research institutes." Compensating for the free market's difficulty in distributing the profusion of goods and services it generated, governments were beginning to make sure that everyone had a basic standard of living, above the poverty line. Eventually America might provide all its citizens with "the kind of medical care that comes as a matter of right to citizens of many other countries."[17]

Some people, seeing how World War II had provided work for everyone, had resorted to a scheme of permanent military mobilization to replenish the diminishing supply of work: "If we could bring ourselves to stop wasting fifty billion dollars a year on . . . defense we would confront the Keynesian utopia almost immediately."[18] However, try as our governments might, spending prodigiously into the future, they would not be able to avoid "the Keynesian utopia" indefinitely: "No matter what we do about improving the conditions of our own people, about expanding the public sector . . . we are still going to be right up against Lord Keynes's future."[19]

Since the steady reduction of available work was inevitable, it made sense to Hutchins to meet Keynes's future straightforwardly. Before the 1950s, generations of Americans had understood progress in terms of increasing freedom from work and necessity: "To repeal the primordial curse is almost by definition to return to Paradise." However, during Hutchins's career at the University of Chicago new obstacles had been erected—governmental and cultural barriers consisting of new beliefs and values, and new professions, institutions, and government bureaucracies devoted to creating more work. To accept leisure's new freedoms and challenges would now require changes "of the most profound order—in our outlook on life, in our slogans, in our most cherished beliefs, one of the most cherished of which is the doctrine of Salvation by Work."[20]

The prospect of leisure for all, increasing steadily until work became a subordinate part of life, now excited a "certain dread." Moreover, since the Great Depression, America's schools, led by colleges and universities, had so focused on preparing students for making a living and "developing industrial power" that most teachers and students knew no other option. Educators had only a dim memory of the alternative vision, education for leisure, that they had endorsed enthusiastically during the 1920s and 1930s.[21]

However, the current wisdom, the "association of education with earning a living," was proving to be "patently absurd." The idea that enough work would be generated by industry or created perpetually from nothing by government to ensure everyone a "full-time" job "borders on fantasy." That the liberal arts, the traditional foundation of higher education, could somehow be justified by their contributions to the new forms of work being created by modern economies and governments was a fabrication, approaching outright deceit.[22]

The time had arrived for the schools to take stock and regain their bearings. From the time of its founding in Plato's Academy, the university had been concerned with freedom. The liberal arts had traditionally been about what to do with freedom—the "liberal arts" were, by definition, the arts (and skills) of freedom. The etymologies of "school" and "scholarship" reflected this tradition as well, both words being derived from the Greek word for leisure. Until "very recently nobody took seriously the suggestion that there could be any other ideal."[23]

Through the ages, only the aristocrat, supported by serfs and slaves who did all the work, had the leisure necessary for learning and practicing the liberal arts. Of course, such elite education had no place in modern democracies. Fortunately, the modern democrat was blessed with "machine slaves" who could do the work and provide abundant leisure for all. Technology had democratized the Greek ideal, transforming what was once a utopian daydream into an urgent priority.

"Machine slaves" was one of Hutchins's perennial themes. Sharing Walt Whitman's, Frank Lloyd Wright's, and Fannia Cohn's conviction that ordinary individuals can participate in a democratic culture, he wrote:

> The substitution of machines for slaves gives us an opportunity to build a civilization as glorious as that of the Greeks, and far more lasting because far more just. I do not concede that torpor of mind is the natural and normal condition of the mass of mankind, or that these people are necessarily incapable of relishing or bearing a part in any rational conversation, or of conceiving generous, noble, and tender sentiments, or of forming just judgments concerning the affairs of private and public life. . . . That mechanization which tends to reduce a man to a robot also supplies the economic base and the leisure that will enable him to get a liberal education and to become truly a man.[24]

Hutchins conceded that one of liberalism's greatest disappointments was that most people were using their free time to watch television and find other empty amusements. The free market and its entrepreneurs were eagerly exploiting the situation, inventing new ways to waste free time: new products to consume, new passive and worthless recreations. Moreover, votaries of the new religion, "Salvation by Work," had seized on the obvious waste of mass leisure to trivialize the entire liberal project, arguing that the coming of abundant leisure would usher in a great silliness from which only more, new work could save the nation. According to them, workers would always need more work, not more leisure. Hutchins concluded, "No wonder the liberals feel betrayed."[25] It was the university's duty to fight back, competing with television admen and hucksters, promoting the active doing of the liberal arts, and demonstrating their superiority to passive, boring commercial recreations and consumerism.

During the nineteenth and twentieth centuries, "the steady reduction in the hours of labor" had provided the average worker in the United States with twenty or more leisure hours a week. Those who supported and fought for this reform had done so believing that the worker might use the new freedom to "increase his understanding of the significance of his work and to promote his development as a human being." This hope had been at the heart of the American labor movement and the traditional idea of progress—a "foundation stone of liberalism since the earliest time": "Liberals since the dawn of the industrial era have insisted on the reduction of the hours of labor because they had these ends in view."[26]

It was time to renew the American dream by reforming its institutions. It was time to restore the "University of Utopia," which would act as "a paradigm, or prototype, or model of the republic of learning and the political republic for which the Utopians [and America] had traditionally yearned."[27] With *The University of Utopia*, Hutchins intended to remind the nation that there was an alternative to Roosevelt's "Salvation by Work."

Originally, the colleges had been concerned with encouraging and promoting freedom, teaching people to recognize, value, and protect it when it came within reach. Modern universities had failed to do this. Turning their backs on their responsibility to teach students about the uses and value of freedom, they were at least partly responsible for the failure of the vision and for the trivial kinds of leisure developing. New intellectual fads, "scientism and positivism," and new academic "cults of skepticism, presentism . . . and anti-intellectualism"[28] ignored or dismissed the possibilities of freedom, concerned only with causality. Academics had been distracted, caught up in their own specialized fields and interested only in data, statistics, techniques, and proximate rather than final causes. However,

> the aim of liberal education is human excellence. . . . It regards man as an end, not as a means; and it regards the ends of life and not the means to it. For this reason it is the education of free men. Other types of education or training treat men as means to some other end, and are at best concerned with the means of life, with earning a living, and not with its ends.[29]

The university had blundered down a dead-end street, pretending to prepare people for work while acquiescing in the "economic rationalization of life." Instead of recommending and teaching about liberation from work and necessity, the university had chosen voluntary slavery, following along with the drift of American culture and politics, inventing new kinds of work and new "necessities," ignoring the ancient wisdom that "work is for the sake of leisure."[30]

To redeem its soul, the university had to become, once again, freedom's model. However, recognizing, valuing, and protecting freedom was only part of the university's responsibilities. The university also had the duty to teach students, and model for the nation, the correct use of the refined freedom of leisure. In modern times, some had attempted to banish perennial claims that there was a right way and a wrong way to use freedom. The idea that humans had certain absolute responsibilities and the claim that certain values, such as freedom, were better than others and were universally valid seemed passé to the many relativists in academia. But Hutchins insisted that freedom was a universal value (who would rationally choose to be a slave?) and that freedom entailed other perennial virtues—indeed "a hierarchy of values."[31]

Like Aristotle, Hutchins reasoned the following: Humans had the potential to be rational and social animals. Reason and sociableness were essential human attributes. But all people had to be taught these things. All of us are born selfish and ignorant—traits that ensure our alienation from each other and our slavery to the natural world, other humans (tyrants and bosses), to necessity, confusion, and chaos. Hence, schools are essential to teach people perennial lessons about how to live together freely and to think. Communication and community are the essence of what the university had always taught. Rhetoric and forms of dramaturgical communication associated with the arts and humanities, as well as the intellectual virtues of analysis, criticism, and creativity, were among the university's foundational subjects.

In addition to "intellectual virtues," the "social virtues" necessary for humans to live together in civility, "justice, prudence, temperance and fortitude," also had to be taught.[32] As they were put into practice throughout life, social virtues became habits of tolerance, veracity, openness, attentiveness, responsibility, and mutuality.[33] Such habits were essential to the functioning of all cultures. Like intellectual virtues, social virtues and habits of civility are universal values. They were not culturally relative, because without them communities and cultures fall apart—no agreement about what to value or believe in could ever be achieved or maintained, thus no cultural values of any sort could be rationally accepted and freely shared.[34] In the absence of these perennial virtues, no cultural value could exist (relative or not), no democracy could survive. Thus, "moral and intellectual virtues are interdependent. . . . The great and specific contribution that a college or university can make to the development of [social] virtue is in supplying the rational basis for it, that is, in developing the intellectual virtues."[35]

The life of the mind in its search for meaning, purpose, and direction and for order and coherence in life required the consistent practice of both the intellectual and social virtues. Habitual intellectual activity, as well as active participation in the other liberal arts (music, art, natural science, and sports) in community were the prerequisites for the pursuit of happiness. At the end of the chain of means and ends, of lesser activities defined mainly by their purposes (such as work), were the ends taught at university—thought, communication, and community engagement—that were worthwhile, meaningful, and complete in and for themselves.

In contrast to popular misconceptions about higher education, the University of Utopia was not reserved for an elite few; nor did it perpetuate the fiction that the liberal arts prepared students for work or professions. Most importantly, education and the practice of the liberal arts were not limited to a few years of late adolescence. The University of Utopia modeled a way of life that was destined to fulfill the promise of freedom for the entire nation, for entire lifetimes.

After graduation, a lifetime of learning follows for the citizens of Utopia. Governmentally supported adult education programs, university extension classes, museums, libraries, theaters, and community colleges would facilitate the transformation of the larger culture into something very like the University of Utopia. However, the initiative and responsibility would shift to mature citizens who would assume the responsibility for their lifetime of learning. Business groups, neighborhood organizations, churches, clubs, choral groups, and families would do their part to promote discourse and the independent practice of the liberal arts, free from governments as well as corporations:

> The Utopians believe that education is a conversation aimed at truth. Their object is to get everybody to take part in this conversation. . . . The educational system is a paradigm of the conversation through which learning is advanced and through which a democracy works. . . . It never occurs to any Utopian that his education should stop when he leaves college. . . . [T]he whole country is dotted with centers of education for adults . . . the object of these groups is not to confer social prestige or vocational advancement upon the members. It is to continue the intellectual development, the liberal education, of the individual. . . . The Utopians have the conviction that intellectual activity and the discussion of the most important theoretical and practical problems are indispensable to a happy life and the progress, and even the safety of the state.[36]

The Rise and Fall of Leisure and the Liberal Arts

Hutchins's career is itself a paradigm, of both the University of Utopia and of the fate of the liberal arts in the United States during the twentieth century. His story is an ideal way for the historian to outline the development of leisure-centered education during the 1920s and 1930s and trace its decline in the face of the ensuing "economic rationalization of life" and rise of "Salvation by Work."

Hutchins began his career as a "boy wonder," or "booby shocker," destined it seemed to become one of academia's visionary leaders. After finishing Yale Law School, he joined its faculty, becoming dean in 1927, when he was only twenty-eight years old. After two years he moved on to become president of the University of Chicago, the youngest person ever appointed to head a major university. From the beginning of his career, he thought of himself as a reformer, concerned with preserving the core values of the liberal arts but at the same time adapting the university to the new challenges of the twentieth century.[37]

Soon after arriving in Chicago he wrote in the *Rotarian* that there was "Something New in Education." During the Depression, higher learning in America faced two new challenges, both directly related to rapid advances in technology, that were steadily reducing the amount of time needed to earn a living. The "principle difficulty" facing educators was that more students were showing up on high school and college campuses than ever before. The other challenge was that "we may also be quite confident that the present trend toward a shorter day and a shorter week will be maintained. We have developed and shall continue to have a new leisure class." He proposed to meet these two challenges by restructuring the undergraduate curriculum at Chicago, democratizing the Greek and Western traditions of education for leisure.[38]

Hutchins was riding the crest of a wave of interest in education for leisure that had built among educators though the 1920s. The vision of a nation of literate people, schooled in the liberal arts, able to engage in intelligent, active, and "worthy uses of leisure" filled educational journals. Prominent individuals such as Dorothy Canfield Fisher, John H. Finley, and Lawrence Jacks toured the country, speaking about the leisured future to packed houses.[39]

It was Hutchins's fate to begin promoting education for leisure during a time when the future looked brightest, just before the competing visions of vocational education and Roosevelt's dream of Full-Time, Full Employment gained ascendancy, gradually to eclipse and then obscure Hutchins's vision and efforts. Thus, he was destined to fight against the odds and against what was becoming the prevailing wisdom among educators after World War II— something that he seemed to relish.

Roosevelt's New Dream: Education for Work

Nowhere was Roosevelt's new vision of Full-Time, Full Employment and "Salvation by Work" more influential than among American educators. In 1935 Roosevelt's Committee on Economic Security (CES) submitted a report to the president that included an indictment of America's educational system. It was "tragically evident" that the schools had failed the nation. A good education was no longer a guarantee of a good job. The committee recommended that "education, to fulfill its purpose, must be related much more than it has been to the economic needs of individuals." Reform was needed so that less "schooling" (general education and liberal arts) and more "education" directly related to future employment were offered.[40]

Rexford Tugwell and Leon Keyserling were central figures in the administration and attempted to persuade American educators to follow Roosevelt's lead. Arguably, Tugwell was the most influential person in the country in planning for a "socially managed economy."[41] He envisioned a "third economy" in which jobs were created by government whenever the free market failed to sustain Full-Time, Full Employment. Government officials, researchers, visionaries, and a range of new professional groups (particularly educators and academics) would be charged with identifying new needs for the people: problems to solve, collective goals, national purposes, and public goods. Then government would set about solving the problems and meeting the needs: planning, passing legislation, finding funds, creating public agencies, and recruiting professionals and private contractors.[42] Tugwell saw such elite workers in the professions, academia, and government as being in the vanguard of the third economy, acting as what may be called "metaworkers"—workers working on work—given the responsibility for creating more work for people to do. World War II, and then the defense industry, later emerged as archetypes for the new social and national purposes that Tugwell envisioned as foundations of the third economy.[43]

The schools had a vital role to play in Tugwell's third economy. He called for a "new spirit" in education, a "revolution in teaching," "an entirely new kind of school" that would establish "a vocational heart to the educative process."[44] Arguing that "we can substitute technological replacement . . . for technological unemployment," Tugwell distinguished old-fashioned vocational education, which tried to prepare students for existing jobs, from the new "vocational heart of the educative process," which would be forward looking, imagining new kinds of work and doing basic research that would develop whole new industries to solve "new problems" facing the nation that experts would be trained to identify. "Public policy" centers would form at universities across the nation.[45]

Old notions about the liberal arts being worthwhile for themselves were simply antiquated—holdovers from an aristocratic past still reeking of "priestly" and elitist arrogance. Modern realities called for the "sloughing off of cultural . . . pretensions." The value of an education had to be established on its utility—the only "virtue" that fit modern needs was usefulness. The pragmatic model was the only one that fit a democracy.[46]

The schools were to be integral parts of Tugwell's new social engineering. Even though variously called "development planning," "development economics," and a "socially managed economy," the educational project of Tugwell and Roosevelt was clear:

> Once we discover the future in the idea of [social] management the remaining things to be done will fall more clearly into the category of usefulness, and the [parts of the curriculum] to get rid of will appear in their true colors. The vague defense that they are "cultural" will lose its force. This is the value of "instrumental education," that it is instrumental to a scheme of society.[47]

The "scheme of society" would be planned out by government and professions (in both the physical and social sciences). Social managers, with government appointments or working within the new professions or at the universities, would determine for all the people what problems needed to be solved for the sake of the common good. They would determine what was needed "scientifically" through the "constant use of planning and shaping activities."[48] Thus, they would construct *utility* whenever more of it was needed. Political leaders would help define and redefine need and, working in the political arena, find funding to create the jobs to meet the needs that had been identified.

Tugwell had several names for his educational project, among them "dignification of vocationalism" and "generalizing vocationalism."[49] Perhaps the most powerful, and certainly the most enduring, of the politically successful reasons for social planning and the growth of governmental programs has been, and remains, "jobs, jobs, jobs."

In *American Education: The Metropolitan Experience, 1876–1980*, the historian Lawrence Cremin noted that education was transformed during the twentieth century.[50] Education was politicized by being recruited into the service of politically defined social goals. Whereas during the nineteenth and early twentieth centuries, educators had "harnessed education to republicanism and Christian morality," educators in the twentieth century revolutionized the schools by putting them and their curricula into the service of vocationalism, the century's salient social and political goal, and a new Tugwellian variety of utility-generating, self-constructing pragmatism that emerged as the century's dominant philosophy.[51] Education no longer had meaning in and for itself, as it had for millennia. It no longer served traditional (republican) virtue—those free arts of living together in community that Hutchins championed. In the twentieth century, education was directed to utilitarian ends defined not by nature (by "natural needs") or even the market place but by politics and government serving the new economic imperatives: growth and the reproduction of work.[52]

During World War II, with the potent social goal of winning the war emphatically established in the political arena, Tugwell's "generalizing vocationalism" nearly eclipsed the liberal arts in the schools. In the universities, government funding went primarily to the physical sciences, initiating a system of funding that still endures—much of higher education has been recruited into the service of politically defined social goals along the traces Tugwell and Keyserling laid down. Wars and defense contracts since then have deeply engrained that system into the life of American universities.

Robert Hutchins Responds: Reconstruction and Reform

Even before World War II ended, Robert Hutchins began to look forward to "reconstruction," to the rebuilding after the war that would offer American education a fresh start. With the war, Tugwell's new "vocational heart to the educative process" had begun to beat strongly. Hutchins responded, defending education's perennial values and attacking the new educational "cults" in vogue.[53] The colleges might have been legitimately recruited in the service of winning the war. But when things returned to normal, American education, if it was to survive in recognizable form, must reconsider its direction and purpose.

Hutchins's remedy was consistent, simple, and to the point. American education had to return to its primary task: education for freedom. Such a return was of supreme importance for the nation because "the alternatives before us are clear. Either we must abandon the ideal of freedom or educate for freedom."[54] Like Walt Whitman and so many others in the liberal tradition with whom he identified, Hutchins also understood progress to be the advance of freedom in stages:

> Freedom is not an end in itself. . . . We want to be free for the sake of do-ing [and being] something that we cannot be or do unless we are free. . . . We [first] want our private and individual good, our economic well being. We want food, clothing, and shelter, and a chance for our children. Sec-ond we want the common good [which is the proper role of government]: peace, order, and justice. But most of all we want a third order of good, our personal or human good. We want, that is, to achieve the limit of our moral, intellectual, and spiritual powers. This personal, human good is the highest of all goods we seek.[55]

In keeping with the long tradition, Hutchins argued that the three stages were hierarchical and together, ordered as means and ends, defined progress. The first two were means to the last, and best, human good—the pursuit of happiness in the development of "our moral, intellectual, and spiritual powers."

With Whitman and others in the liberal tradition, Hutchins also recog-nized that there are no guarantees that freedom will not be squandered—forgotten or wasted on foolish or selfish things. Like Whitman, he often la-mented that the nation seemed prone to shy from freedom when it came within reach.[56] It was the nature of freedom that humans could refuse it or give it away. When freedom was at last misspent, slavery would surely return, and the "foun-dation stone of liberalism" as well as the American dream, would be lost.[57]

American universities had been misspending freedom prodigiously. Begin-ning in the first few years of the twentieth century, "the great criminal [Charles William] Eliot who was president of Harvard applied his genius, skill, and longevity to the task of robbing American youth of their cultural heritage."[58] Scrapping the traditional curriculum based in the classics, Eliot had instituted an elective system whereby students were able to select courses that they were interested in and that they believed might be useful in their careers.

Hutchins agreed that during the nineteenth century higher education had declined; it was taught largely by rote and by pedants with little or no regard for life beyond their ivory tower.[59] However, Eliot and his ilk had gone too far. Instead of reinvigorating the liberal arts by reestablishing intellectual virtue as the center of higher education and instead of showing the relevance of the classics (the "great books") to the advent of technology, "machine slaves," and democratic leisure, Eliot had simply released students to their own devices. His was a criminal neglect of the responsibility that educators had accepted for mil-lennia to teach students the lessons that were the essence of the liberal arts: how to be free. With the center lost, with no direction and no sense of purpose, stu-dents and their professors had floundered. License was confused with liberty. Chaos at the universities had ensued.

Into the vacuum had rushed various "cults." Scientism was one of the most dangerous because it denied freedom. The fields of academe were filling with myopic specialists who cynically assumed that ordinary people could never live as free, intelligent, and social beings. Such specialists focused their work and teaching on "sociological determinism" or "economic determinism."[60] Instead of believing that humans, by nature, might aspire to be free creatures, modern specialists had presupposed that they are, by nature and universally, driven by selfish, acquisitive, competitive, economic, class, sexual, or unconscious motives and that neither education nor progress could free them or prepare them to live together in anything other than perpetual conflict.

Without a clear purpose, proponents of scientism had lost their bearings. The social and physical sciences, and the new professions based on them, could discover all kinds of "useful" knowledge and handy techniques, but for what?

> The goals of human life and of organized society . . . cannot come from science. Our most disturbing questions, moreover, are questions about ends. Science is about means. We cannot rely on science to tell us how to get a better society unless we know what is good. If we know where we want to go, science will help us get there. If our problem is where to go, science cannot help us. When we don't know where we ought to go we shall find, as we are finding to-day, that science makes our wild lunges in all directions more dangerous to ourselves and to our neighbors than they would be if we were ignorant of it. The technology with which science has equipped Hitler gives him a capacity for mass destruction which is unexampled in history.[61]

Other "cults" had followed scientism: skepticism, presentism, and antiintellectualism.[62] Inevitably, these "cults . . . will lead us to despair, not merely of education, but also of society" because they denied the quintessential assumptions of the academy: that humans could be free and could learn to communicate and live together convivially, in community.[63] Skeptics recognized no such stable truths. For them, all is flux and pandemonium ruled. Communication was just so many inarticulate grunts.

The new cults lived a parasitic existence at the university. Professing *nothing*, cult professors still held on to their positions, content to feed on the goodwill and reputation their schools had built for millennia—a reputation founded on the age-old claim that *something* was being taught at university. For protection, cult professors were now hiding behind the "patently absurd . . . association of education with earning a living."[64]

As a result of Eliot's crime, academic departments multiplied. Such vocational fields as journalism (even cosmetology and mortuary science) sprang to life as academic departments. Legitimate departments subdivided, producing specialists with no idea what other academics were doing. Academics had ceased to be colleagues who shared anything—all hope for a common language had been lost in a sea of jargon. Instead of teaching and modeling freedom, discourse, communication, and civility for the nation, the university had come to reflect its surrounding culture: keenly competitive, selfish, quarrelsome, petulant, and confused.

Summing up his critique of the direction of modern scholarship, Hutchins wrote:

> The crucial error is that of holding that nothing is better than anything else, that there can be no order of goods and no order in the intellectual realm. There is nothing central, nothing primary. . . . The course of study goes to pieces because there is nothing to hold it together. Triviality . . . [and] vocationalism take over.[65]

Attacking all claims about *anything*, about Truth or the essentials of human nature, modern educators taught and advocated, zealously, *nothing*.

Role of Government

It is difficult to label Hutchins conservative or liberal. Perhaps because of his views about wealth redistribution and international relations, he is often included in a mythology that has imagined a socialist, "world government" conspiracy growing up after the war. But the paranoid-style caricature has little to do with the man. He had strong ideas about the role of government in protecting basic liberties (such as the freedom of speech), regulating the economy, promoting economic equality, and supporting public institutions that served the people in their freedom. He endorsed governmental regulation of the economy for the sake of the "common good" and a social order "based on charity."[66]

Nevertheless, he recognized the dangers involved when governments try to do too much, grow too large, and begin to curtail freedom rather than protect, promote, and serve it. Unlike most run-of-the-mill conservatives, however, Hutchins was not worried about government's limiting of economic freedom. He feared, rather, that government, obeying the new imperatives of economic growth and in furtherance of the "economic rationalization of life," had become capitalism's servant and was curtailing the higher uses of individual freedom that were to be found beyond both politics and the marketplace.

Time and again he explained that neither the economy nor the "state is . . . an end in itself."[67] For him, both were means "to the virtue and intelligence, that is, the happiness of the citizens." "The economic rationalization of life" threatened all when government began serving the advance of the economy rather than freedom, which was "the highest good of the individual and of the whole society." The "economic rationalization of life proceeds in the face of the basic law of human society," creating a topsy-turvy world in which economic means are elevated as ultimate ends and promoted, illegitimately, by government.[68]

Because the "political order" had been made "subordinate to the economic order," government had not only neglected "the moral, intellectual, and spiritual goods of the citizens"; it was erecting bureaucratic and ideological barriers against them. Government had abandoned authentic progress and, by so doing, imperiled true freedom. By supporting the "economic rationalization of life," governments were helping forge new chains holding citizens back from realizing their full, free humanity for which they were destined.[69]

Because technology was irreversible and would continue to replace humans with machines, work time was bound to decrease sooner or later. Governments could postpone the day of reckoning but not indefinitely. Instead of chasing the "Salvation by Work" phantom, desperately shoring up work by making a devil's bargain with capitalism, government should accept and support the coming new freedom, funding schools, libraries, museums, parks, community centers, nonprofit organizations, adult educational facilities, and other parts of the public sector that would serve the new leisure as it grew. This was government's true calling and would be its ultimate achievement.

Throughout his life, Hutchins argued that "we are in the midst of a great moral, intellectual, and spiritual crisis."[70] He wrote, "Our country has long been afflicted with problems which . . . must be solved if the nation is to persevere. . . . These problems are not material problems. . . . No, our problems are moral, intellectual, and spiritual."[71]

Undaunted by critics, through mid-century Hutchins continued to urge the schools and other public institutions to follow the University of Chicago's lead. Speaking at a conference of librarians in 1950, Hutchins claimed that "the public library is the most important agency in American education."[72] Continuing his career-long focus on leisure's challenge and promise, he began his proof by making many of the same points that he had made throughout his life: mechanization is irreversible, increasing leisure is inevitable, vocational education "is clearly irrelevant," and education in service to the people's leisure might help realize the Greek and American ideal of a democratic culture. He said, "It follows that democratic education must be truly universal. Our problems are those of democratic citizenship and the right use of leisure."[73]

However, Hutchins had begun to fear that "the world is in imminent danger." Two dangers loomed: destruction by fire or ice—a nuclear holocaust or terminal boredom. The library was vital because the "primary . . . recipients of . . . education must be adults." And it was adults who were confronted with "the great paradox of our time: The trivialization of life."[74]

> Without purpose, without faith, [adults] will become the victims of universal boredom as leisure and life lengthen. Adult education is necessary to save them from the suicidal tendencies that boredom eventually induces. Television and the comic book, though they are sufficiently shocking, are no longer sufficient to arouse them. Since they cannot read or listen, since

they have no tradition, no ideas, and no ideals, they cannot appraise what is said to them, they cannot resist skillful propaganda.[75]

Americans must be taught and encouraged to engage, communicate, and struggle actively with others in their communities about matters vital to the maintenance of their humanity: justice, progress, love, beauty, God, liberty, and good and evil (a listing of 102 great ideas of Western civilization eventually filled Mortimer Adler's *Great Ideas: A Synopticon of the Great Books of the Western World*).[76] Humans must "use their heads, [or] they will go crazy; that is, they will cease to be rational animals and will no longer be men." Then they would be easy prey for tyrants and demigods who could easily incite them with hatred and prejudice.[77]

Hutchins agreed with William Ellery Channing: "The object of education is to prepare for more education." Libraries were the best places to promote continuing adult learning within the community and to sustain "the great conversations" essential to democracy's survival: "The kind of education that we should have for adults, then, is a kind that gives meaning and purpose to life. It is a kind that promotes communication. It is a kind that symbolizes and advances the Civilization of the Dialogue."[78]

The second "imminent danger" facing the nation was that "we might all go up in one great explosion." However, that threat would never be addressed "by military means." Concluding that "there is no defense against the atomic bomb," he pressed for his and Aristotle's solutions—thought, communication, and civility.[79] The need to learn and practice intellectual virtue and civility, and to establish the "Civilization of the Dialogue," had become international necessities:

> The most we can hope for is to induce all men to be willing to discuss all matters instead of shooting one another about some matters. The only civilization that is possible for us is the Civilization of the Dialogue, which conceives of history as one long conversation leading to clarification and understanding.[80]

Models for a "Civilization of the Dialogue": Two Years and Out at Chicago

Hutchins's original efforts to reform the undergraduate curriculum at Chicago were directed toward the same ends he envisioned for libraries. It was Hutchins's original vision to streamline university education by jettisoning vocational education—both the old and the new Tugwellian varieties. He argued that not only were most professors simply unable to teach students about the jobs they would eventually hold, but by the time students graduated, most of the "techniques and information" they had managed to piece together at college were out of date.[81]

By refusing to do the impossible, educate for jobs, the colleges could concentrate on teaching intellectual virtue through a clearly defined, coherent liberal arts curriculum, finishing the job in two rather than four years—students were told exactly what they needed to know and how to go about learning it. Matriculating students were free to go at their own pace, attending classes as they wished and reading on their own, directed by professors. The paradoxical result was that lectures were better attended. At the end of two years, or before if students felt they were ready, general examinations were given by college boards, not by professors who taught classes. After passing the examinations and receiving their bachelor degree, students were encouraged to leave the university and get on with the business of making a living and to begin their real education as adults within their communities. Others, pursuing additional professional education with a long-standing university presence, such as law and medicine, might enroll in graduate school two years earlier than usual.

Soon after inaugurating the new curriculum, Hutchins reported that the "scholastic aptitude" of Chicago students granted a bachelor of arts degree after two years' study was better than that of those in prior graduating classes. Subsequently, and until a year after he left Chicago, he and his deans keep close track of how Chicago graduates compared to national averages, consistently claiming that national standard examinations (such as the Graduate Record Examination) showed that Chicago graduates had not suffered in the least because of the lack of junior and senior years.[82] Nevertheless, other graduate schools began to discount Chicago's undergraduate degree (some at the University of Wisconsin called it a Bastard of Arts) toward the end of Hutchins's term.[83]

In turn, Hutchins continued to be highly critical of the new kinds of vocational and professional education that were establishing beachheads in colleges such as the University of Wisconsin during mid-century.[84] Schools of journalism, business, and so on, were prime examples of making "the political order subordinate to the economic order." Hutchins asked, "Why should the state use taxes to pay for the material advantage of some—why shouldn't industry shoulder the burden of preparing people for their jobs as part of the expense of doing business?"[85] Tax-supported schools and colleges had no business training students for jobs—doing with tax money what corporations, businesses, and the newly emerging "professions" such as cosmetology (Hutchins's favorite whipping boy) should have to pay for in a free market:

> I have not been able to reconcile these conclusions [that public institutions should train and recruit for professional and industry jobs] with the theory of free enterprise under which, one would think, the business of making an occupation attractive and training neophytes to practice it should devolve upon the enterpriser and not upon institutions supported by taxpayers or philanthropists.[86]

The university would eventually lose its soul prostituting its curriculum to a *"laissez-faire* world where education is primarily pecuniary."[87] Moreover, why should the university further confuse the political order with the laissez-faire world by assisting government in creating more work for more people to do—training students for public jobs and facilitating the growth of professions and bureaucracy? Perpetually discovering new "needs," finding new work, and then producing workers to support both the permanent growth of government and the economy were fool's errands.

Recentering Education: Adult Education and *Great Books of the Western World*

By mid-century, Hutchins was under increasing attack from educators and academics, including the faculty at Chicago. With the nation's colleges and schools ignoring Chicago's model and embracing ever more fervently the myth that a liberal education prepares people for work, Hutchins turned first to public institutions such as museums and libraries and then to private, nonprofit organizations and foundations; the private sector; and volunteers (community groups and businessmen) to keep his and the original American dream alive. Surely it is saying too much to claim that Hutchins attempted to privatize higher education; however, he did see private and nonprofit organizations and volunteerism playing a larger role in the coming "Civilization of the Dialogue."[88]

Encouraging students to leave college after two years and transferring the burden of vocational education to private and nonprofit agencies were parts of his strategy to shift the focus of higher education from adolescents to adults; he envisioned the University of Chicago becoming primarily an adult education center. Hutchins sought to wean adolescents as soon as possible from their alma maters, converting large parts of the university to the service of self-motivated adults. He also began to turn to film, television, and books that he imagined would serve the educational needs of an increasingly free people more efficiently than a university increasingly committed to "the economic rationalization of life." As a logical part of his efforts at Chicago, Hutchins, together with Mortimer Adler, helped raise considerable private funds to support the Fund for Adult Education; the Adult Education Association, which Dorothy Canfield Fisher had headed in the late 1920s; the American Foundation for Political Education; and the Great Books Foundation. He was also a pioneer in the use of film and television as adult educational resources.[89]

Reporters were fond of quoting Hutchins's "wisecracks" (what *Time* magazine finally labeled "Hutchinsisms"), among them "Under the impact of television, I can contemplate a time in America when people can neither read nor write, but will be no better than the lower forms of plant life."[90] Nevertheless, he tried to adapt the technology to his vision and actively competed with commercial television. Throughout his life he was confident that most people would eventually become so bored with commercial entertainment, and so sated by entertainers trying to retain audiences with increasingly daring titillations, that they would turn in desperation and revulsion to active, community forms of recreation—to reading the great books and to talking with each other. Boredom and its toxic effects were among Hutchins's favorite speech topics, and he began to portray the "American Dream" as the antidote for boredom:

> If Aristotle was correct in saying that all men by nature desire to know, then we must assume that the ball game, the television set, and the beer can will eventually cease to convey the full meaning of the American Dream. For the first time in human history, I say, we are all of us going to have the chance to lead human lives, to make the most of ourselves, and to make the most of our communities, too. Man is distinguished from the brute creation by his mind. Human communities are distinguished from those of gregarious animals, like wolves and bees, by their *deliberate* pursuit of the common good.[91]

Historian Mary Ann Dzuback concluded that "the Fund for Adult Education reflected Hutchins' concern for the kind of education that would absorb adults' leisure time." She also found that the fund "provided much of the initial financing for educational television stations and for programming . . . [and pressured] the Federal Communications Commission to reserve channels for public television."[92]

The Adult Education Association also supported the Great Books groups for adults that Hutchins and Adler had initiated in the Midwest in the 1930s and 1940s. Hutchins described one of the first classes, organized in 1933 in Highland Park, Illinois, and in continuous operation for seventeen years when he wrote:

> It deals with the tradition in which we live. It deals with the highest aspirations and achievements of mankind. It is—and it teaches—communication, and with all kinds of people. A Great Books class is a lesson in democracy because every kind of person from every walk of life is in it. The Great Books class symbolizes the Civilization of the Dialogue.[93]

Hutchins left detailed descriptions of why and how the groups worked. One of the biggest advantages was that, compared to alternative forms of higher education, the Great Books classes were real bargains; the only cost involved were the books, available initially for sixty cents each from the Great Books Foundation—or as Hutchins often quipped, the trouble it took to check them out of the library. Once under way, the groups became self-running and self-propagating. Hutchins and Adler assumed that literate adults would be able to read and understand the great books on their own—they needed no priests or academics to interpret for them. He and Adler insisted that the great books were important because they raised perennial questions about the human condition, not because they provided the right answers. Various authors had various ideas about perennial questions of justice, love, happiness, and so on. One of the key selling points of *Great Books of the Western World* was Adler's tour de force, the *Synopticon*, an index of hundreds of history's great ideas, or questions, for the groups to use as reference.

The groups were based on the Socratic method. With no Socrates present, the questions were provided by the *Synopticon*, the discourse by the groups. Hutchins explained that the discussions need not be a dry rehash of antique books and thought. Indeed, group leaders were reporting that the groups began striking out on their own before they had covered what the writer for the day had to say, testing the ideas and questions raised by the readings with reference to current personal, community, and national goings-on. This was Hutchins's ideal: the "Civilization of the Dialogue."[94] He once asked an audience of librarians:

> How can you discuss a question if there is no specialist in the room who knows the "right" answer? It is true that most of the leaders in the Great Books program are laymen. The extension of the program on its present scale would have been impossible otherwise. It is also true that the primary requisite for a Great Books leader is the ability to conduct a discussion. . . . A professor may spend all his life telling the people in front of him what he knows. A Great Books leader is not there to tell what he knows but to get the members of the group to talk as intelligently and logically as possible about the books. Lawyers educated by the case method are likely to be better leaders than professors who have lectured all their lives. One of the best leaders we have is a locomotive engineer in Rogers Park.[95]

Facing what *Time* called a "sizable rebellion in his faculty," Hutchins helped form the Great Books Foundation to take over the "great books" classes from the University of Chicago.[96] In 1947 the foundation began publication of sixteen of the great books (60 cents each, $7.50 for the set).[97] The university's vice president, William Burnett Benton, formerly a Madison Avenue ad executive and then head of the university's Encyclopedia Britannica subsidary, called the great books initiative and new foundation "the backfire approach in bringing educational ideas to the public against the invested interests of education."[98]

In the *Encyclopedia Britannica*, Hutchins found a new way to promote "his favorite crusade: adult education," free from what he believed were the constraints of the educational establishment.[99] In the fall of 1946, under siege at the university, Hutchins turned over his duties at the university to its new president, Ernest C. Colwell. Taking the title of chancellor of the university, for six months Hutchins moved his office to the Chicago Loop to work full time at Britannica. By June 1947 Britannica had announced its own project, a $200, fifty-four-volume set of 432 *Great Books of the Western World* (which would include

Hutchins's introduction, "The Great Conversation," and Adler's *Synopticon*), all of which appeared by 1952.[100]

Time reported in 1962 that no enterprise in the United States had been more successful in "cashing in" on the fact that adults with "more leisure and bored with the regular fare on TV, were looking for something more substantial." Reviewing the first decade of Encyclopedia Britannica's effort to find a "culture market" for the books, *Time* reported that the company had enjoyed surprising success: 153,000 sets had been sold.[101] In 1959 the *New York Times* had reported that there were 2,200 groups nationwide with 35,000 participants.[102] With Hula Hoops and drive-ins, the great books became something of a 1950s fad.[103]

After the first few years, when sales became sluggish, master encyclopedia salesman Kenneth M. Harden was recruited to move the sets. Against Hutchins's wishes at first, Harden began to sell the books to "everyman . . . the butcher and the baker" as well as to organizations, business people, and "eggheads." He marshaled his door-to-door salesman army, training them in innovative methods: instructing customers in the use of the *Synopticon* and in how to organize their friends; offering sets of books for ten dollars down and ten dollars a month; and throwing in a bookcase, Bible, and dictionary to boot. Inspired by Hutchins's vision, and by a healthy profit, Harden and Britannica had begun to privatize *adult* education, claiming that the only expense to the customer would be the books—the community, and leisure, would do the rest. As part of their pitch, salesmen offered the vision of similar groups around the nation, growing to form a citizenry of functioning autodidacts who would no longer need to rely exclusively on colleges or defer to cloistered groups of trained academics or mass media.[104]

Salesmen were instructed to sell the books by selling Hutchins's vision. *Time* reported that salesmen used the "hard sell"; they "talked earnestly of the importance of a liberal education for children, and displayed Great Books reading lists for youngsters."[105] At the beginning of the project, Lynn Williams left a vice presidency at Stewart-Warner (a leading auto industry company) to "sell the books to the masses—paperbound, at popular prices." He envisioned fifteen million sets sold and a day when "Aristophanes' Birds outsells Betty MacDonald's [best-selling book *The Egg and I*]."[106] Britannica had begun to do for the liberal arts tradition what Kellogg's had done for cornflakes, create a market and new interest by vigorous advertising and marketing. A true believer, Hardin insisted that he and his sales force were playing a win-win game: "[Salesmen] are not just making money. They are carrying the banner." For a brief while at least, some reporters at *Time* seriously suggested that "Spillane v. Spinoza" might become a real marketing contest.[107]

As he was leaving University of Chicago to become director of the Ford Foundation, Hutchins advised the university's trustees: "If you are going to present education as it is . . . you've got to present it as a mess. But why not do this: Why not sell the idea of a liberal education?" The *Time* reporter concluded,

"With $250 million [of the Ford Foundation's money] behind him, Robert Hutchins might turn out to be as good a salesman of his ideas as ever."[108]

Topic for Debate: To Save the Nation from Leisure, Should the Government Create Work?

In 1967, in the annual update of *Great Books of the Western World*, Hutchins and Adler published *The Great Ideas Today: Work, Wealth, and Leisure*. In this volume they put into practice what they had extolled as a fundamental intellectual virtue: an open, informed, and civil debate about important current issues. Turning from their primary concern and expertise, higher education, they opened debate on the most pressing domestic issues facing the nation: the economy and chronic unemployment.

In the introduction, Hutchins set the stage. John Dewey was right that the nation could count on continued scientific progress. Science and capitalism would continue to replace humans with machines and more efficient techniques. The question that science could not answer, however, was "What will people do if there are not enough jobs?" At least three points of view were possible. Conservative economists felt that advances in technology would create new work automatically—steady economic growth would be a reliable source of new jobs if only governments got out of the way. Others believed Roosevelt was right: the government had to take the responsibility of assuring everyone a "full-time" job whenever the private sector failed to do so, as it had done all too often in the past. Others, traditionalists such as Hutchins and Adler, maintained that leisure was, and should continue to be, the proper avenue for progress; instead of intervening in the economy to create more work, governments should allow work to recede and support free citizens in their pursuit of happiness.[109]

Hutchins and Adler allowed their opponents to speak first. Yale Brozen, economics professor at Chicago, argued that all was well. The economy, on its own, was fully capable of providing everyone a "full-time" job: "Technological change has created more jobs than it has destroyed." Indeed, since World War II, the "average workweek has shown little tendency to decline despite a marked rise in real hourly earnings." Because "the average workweek will tend to fall two to three hours in the next decade . . . the preferred workweek" would soon arrive. Soon, work time would stabilize and leisure would be less of a problem.[110] Thus, Brozen represented what was becoming an increasingly accepted view of human progress: increased free time as either unemployment or leisure were things of the past because the economy would grow forever, automatically creating new goods, services, wealth, and new work previously undreamed of. Leisure rather than the economy would arrive at a "stationary state."[111]

Next to speak were two among the group becoming known as "liberals," Adolf Berle and Robert Theobald.[112] Both were certain that the views Brozen expressed were utopian and impractical. History did not teach that all is well if government left the economy alone. History taught that over time the economy failed to provide enough jobs. It suffered cyclical periods of instability. It had failed, and was presently failing, to grow fast enough to support full employment—technology took jobs faster than it created them. Depressions and recessions would continue to throw people out of work.[113] Indeed, there was no guarantee that economies on their own would ever provide full employment. They might very well, as John Maynard Keynes had argued, settle into a condition of chronically high levels of unemployment.[114]

Berle, a former member of FDR's brain trust, maintained that government must continue to take action to counter the economy's very real tendency to shed work time: "Nor is the conclusion warranted that more rapid growth of the American economy will by itself resolve [chronic unemployment]. . . . Without some added element . . . the result will be steadily growing unemployment."[115] He claimed that there was a "double need, first to supply the income to [the] growing segment of unemployed and second to assign them tasks . . . our problem is to organize the work as well as the finance . . . to provide the tasks . . . [and] to pay for them."[116]

Berle argued that to provide enough work to go around, government (politicians, professionals, and bureaucrats) must continue to assume the responsibility of identifying new "needs" and "problems" confronting individuals, communities, and the nation. The free market was simply not up to the task. "There is not a shortage of unsatisfied needs and wants. These exist but under present organization they merely go unsatisfied. . . . Even a cursory glance suggests the vast area of work that *ought* to be done . . . [but has not yet] crystallized into available jobs."[117]

Berle offered what he believed was the new, enduring economic principle of government action:

> Wherever there are unfilled needs or wants, there are potential jobs for the men and women now or later to be unemployed. These needs or wants may be met either through private enterprises employing men and women and selling their product or service for profit, or through public organization–provision by the state, the communities, or by public corporations or enterprises, paid for by public funds.[118]

As its special concern, government ought to begin to create work "in services provided by human beings." To meet their responsibility, government officials and professionals (those metaworkers Rexford Tugwell described) would have to fabricate jobs that "will run the entire gamut, from street cleaning and home care to teaching, music, acting, and the fine arts." In service to a universe of "unfilled wants and needs [at] a far higher level [than food, clothing, and shelter]," such jobs would introduce an entirely new kind of work into the marketplace. Berle dreamed of converting previously free activities, such as the liberal arts, into jobs. For the sake of the economy, he rightly predicted that government would begin to colonize what generations of Americans had previously understood as the realm of freedom, transforming into work those very activities Hutchins understood to be the consummation of human liberation—activities that Hutchins believed must, by definition, be done freely and for themselves.[119]

Thus, Berle represented Roosevelt's revolution: government had to take responsibility for creating enough work to provide all with "full-time" jobs by expanding government and doing all it could to support the permanent growth of the economy.

Adler and Hutchins had the last word. Modeling the "Great Conversation," they consulted what they considered the best minds of Western civilization—Plato, Aristotle, Aquinas, John Stuart Mill, Immanuel Kant, Thomas More, Karl Marx, Adam Smith, and Henry David Thoreau. Brozen and Berle, and other Americans who had begun to share their views, had departed from the Western tradition with their support of the unlimited creation of wealth. The economic growth principle they promoted assumed that more wealth, without limit, was good. However, one of the most prominent themes running through the great books was that piling up too many possessions was a sure sign of ignorance, was dangerous, and was often fatal. Having and pursuing too much was bad for the soul, of individuals and of nations. Remaining concerned primarily with economic matters after having secured the basic necessities was to become what Plato called a voluntary slave. Through the millennia of human history, the pursuit of unlimited wealth was understood to be inimical to happiness.[120]

Authentic progress, as it was understood through the ages, had always been defined by the eventual satisfaction of human material needs. Governments who defined new needs and problems for their people and businesses that spent billions trying to persuade the public that they needed things previously unimagined were recent developments, products of a new view of the world. Agreeing with John Kenneth Galbraith's description of modern America as "the affluent society," Hutchins and Alder noted that compared to other nations and other times, America had already reached a point of "undreamed of abundance in the wealth that is now produced by industry." The problem facing the nation was not how to keep the economy and government growing so that everyone had "full-time" jobs; the real problem was "the proper use of wealth and its place in the pursuit of happiness."[121]

Through the ages, wealth was seen to be important because it freed humans for leisure. But the modern age faced a quandary: free time had come to be identified either with unemployment or the great silliness of television and consumerism. Turning again to the classics, Hutchins and Adler reexamined modern work and leisure. Consistently, the great books portrayed leisure as the opportunity for *activity*—a body, mind, and soul enlivened by the Truth were what Plato and Aristotle had in mind for leisure. Hence, the modern distinction between work as active engagement with the world and leisure as passive, nonaction was based on a profound misunderstanding of freedom. The perennial distinction between work and leisure was that work was activity required to make a living and leisure was activity that was its own reward. Leisure was best understood as a verb (as Aristotle had used the word)—"to leisure" was to give vigorous expression to human virtue in activities that are self-contained and satisfying in themselves. Habitually putting virtue into practical action (*praxis*) defined happiness (Aristotle's *eudaimonia*).

Once again Hutchins and Adler explained how modern "machine slaves" put the Greek ideal within reach of every man and woman and attempted to clarify terms:

> Work . . . can be considered as having two forms: subsistence-work and leisure-work. The first of these has its compensations outside of itself, in its product or reward . . . [and] is being eliminated by machinery. . . . [L]eisure work is intrinsically rewarding . . . it is the activity of our free time.[122]

Even though subsistence work may contain elements of leisure work (parts of subsistence work may be intrinsically enjoyable), this was

> no justification for confusing these important parts of life as though they were not profoundly different from one another. . . . Subsistence-work is pursued for the sake of economic goods that it obtains. . . . Both wealth and work are sought as means to an end beyond themselves. That end, in the most general sense and also the most ultimate sense, is happiness, and happiness is achieved in and through leisure activity.[123]

Four years earlier Adler had written in *The New Capitalists* that history was filled with examples of wealthy people who, failing to "distinguish between the means to a good life and the living of a good life once adequate means are assured," continued to produce and pile up "more of the means— *i.e.*, more wealth." If only humans would learn from the unfortunate examples of the past, modern capitalist societies "would cast out the irrational doctrine of full employment"—what Hutchins had called "Salvation by Work" in 1953. In an "enlightened" nation, as individuals became wealthier they would naturally choose to work less and pursue happiness, refusing the irrational course of making work for its own sake. They would need less from the economy and less from government.[124]

But why did this course of action, so evident from even a cursory reading of human history, seem "unrealistic" to so many people in the modern world? Adler answered that a new, competing view of progress had emerged. Instead of expecting technological progress to free us, we now

> *delude ourselves that the purpose of technological advance is to provide full employment.* So long as we cling to this nonsense, it seems futile to begin

educating children and adults alike to comprehend the limited . . . extent
to which human toil is either necessary or capable of producing wealth in
an industrialized society.[125]

In a final rebuttal to Brozen and Berle, Hutchins and Adler turned from
European great books to the American dream. They included six chapters of
Henry David Thoreau's *Walden* in their new *Great Ideas Today* volume, observing that Thoreau agreed with Aristotle and the other great book authors
that "wealth can become . . . an obstacle to the pursuit of happiness. It does
so when it interferes with leisure." The purpose of Thoreau's sojourn into the
woods was "to set time for leisure. . . . [H]is experience provided [the traditional
American] perspective on the meaning of work and leisure."[126]

Labor Turns from Shorter Hours
to Full-Time, Full Employment

After World War II, labor renewed the call for shorter hours. Using familiar arguments, some of which were over a hundred years old, laborites called for reducing weekly work hours to below forty to combat unemployment, create jobs, promote health and safety, and stimulate economic demand to make sustainable growth possible. Briefly, labor leaders challenged FDR's dream of "full employment" at forty hours a week (Full-Time, Full Employment) returning to labor's original vision of Higher Progress. The unions presented shorter hours and higher wages yet again as the roadmap for America's future.

Throughout the war, the American Federation of Labor (AFL) had reaffirmed its commitment to the thirty-hour week as its "ultimate objective," explaining that the only justified delay was winning the war.[1] As the war was drawing to a close, and with the prospect of depression returning when America's soldiers reentered the labor force, the AFL in its 1944 convention called once again for a legislated thirty-hour workweek—a call echoed throughout the nation by local union affiliates.[2] William Green repeated his claim that thirty hours was "an economic necessity . . . the only practical way" to avoid the return of chronic unemployment.[3] The AFL weekly news service concluded in 1946, "The 40-hour week, once labor's proudest boast, is doomed to be discarded within the foreseeable future. The 30-hour week is bound to come, opening up new opportunities for employment, and a fuller life for the working masses."[4]

As labor resumed the struggle for progressively shorter hours, President Truman and Congress reiterated Roosevelt's vision of Full-Time, Full Employment. As it was originally presented, the Full Employment Act of 1946 came close to making compensatory (countercyclical, or stimulus) spending a federal mandate and a forty-hour-week job a new individual right—enshrining

Roosevelt's dream in law.[5] Truman also adopted FDR's wartime rhetoric, arguing that the newly forming Cold War and the beginning of permanent military
mobilization trumped labor's call for work reductions—Eisenhower and others
had linked France's poor showing during the war to its short workweek.[6]

However, as amended, the bill became more of a series of guidelines, establishing the Council of Economic Advisors and requiring the president to
submit an annual report on the economy. Congress also directed the president
to predict unemployment rates and take steps to promote "full employment."[7]
Subsequently, the political rhetoric of jobs, jobs, jobs, as well as governmental policies and research about unemployment, with few exceptions has assumed the forty-hour week as the standard, branding anything less part-time
employment.

Most exceptions occurred when labor leaders tried to reintroduce shorter
hours into the national debates about unemployment after the war. Just as they
had done during the Depression, laborites challenged the theory that economic
growth, on its own, would sustain Roosevelt's Full-Time, Full Employment, repeatedly warning that chronic levels of high unemployment (above 5 percent)
and extreme market cycles would plague the economy without the shorter-
hours governor and that a national full-employment strategy had to contain a
flexible definition of full-time jobs. More importantly, labor also continued to
maintain that shorter hours were a "part of general national progress," and as
Samuel Gompers had observed early in the century, "freedom is synonymous
with the hours for leisure,"[8] A resolution passed in 1959 by the American Federation of Labor–Congress of Industrial Organizations (AFL-CIO) Executive
Council provides a representative example:

> [Whereas] the time has come for wide-scale reduction in hours of work so
> that more people may be employed[:]
> ... [T]here is persistent unemployment of 5 percent or more. ...
> ... [T]echnological change and the accompanying increasing produc-
> tivity are gaining momentum. ...
> Unless some of the benefits of the accelerating rate of technical
> advance are taken in the form of shortening of time at work ... unemploy-
> ment will mount steadily. Technological progress is making shorter hours
> not only possible but essential. ...
> Today ... there is ... a general recognition that the present 8-hour
> day and 40-hour week ... should and will be reduced as part of general
> national progress. ...
> ... [T]he plain fact is that other ways [of combating unemploy-
> ment] ... are not doing the job. ...
> ... [W]ithout a reduction in hours as a key element in an anti-unem-
> ployment program, the other measures ... are not adequate. ...
> *Resolved*, That shorter hours of work must be attained as a vital means
> of maintaining Jobs, promoting the consumption of goods and converting
> technical progress into desirable increased employment rather than into

increased unemployment. Our economy should and can support concurrently both shorter hours and production of additional goods and services.

We call upon Congress to take as rapidly as possible the steps needed to amend the Fair Labor Standards Act to provide for a 7-hour day and a 35-hour week.[9]

Up until the mid-1950s, labor made some gains in reducing work hours in some industries. Compared to the advances made before Roosevelt's new vision gained ascendancy, however, progress was slow. Workers in the printing trades, together with some textile, telephone, mine, rubber, rail, and maritime workers, were able to reduce their hours below forty a week or mounted serious campaigns to do so. After the war, Kellogg's workers in Battle Creek, Michigan, voted more than three to one to return to six hours; Goodyear workers in Akron, Ohio, struck to reestablish their six-hour day. The International Ladies' Garment Workers' Union (ILGWU) continued its leadership, winning a thirty-five-hour week by the mid-1950s. Led by Harry Van Arsdale, Manhattan's Local 3 of the International Brotherhood of Electrical Workers (IBEW) held labor's salient for a while, striking for and winning a twenty-five-hour workweek in 1962.

Even though national averages remained nearly static, supporters were enthusiastic, reasoning that general progress had always followed small numbers of unions that advanced. Prominent national labor leaders, including George Meany, promised to continue the fight. Meany's famous retort, "More!" to a reporter's question about what the unions wanted, was followed later by his more complete explanation: "If by a better standard of living we mean not only more money but more leisure and a richer cultural life, the answer remains 'more.'"[10]

Public interest outran actual accomplishments as well. On the basis of labor's rhetoric and the few gains being made, the American press confidently predicted that an age of mass leisure was imminent. Institutes were created, such as the Center for the Study of Leisure at the University of Chicago, to make preparations. Dire warnings were issued about the "problem of leisure" and the looming plague of boredom. Pundits and economists tried to analyze what appeared to be an unstoppable groundswell, most emphasizing unemployment as the workers' primary concern. Reporters and researchers also noticed that women were among the strongest supporter of shorter hours—of the six-hour days in Akron and Battle Creek in particular. Occasionally, analysts recognized that what workers wanted was what the press was so loudly predicting for America's future—the shifting of life's balance from work to leisure. Researchers with the United Rubber, Cork, Linoleum and Plastic Workers of America found that, after women, the strongest supporters of six-hour days were "those who feel that shorter hours should be a primary goal of labor" because it was an integral part of the nation's progress. As evidenced by the AFL-CIO Executive Council 1959 resolution, labor still believed in Higher Progress and recognized "that the present 8-hour day and 40-hour week . . . should and will be reduced as part of general national progress."

Traveling to Battle Creek and Akron in the late 1980s and through the early 1990s, my students and I interviewed hundreds of employees who had worked the short day.[11] Most of them said that they liked the six-hour day primarily for practical, everyday reasons: it gave them a chance to do things other than work their jobs. Just as their forebears had been repeating for a century and a half, they consistently spoke in terms of freedom—of being able to, having the opportunity to, getting to do things that were important to them. The majority of responses to our question "Why did you prefer to work six hours?" confirmed that a bedrock radicalism and working-class identity persisted in the two cities, connected inextricably to the shorter-hour process. Just as at the origins of the American labor movement, when the Lowell women and their New England brothers fought for the ten-hour day, shorter hours in the form of the six-hour day continued to offer the possibility of experiencing and constructing a freer, more humane, and enjoyable alternative to the capitalist "selfish system"— "beyond the influence of factory bolts and locks."[12]

Not satisfied with so obvious an answer, my students and I pressed for other, what we then thought must be more important reasons. The Goodyear and Kellogg's employees would generally oblige and talk about unemployment, job security, working conditions, and health and safety. Some would repeat labor's argument that shorter hours stabilized the economy, slowing unsustainable growth and providing additional free time to cultivate new markets and new consumption. There is no doubt that such things were important, but they were seldom the first things mentioned.

Women and men who worked for the two companies would often speak of their children and their nation's future. They expressed the hope that America would progress to the point where more people, their children included, would have more time to spend with their families and communities; in nature, education, and sports; and on culture and the myriad free activities they were finding to do. For many of these workers, the two extra free hours a day had become a time for exploration and experimentation—for finding new ways to live together, to grow and develop, that they thought had value apart from and in addition to new consumer goods and higher material standards of living.

Other workers who reduced their work hours below forty before the 1960s were reported to have had similar experiences with, and expectations about, their new leisure. David Dubinsky, president of the ILGWU in the 1950s, observed that increased leisure was important for union members because

[they are able to be] better parents, better husbands and wives when they are not chained to the workshop, when they have some time in the day which they can call their own. They can be better citizens as well, and take an active part in community affairs, recreational and cultural opportunities.[13]

Dubinsky declared that by winning the thirty-five-hour week his union was continuing in the "spirit of Samuel Gompers," leading the way to progress as "a continuous upward spiral in the well-being of union members, commensurate with an increase in industrial productivity." He boasted that the ILGWU was continuing to build educational and recreational facilities to support the new leisure: "Thus, today the workers' union tries to help its members enjoy wisely the leisure brought by the 35-hour week secured by union effort."[14] He offered a long list of union programs that were popular with the rank and file. They were popular, he judged, because they offered what TV viewing and most commercial entertainments lacked: "human fellowship." Pointing out that the ILGWU's Broadway play *Pins and Needles* had won international acclaim, Dubinsky reported that local unions around the country were providing a variety of similar do-it-yourself cultural opportunities: art classes; choral, orchestra, and drama groups; regular parties, dances, picnics, outings, and trips; and amateur sports.[15]

Building on Fannia Cohn's efforts, the ILGWU had begun to offer instruction and counseling in the arts of living together in communities and families: "Outstanding specialists in social hygiene, psychiatry and marriage problems give lectures on their specialties to aid members in their difficulties and help them to benefit from modern discoveries in human relations."[16]

According to reports published by the ILGWU's Education Department, these programs were well attended, often oversubscribed. Union officials such as Mark Starr were confident that they were meeting a real demand for a range of active leisure opportunities that commercial recreation and amusements were ignoring, particularly those that involved what Dubinsky called "human fellowship." They also claimed to be making progress in the arts of living together, helping build the skills necessary for successful human relationships—accomplishments that were even more important than the material progress the nation was enjoying.[17]

Moreover, in his study of African American members of the United Automobile Workers (UAW) in Detroit, David Lewis-Colman pointed out:

> Through leisure activities, the CIO tried to reduce the racial, religious, and ethnic antagonisms in the working class that had stymied industrial unionism for generations. [The CIO's] leisure activities sought to emphasize the common class bonds of all workers and promote union loyalty. . . . The UAW sponsored picnics, choral groups, and sports teams . . . [and often brought] together black and white autoworkers who had kept their private lives distinctly separate. The union-sponsored interracial social interactions could have proven a powerful tool in reducing the racial antagonism [had they been more extensively used].[18]

Defending the twenty-five-hour week, won in 1962 by New York's construction electricians, Harry Van Arsdale quoted prominent authorities, such as the physicist Boris Pregel, who predicted that the four-hour workday would be the national norm by 1970: "Automation is going to result in a new kind of eight-hour day—four hours of work and four hours of formal study in colleges or adult education centers."[19] The electricians' educational and recreational facilities, like those of the ILGWU, had become symbols of their vision of Higher Progress. The "vitality" and "breadth" of the union's "cultural programs"

> represent for the membership a perfect vision of what America is meant to be. Here is a vehicle built with their own sweat and imagination that provides passage to a more thoughtful, more lively life not only for the working men and women who make up the union, but for their children as well.[20]

A Freedom Too Far: Retreat after 1956

In the last chapter of *Our Own Time: A History of American Labor and the Working Day*, "The Hours Stalemate since 1939," David Roediger and Philip Foner provide an excellent account of labor's shorter-hours initiatives, successes, and failures.[21] While agreeing with the economist John Owen that "'no net change' of consequence"[22] occurred from 1948 to 1975, they nevertheless make a strong case that labor's few successes and the widespread interest in "mass leisure" were important, "substantial" developments. However, they conclude, "The progress of the shorter-hours movement between 1945 and 1956 was not great by comparison to pre–World War II standards, but it was substantial by comparison to the stasis and retreat of the post-1956 years."[23]

Moreover, workers who worked less than forty hours before 1956 were not able to hold what they had won. Ronald Edsforth points out that, after the abortive rank-and-file auto worker initiative of the 1950s and early 1960s, "UAW leaders ha[d] not renewed the labor movement's historic struggle for work time reform."[24] That labor's progress was met with fierce opposition was hardly new. What was new was the failure of labor's leadership to adequately support and actively extend the shorter-hours salient made before 1956. Also new was the failure of labor's traditional allies to lend their full support. Instead of following the examples of middle-class moralists and reformers who for over two centuries had contributed inspiring visions of what increasing leisure presaged, former supporters of shorter hours and Higher Progress such as the sociologist David Riesman and Arthur Goldberg, John F. Kennedy's secretary of labor, began to write and speak of "the problem" of leisure.[25]

While paying lip service to the reform, the AFL and major CIO unions such as the UAW and United Steelworkers (USW) made little actual progress, keeping their "shorter-hours commitments largely confined to paper." Walter Reuther opposed the Rouge River auto workers' bid for the thirty-hour week with no pay cut ("30 for 40") as "subversive."[26] For him, the choice between more money and shorter hours was no real choice at all—the need for wages always outweighed the desire for leisure: "When we get to the point that we have got everything we need, we can talk about a shorter work week."[27] John L. Lewis told mine workers, "If you want to stop eating so much and loaf more, we can get you the six-hour day."[28] Branding additional leisure as loafing, subversive, and only for "the women" became commonplace among union leaders and labor's traditional allies—an important rhetorical shift that imperiled shorter-hours advances even more than business and conservative political opposition.

After World War II, the *American Federationist*, once bristling with articles about the thirty-hour week and the promise of leisure, remained virtually silent on the subject. The *IUD Bulletin* (published by the Industrial Union Department [IUD] of the AFL-CIO) offered limited coverage. In both publications, labor's turn from shorter hours to Roosevelt's new dream was evident. Labor's publications began to fill with the rhetoric of jobs, jobs, jobs and with articles about the importance of economic growth sufficient for Full-Time, Full Employment, the need for government spending to stimulate the economy, and the necessity for new government programs and jobs to absorb whatever unemployment remained. The IUD defined labor's emerging, postwar position in a 1956 Labor Day message. With no mention of shorter hours, the *Bulletin* proclaimed, "National policy must be geared to an expanding economy, to full employment and to rapidly rising living standards."[29]

Historians have offered a variety of explanations for labor's retreat from shorter hours after mid-century: the ouster of communists and union radicals; the "countermarch of labor legislation,"[30] such as the Taft-Hartley revisions of the National Labor Relations Act; the legacy of the Depression and war; pent-up consumer demand released after the war; changing demographics; changing leadership; consumerism; and alienated or commodified leisure. The most convincing explanation, however, is that labor abandoned shorter hours because it came to favor Roosevelt's new dream of Full-Time, Full Employment and the Keynesian governmental policies and strategies that this new ideology entailed. Ron Edsforth notes that Reuther and other UAW leaders' lack of support and abandonment of the cause was because of their turn "to a labor-oriented form of Keynesian liberalism that stressed national economic planning to create full employment and sustained economic growth."[31] Roediger and Foner confirm that labor's "alliances with liberal Democrats in support of Keynesian economic policies were much preferred [over shorter hours] . . . by UAW and USW."[32]

Nevertheless, because shorter hours remained popular for a substantial number of workers, labor leaders publicly supported the issue.[33] They did so, however, mainly to avoid alienating union members and to improve their chances in negotiations with management and politicians for things they wanted more.

John F. Kennedy took labor's rhetoric seriously, however. Campaigning among steelworkers in the 1960s, he told the union, "In the face of the Communist challenge, a challenge of economic as well as military strength, we must meet today's problem of unemployment with greater production rather than by

sharing the work"—an observation he often repeated.[34] Arthur Goldberg, The-
odore Sorensen, and Walter Heller (chair of Kennedy's Council of Economic
Advisors) opposed shorter hours throughout Kennedy's administration, arguing that the most desirable way to combat unemployment was with economic
growth and by developing government programs to put everyone to work at
forty hours per week.[35] Paul Samuelson, head of a task force on the economy appointed by Kennedy, warned, "If we don't produce a better environment of economic demand capable of absorbing large numbers of those now unemployed, I
predict an increasing and more successful agitation for a shorter work week."[36]

Nevertheless, the administration, together with labor leaders, felt the need
to assure the public that it remained in favor of the historical shorter-hours
process. Heller spoke of "the natural reduction of the work week in the course
of time, as the economy grows—that we welcome."[37] Just before his death, Kennedy predicted that because of automation "we're going to find the work week
reduced . . . we are going to find people wondering what to do."[38] He continued
to speak of progress in terms of shorter hours, assuring his audiences that the
process would resume "by the end of this century, perhaps sooner."[39] Pointing to the new recreational facilities of California's multiuse Central Valley
Project, he urged "the present generation of Americans" to continue to provide
adequate public recreational resources for the future.[40] Extrapolating from the
president's remarks, Tom Wicker at the *New York Times* predicted that the administration was about to endorse labor's bid for a thirty-five-hour week, forcing Kennedy to explain his remarks:

> What I was talking about was that inevitably as the century goes on . . .
> as machines increasingly take the place of men, that we will have more
> leisure, and therefore we should take those steps in the field of conserva-
> tion, resource development, and recreation, which will prepare us for that
> period. But that is not talking about today or tomorrow.[41]

In a special message to Congress on tax reduction and reform in January
1963, Kennedy argued, "The most urgent task facing the nation at home today
is to end the tragic waste of unemployment . . . [by stepping] up the growth and
vigor of our national economy. . . . The chief problem confronting our economy
in 1963 is its unrealized potential—slow growth . . . persistent unemployment."
Kennedy then proposed what Nelson Lichtenstein called an "across-the-board
tax cut that delivered a lopsided stimulus to corporations and the wealthy."[42]
Kennedy added, however, "It would be a grave mistake to require that any tax
reduction today be offset by a corresponding cut in expenditures." The alternative to his proposals, he observed, was that "pressure for the 35-hour week"
would mount and might prove inexorable.[43] The workweek had to remain stable to meet the new challenges facing the nation: the Soviet threat, international
competition, the space program, and the growing national debt.

Labor Follows the Politics of Jobs, Jobs, Jobs

Facing political opposition from Kennedy and then Lyndon Johnson, labor continued its turn from shorter hours and Higher Progress to Full-Time, Full Employment and meaningful work. Three events mark this turn and illustrate the divisions within the unions over the issues: the AFL-CIO's 1956 Conference on Shorter Hours and the 1963 and 1979 congressional hearings on proposed amendments to the 1938 Fair Labor Standards Act—amendments to lower weekly hours to thirty-five.

Shortly after the merger of the AFL and CIO in 1955, George Meany called the unions together to discuss shorter hours. Meany began the conference with a powerful, memorable claim: "The progress toward a shorter work day and a shorter work week is a history of the labor movement itself." But he turned immediately to emphasizing the importance of increasing wages to match increased productivity, noting that without adequate demand unemployment was bound to grow and recalling that the "depression of 1929 . . . came because production had outrun the power that was in the pay envelopes."[44] As he continued his speech, it became clear that he was less than enthusiastic about the prospect of further reduction in work hours: "I know one of the items on the agenda is this question of leisure. Well, I don't think that there is any great objection to having more leisure time if you have something to do with it, and if you have the type of income that will allow you to enjoy yourself." He concluded that "keeping the economy going by maintaining purchasing power" was labor's primary concern, but "if this leads to more leisure for the American people as a whole, labor will help to bring this about."[45]

George Brooks, research director of International Brotherhood of Pulp, Sulphite and Paper Mill Workers, followed Meany's turn from shorter hours. Brooks agreed that once, when hours were long and work difficult, increased leisure was important. However, he concluded, times had changed: "Workers are eager to increase their income, not to work fewer hours."[46] The only reason for reducing work hours was to protect against unemployment.[47] After reading his prepared text, Brooks continued extemporaneously, declaring that the lack of enthusiasm for shorter hours was "desirable" since work "will probably be the most meaningful thing people do" and most workers had no good use for additional free time.[48]

Several speakers echoed his remarks.[49] Otto Pragan of the International Chemical Workers Union agreed that, historically, shorter hours had been a "social movement spearheaded by the whole labor movement and the liberal forces in the United States," founded "on economic as well as moral grounds." However, the "moral grounds" had been superseded and the liberal forces directed elsewhere. Support for shorter hours remained only in a "few selected industries for specific reasons related to the economic growth."[50]

Meany, Brooks, and their allies were met with strong opposition. Sylvia Gottlieb, research director for the Communications Workers of America replied:

I want to take issue with Mr. Brooks' conclusion that there is no evidence of a desire for a shorter workweek. . . . [T]hat is not the case certainly among a large segment of female workers employed in the telephone industry. . . . We estimate that there are roughly 300,000 telephone operators in the U.S. Almost without exception, when they are asked what is the one thing they want in collective bargaining this year their response is a shorter work day or a shorter work week.[51]

E. W. Kenney observed that the "International Woodworkers at their conventions year after year have gone on record for establishment of the six-hour day." Moreover, "it split our union considerably when it came up for negotiations."[52] Jack Barbash, research director for the Industrial Union Department of the AFL-CIO reported that the hours issue was still "a terribly important thing in the collective bargaining picture. I would guess there presently isn't a union engaged in collective bargaining in which the question of shorter hours is not an important consideration."[53]

Frank Honigsbaum, director of research for the International Brotherhood of Paper Makers argued that, instead of becoming the "most meaningful thing people do," jobs created by automation were more "likely to be uninteresting and boring." Barbash also disputed Brooks's claims about "meaningful" jobs by pointing out that the eight-hour day was "as socially and culturally oppressive" as a sixteen- or eighteen-hour day. "Meaningful work" was largely a middle-class fiction. He added that Brooks was "excessively cynical . . . and pessimistic about workers' interest in the reduction of hours. . . . [I]t is of great importance to workers and to unions." He concluded that shorter hours remained a "wholesale social movement of great consequence" and that increasing leisure still promised a richer and fuller life.[54] Higher wages and shorter hours, together, should remain labor's primary objective.

Brooks, stung by accusations that he had joined the bourgeoisie, retreated somewhat but continued to deny that the shorter-hours issue was still as important as higher wages or still represented an ongoing "social and cultural" movement. He added, "One final point: I would avoid any ethical judgments about the morality or desirability of shorter hours."[55]

1963

The week of President Kennedy's assassination, the House of Representatives' Select Subcommittee on Education and Labor, chaired by Elmer J. Holland (D-PA) began to hear testimony on a series of bills (HR 355, 1680, 3102, 3320, 9074) introduced by a group led by Congressman Holland and Senator Joseph S. Clark (D-PA). The bills would have amended the Fair Labor Standards Act of 1938, reducing workweek maximums to thirty-five or thirty-two hours and increasing overtime penalties.[56] The press largely ignored the hearings, concerned with the death of the president. Nevertheless, the hearings were an important milestone illustrating labor's turn from shorter hours.

Holland began the hearings by recalling that Kennedy had called unemployment the nation's most serious economic problem. Unemployment had remained above 5.5 percent for the past five years despite healthy economic growth, casting doubt on the theory that the nation could grow itself out of chronic unemployment.[57] The hearings became a sounding board that resonated with the growing concern in the nation that unemployment had become immune to economic expansion. A variety of witnesses confirmed Holland's fears. Leon Keyserling, having served as chair of the Council of Economic Advisors under Truman and Eisenhower after his influential role in FDR's administration, explained:

> Unemployment continuing to rise despite . . . the economic upturn . . . vindicates what I have been saying for 10 years, that unemployment is rising chronically and is going to continue to rise chronically . . . unless there are very profound changes in policies dealing with the problem.[58]

Keyserling's Keynesian solution was to increase economic demand by ever-faster government spending. However, other labor leaders and economists pressed their argument that shorter hours were a necessary part of the unemployment solution. Robert Kirkwood, director of the United Electrical, Radio and Machine Workers of America reiterated labor's traditional argument that shorter hours were necessary for sustainable economic growth, making William Green's point yet again that automation forced the choice between unemployment and leisure. Jimmy Hoffa of the International Brotherhood of Teamsters made similar remarks.[59] Andrew Biemiller, director of the AFL-CIO Department of Legislation, took issue with Keyserling, noting that even the rapid growth of government (accounting for nearly half the new jobs recently created) had proved unable to bring unemployment down to acceptable levels. Lazare Teper, economist and director of research for the ILGWU, attributed the lack of job creation in a growing economy to working hours having "remained virtually static" since 1947—an unprecedented development during a period of increasing productivity and economic growth. He also pointed to an ALF-CIO report that showed it took "twice as much GNP [gross national product] to create one job today, as it did in 1958–60."[60] Eli Ginzberg, economics professor at Columbia and director of President Eisenhower's Conservation of Human Resources Project, agreed that the consumer demand necessary for sustainable economic growth still depended on increasing leisure: "In short, the expanding part of the economy . . . depends upon consumers having not only money but time. . . . [A]s an economist, I want to stress the fact that a tremendous part of our economy depends on people having leisure."[61]

Such arguments were countered by businessmen, economists, and committee members opposed to the legislation. Ginzberg noted that the Kennedy administration "viewed with alarm any downward reduction in hours," an observation confirmed by several witnesses.[62] Clyde Dankert, professor of economics at Dartmouth, warned that "the 35-hour workweek is a luxury which we cannot yet afford" and that America would lose the respect of "undeveloped nations" if the legislation passed.[63] A Texas business executive described increased leisure as a "useless waste of our national man-hour resource," which instead ought to be spent growing the economy or on constructive government programs—a sentiment shared by several witnesses.[64]

Ben Seligman of the Retail Clerks International Union pointed out that economists and businesspeople were expressing "their horror at the thought that workers might enjoy somewhat more leisure," believing it simply a waste. He noted that electricians in New York were vilified for their five-hour day, "savagely attacked for selfishness and lack of patriotism . . . [even though] well over a thousand new jobs were created."[65]

Still, supporters of the bills continued to defend shorter hours as the realization of the American dream of Higher Progress. Ginzberg argued that leisure had "given many constructive dimensions to our society" and had already improved "family relationships and community relationships." Economists and others opposed to the legislation had confused "recreation," the aimless, wasteful use of free time, with "leisure time activities" that "can be very important for a progressive democracy. The more people participate in philanthropy, church affairs, politics, the better . . . [and the more they find] satisfactions in their nonwork areas of life."[66] Kirkwood, taking issue with the businessmen's rhapsodic portrayals of work, argued that "companies are making automatons of their employees"[67] and stated:

> Greater leisure is an absolute good these days, not an evil, as some companies would have us believe. Greater leisure is necessary as a release from the great monotony and tedium of the rapid pace of work that is the lot of millions of workers. . . . Greater leisure is necessary to give workers an opportunity to broaden their horizons.[68]

Kirkwood quoted Justice William O. Douglas, who had recently spoken about the promise of leisure. Douglas, repeating an argument that many others had made, pointed out that the ancient Greeks had constructed their Golden Age on the foundation of leisure. Technology was making a *democratic* Golden Age possible. Machines were taking the place of human slaves, doing the nation's necessary work and making it possible for "all people" to follow the Greek ideal: "In our society we must find ways for all people to improve their minds, bodies, and souls with the new slaves [of] automated machinery."[69] However, Kirkwood lamented, "the only thing the working people are getting today out of automation is unemployment."[70]

James Cary, president of the International Union of Electrical, Radio, and Machine Workers, followed Kirkwood. In the face of "savage" criticism directed at New York's electricians for their twenty-five-hour week, Cary remained unapologetic. He explained that the "calamity howlers," business, and a "reactionary press" had condemned labor's progress for over a hundred years. He continued to insist that the new leisure his union's members enjoyed was vitally important, rejecting the claims of businessmen that leisure was a trivial waste of time. He agreed with Kirkwood (and with Gompers and generations of laborites) that automation still held out "the hope for a new freedom."[71] The machine still "could be man's liberator," offering "the potential for a glorious new day."[72] His union continued to support the progressive shortening of work hours as the realization of America's promise of freedom:

> We support the shorter workweek, the shorter work year, the shorter work life not only as a means of helping to restore full employment, but also because we think that man should be given maximum personal use of his lifetime. . . . [W]hat greater blow could be struck for personal freedom than to tell each man that his personal time will be increased by a week each year, an hour each day, or 2 or 3 years in his lifetime?[73]

Legislative action had to be taken, however, to make sure that the new machines provided the new freedom of shorter hours rather than doom the nation to chronic unemployment.

However, most supporters of the legislation followed Meany and Reuther, abandoning labor's traditional, positive defense of leisure as the essence of progress to rely exclusively on the unemployment benefits of a thirty-five-hour week.[74] Even ILGWU's Lazare Teper, ignoring his union and its leaders' eloquent and long-standing defense of shorter hours as the gateway to Higher Progress, spoke only of economic benefits: "The need to limit the workweek in order to provide job opportunities . . . was paramount."[75]

1979

The 1963 congressional hearings ended with the bills and amendments related to the Fair Labor Standards Act of 1938 dying in committee. In October 1979 Representative John Conyers (D-MI) renewed attempts to amend the act.[76] By this time, labor had come to rely almost completely on an unemployment defense of a thirty-five-hour maximum. What labor had always seen as the conjoined-twin constituents of progress—shorter hours and higher wages— had divided, the one emerging as labor's cardinal objective and the other relegated to a subordinate role. Throughout the extensive hearings in 1979, leisure was seldom defended on its own merits, the dream of Higher Progress in an expanding realm of freedom virtually absent. The only voices reminding Congress of what awakened the labor movement in the first place and sustained it for over a century were those of the historians Philip Foner and Bill McGaughey. McGaughey's words were among the last recorded by the committee:

If the economy kept rolling along . . . it would turn up, on its own, all the things which we would want in life—an abundance of food and other materials, enough free time to enjoy them, opportunities for a variety of rich experiences, wisdom, beauty, good health, good entertainment. . . . Once life's minimal . . . requirements are met, what does further economic progress bring? These and other precious things? No, our experience has been quite different. All that sacrificing of leisure for a "higher standard of living" has not produced material or spiritual satisfaction, but mass-market consumer manipulation and deception, weakening of thought and will, deepening symptoms of decay in our institution-blighted lives. Our reward has . . . not [been] riches or happiness. . . . Bureaucracy has increased. Bureaucratic institutions have an enormous appetite to appropriate our time, our money, our energy, our lives. . . . This is a world governed by Parkinson's Law: "Work expands so as to fill the time available. . . ." Recognizing it we may perhaps substitute our own goals for the bureaucracy's . . . [the] goal of freedom—the shorter workweek. Let the economy take form around that possibility. A new, leaner economy will emerge. [However,] people at last will have time to do what they would want to do with their lives.[77]

Farewell the Working Class

In 1965 under a headline proclaiming "Union Labor: Less Militant, More Affluent," *Time* magazine quoted long-time radical labor leader Sidney Lens as saying, "The labor movement is really a carbon copy of capitalism." The reporter then added, "It is more than that: it is capitalism," going on to describe labor's "spiritual sag" and loss of vision. Summing up his interviews with George Meany and Harry Van Arsdale, the reporter concluded, "The cause no longer seems to cry out for crusaders . . . [f]or those motivated by idealism."[78]

The reporter explained labor's "leadership lag and spiritual sag" primarily in terms of "America's vast affluence"; labor had been tamed by what historian Steve Frasier and others have called "goulash capitalism." Frasier is one of several scholars who agree with the *Time* reporter that affluence and the lure of consumerism diverted labor, resulting finally in its virtual merger with capitalism.[79]

However, consumerism alone did not tame labor. Workers had always wanted more money to spend and, as recent scholarship has confirmed, found class-identifying ways to consume and use new products so long as they had sufficient time. More important was labor's "spiritual sag"—its loss of the vision of Higher Progress and its abandonment of the quest to establish an alternative to capitalism's "selfish system" and "goulash" on the basis of the steady reduction of working hours.

Labor's interests became identical with management's when it embraced Roosevelt's and capitalism's new projects of eternal economic growth and Full-Time, Full Employment. As a consequence of its spiritual sag, labor also

abandoned its recurrent critique of modern work as tyrannical, enslaving, mechanical, devitalized, dehumanizing, boring, and alienating, turning instead
to embrace the dominant bourgeois morality—what Hannah Arendt called the
modern "glorification of work" and the attendant myths of "good jobs."[80]

Subsequently, having forgotten Higher Progress, labor began to neglect the
unemployment defense of shorter hours as well. Even in the face of what labor
had always deemed "intolerably high" levels of chronic unemployment, labor
and its supporters put their hopes almost entirely on Keynesian solutions and
economic growth.

A Freedom Too Far: Labor's Allies Abandon Shorter Hours

As labor leaders fell into step with the ideology and politics of Full-Time, Full
Employment, labor's traditional allies followed along. David Riesman is a case
in point. Generally regarded as the most prominent and influential sociologist
of his generation and coauthor of the best-selling *The Lonely Crowd*, Riesman,
together with several of his colleagues such as Helen and Straughton Lynd, Paul
Lazarsfeld, George Lundberg, and Reuel Denney, was initially interested in the
coming "age of mass leisure." After World War II, they set about planning for
the transition from a traditional society built on work to one facing substantial
liberation.

In the first edition of *The Lonely Crowd*, published in 1950, Riesman held
a view of "the progressive shortening of the hours of labor" in keeping with labor's traditional vision and consistent with what Robert Hutchins called "liberalism."[81] Moreover, Riesman had discovered a new threat to liberty and leisure
facing the nation, the "other-directed man." The rapid growth of the suburbs,
mass consumption, and conformity at work had created a new breed of American, no longer self-reliant, depending on the mass media and other impersonal
social forces for individual views and life choices. Losing autonomy, average
citizens were also losing community. Communities of authentic companionship, issuing from personal autonomy, were being replaced by the "lonely
crowd"—groups of individuals held together by the ephemera of consumption,
media, and conformity. His eulogists remembered that he had championed
"empathetic individualism that was responsive to civic responsibilities" in the
face of the "conformist tendencies of modern mass society."[82]

Riesman maintained that leisure could help guard Americans from the
emerging threat of conformity:

> The promise of leisure and play for the other-directed man is that it may
> be easier in play than in work to break some of the institutional charac-
> terological barriers to autonomy . . . [and leisure] can increasingly become
> the sphere for the development of skill and competencies in the art of liv-
> ing. Play may prove to be the sphere in which there is still some room left
> for the . . . autonomous man to reclaim his individual character.[83]

However, it would take determined effort to realize the promise of leisure: "We have still to discover the player." Because the "sphere of leisure is blocked in America" it was essential to "develop institutional means to release the American leisure society from some of its chains."[84] Compounding the problem, advocates of consumerism and conformity were finding new, "needless" work to do, rejecting the freedom offered by modern labor-saving machines and making leadership and vision doubly important:

> If the other-directed people should discover how much needless work they do, discover that their own thoughts and their own lives are quite as interesting as other people's . . . then we might expect them to become more attentive to their own feelings and aspirations.[85]

The challenge of leisure represented the perennial challenge of American liberty. It is the "inner-directed man . . . [who] listens to tradition" and "is more steadily guided by the internalized voices of ancestors" and so is better able to meet freedom's [or autonomy's] autotelic challenge:

> We are looking for a quality we can only vaguely describe: it is various and rhythmical; it breaks through social forms and as constantly recreates them; . . . it is at once meaningful, in the sense of giving us intrinsic satisfaction, and meaningless, in the sense of having no pressing utilitarian purpose. It is some such model as this, I suggest, which haunts us when we consider leisure and judge its quality in ourselves and others. It is a model which has been elaborated in our culture, and yet which transcends culture.[86]

However, by the time he wrote the introduction to the 1961 edition of *The Lonely Crowd*, Riesman had changed his mind. Daniel Bell (and others) had taken Riesman and other "prophets of play," such as John Kenneth Galbraith and David Potter, to task for continuing to suggest that leisure "in itself" could be "significant" or "meaningful." Riesman appears to have simply conceded: "We soon came around to agreeing with [Bell] . . . [that] leisure could not carry the burden of making life meaningful for most people. . . . [L]eisure itself cannot rescue work, but fails with it, and can only be meaningful for most men if work is meaningful."[87]

Joining Daniel Bell and a tide of converts, including leaders of "second wave feminism" such as Betty Friedan, Riesman, B. F. Skinner, and other social scientists discovered the need to re-create and restructure work. Leaving behind their traditional support of progressively shorter hours, they began to believe it possible to graft autonomy, mutuality, and equality, qualities they once hoped would grow in the freedom of leisure, onto modern jobs. Riesman and many others who followed Roosevelt's vision of Full-Time, Full Employment had changed their minds about progress.

Riesman recognized that the creation of "meaningful and significant work" would be just as difficult as finding direction in an age of leisure. The new challenge to make work, instead of leisure and play, "significant in itself" and "meaningful itself" was just as much a visionary and utopian-sounding project as mass leisure. He also recognized that the new vision depended on perpetual economic growth, a daunting enterprise that might not succeed.[88]

For generations laborites had seen work's perfection as depending on "the reduction of human labor to its lowest terms."[89] After the 1950s, labor's traditional supporters, progressives, and liberals began to distance themselves from shorter hours, redefining leisure as a problem rather than a promise and embracing the new view that "meaningful work," satisfying in and for itself, took precedence, thus strengthening the position of labor's traditional business opponents who claimed to be job creators. Instead of trying to combat the commodification and trivializing of leisure by building new infrastructures of freedom and imagining new possibilities in the emerging realm of freedom, labor's supporters turned to the "glorification of labor," a problematic enterprise that entailed the permanent erection of new frameworks of necessities in both the marketplace and new government programs.[90]

Participating in a CBS TV panel in the summer of 1962, in the midst of the Cold War, Eric Sevareid argued that the greatest threat facing the nation was the certain increase in leisure for the average American, who was incapable of making good use of it.[91] Arthur Schlesinger agreed: "The most dangerous threat hanging over American society is the threat of leisure . . . and those who have the least preparation for leisure will have the most of it."[92] *Walden Two*, by B. F. Skinner, is one of the last truly utopian novels depicting "labor-saving" machines freeing humans from work for a better life. The evocative phrase "leisure's our levitation" is at the book's center; Skinner also used the centuries-old utopian premise of the four-hour workday. After writing *Walden Two* in 1948, however, Skinner looked beyond freedom and dignity.[93] Whereas in *Walden Two* he illustrated how psychology could become science's ultimate labor-saving device, freeing humans from antisocial and neurotic desires to consume and work after technology had ensured abundance for all, by 1971 he had decided that "leisure is a condition for which the human species has been badly prepared." Mass leisure and its misuse had become serious problems because "there has been no chance for effective selection of either a relevant genetic endowment or relevant culture." For the time being, and well into the future, the "species" would have to be managed by social engineers and professionals who found "meaningful" work for those lesser-evolved creatures around them.[94]

Conclusion

Thus labor and its supporters began to trivialize leisure, assuming that because so many people appeared to be using their leisure badly, no virtuous or important use could be hoped for or even imagined. The modern abandonment of leisure in favor of Full-Time, Full Employment is in part explained by the widespread assumption that ordinary people (and the nation) are incapable of substantial humane and moral growth and will always need the discipline of work at life's center. Like the Puritans of Cotton Mather's day, those who doubt and trivialize leisure today often embrace a work ethic quite different from labor's traditional view that work is a means to better ends. Today many believe, instead, Puritan-like, that human nature is naturally selfish and essentially uncivil, controllable only by the harness of perpetual work.[95]

Labor and its supporters became complicit in management's strategy of promoting "full-time" jobs. With this strategy, corporations and modern conservatives have been able to hold labor and progressives at bay politically, claiming their strategy is the best provider of the most precious of resources, new jobs, using a moral high ground that is now increasingly employed to claim that capitalism's controversial features—selfishness, greed, unrestrained competition, and exploitation of peoples and the environment—are virtues.[96] Donald Trump regularly excuses his controversial projects by claiming he is creating jobs.[97] With many of its leaders repeating with George Brooks that "work will probably be the most meaningful thing people do," labor lost a major part of its essential purpose, ceasing to struggle toward the opening "realm of freedom," no longer fighting for higher wages *and* shorter hours, bread *and* roses, consumerism *and* leisure—no longer looking for liberation "beyond the influence of factory bolts and locks." As Sidney Lens observed, "The labor movement [became] . . . a carbon copy of capitalism."

9

Higher Progress Fades, Holdouts Persist

While increasingly rare, representations of Higher Progress could still be found in the United States after the 1970s. Rank-and-file union workers in locations such as Battle Creek, Michigan, and Akron, Ohio, through the 1980s and into the 1990s held on to the vision. However, after voting twice to reinstate the six-hour day after World War II, Kellogg's workers began to move to eight-hour days during the 1970s, and Goodyear ended its short-day schedule in the 1950s.[1] The controversial change from six back to eight hours sparked a discourse about leisure and work that was a microcosm of the national debates.

The experience of the new leisure had not been uniformly pleasant or rewarding in the two cities. A growing number of the workers, primarily males, found the extra two hours to be a freedom too far after the 1950s. Some reported that they were bored and preferred work to having nothing to do. For others the extra leisure was too much of a challenge to established social and gender roles and at odds with the advent of a primarily economic understanding of progress and standard of living.

Whereas during the 1930s, and even after the reinstatement of six-hour days after World War II, most workers talked about their new leisure in terms of new opportunities and freedoms, after the 1990s those who had chosen to return to eight-hour days most often used a language of necessity. Echoing national labor leaders such as Walter Reuther, Kellogg's and Goodyear workers had begun to speak of the need to work "full-time," of economic necessity that was absolute and impervious to wage increases. For many of these workers, the choice to work less had simply been foreclosed—abundance was no longer a possibility. John L. Lewis and David Riesman branded additional leisure as loafing, unpatriotic, silly, or only for "the girls." Kellogg's and Goodyear workers joined them and also began to echo national leaders such as George Brooks who were beginning to talk of the intrinsic rewards of work. Influenced as well by their companies' attempts to propagandize work as a management strategy, they came to speak of the importance of work remaining at the center of life to ensure a serious, worthwhile, and manly existence. Free time was for those who had nothing important to do, the hangers-on in the community, the ne'er-do-wells who would waste the afternoon at the movies. A reversal in the ways work and leisure were spoken about in both cities had occurred, a change in rhetoric that had very real results. Insisting that money was the only real job benefit, most of the men in the two cities abandoned labor's tradition, higher wages *and* shorter hours, to depend solely on the first.[2]

Women were the clear majority of the six-hour holdouts, and their predominance in preferring the six-hour day was possibly its most commented-on characteristic after the mid-1950s.[3] The division along gender lines was, at least in part, the result of changes in company management styles. In keeping with the new Human Relations management philosophy that gained ascendancy after the 1950s, Kellogg's turned from extrinsic motivators (that is, the higher wages and shorter hours of the six-hour day) to intrinsic ones (attitude, commitment, team work), attempting quite openly and explicitly to convince employees that their job was the most important, meaningful, and serious part of their lives. Kellogg's management formed alliances with senior male workers and, according to its own reports, successfully built a profitable, productive, and tractable workforce.[4]

Male workers often reported that they felt bored or ill at ease with "too much time on their hands."[5] One of the important sources of their discontent was the large number of women at home and around their neighborhoods. Instead of trying to discover ways to relate to the women around them in the unfamiliar, often contested territory, the men under the cover of necessity frequently escaped to second jobs or transferred into eight-hour departments at Kellogg's. Among the best-known examples of such male discomfort, reported widely in the press and mentioned in congressional hearings, were "honey-dew days"—a neologism coined to describe men off work who felt besieged by women suggesting things for them to do.[6]

On both the national and the local levels, laborites began to feminize shorter hours, insisting that it was only because of lack of strength or ignorance of the importance or necessity of work in a person's life that "the girls" held on to the six-hour day—"like a puppy holds on to a root" according to one Kellogg's executive.[7] Men who continued to work six-hour days were frequently called "disabled," "weak," or "sissies."[8]

The new coalition of labor and management, propagandizing work while feminizing and trivializing leisure, broke the long tradition of worker solidarity in support of progressively shorter work hours, dividing men and women, junior and senior employees, and union and unorganized workers. The coalition, with its human relations agenda, also effectively obscured the vision of Higher

Progress that had been labor's ideological wellspring. While the traces of these developments are somewhat obscure at the national level, in the histories of Kellogg's and Goodyear's return to "full-time" work schedules, they are clearly visible.

In the face of pressure to give up six-hour days, an important minority of Kellogg's and Goodyear workers held out, defending shorter hours as just as practical as higher wages, the source of new freedom, and still half of the definition of a higher standard of living. Often branded mavericks by the eight-hour supporters, they adamantly supported labor's cause of a century and a half, reporting that new, valuable opportunities had opened for them. Continuing to speak in terms of freedom, they described how the extra two hours had permitted them to experiment with "how people usually lived" and to "find new things to do" with their families and in their communities. They had discovered something new, however, often reporting that the balance of their life seemed be shifting;[9] as Bill McGaughey put it in his congressional testimony, their lives had begun "to take form around the possibility" of freedom.[10]

The anthropologist Margaret Mead detected a shifting in the balance of American life as well. In 1957 she concluded that the generation that had married after World War II was "shifting the balance from work . . . to the home . . . that has now become the reason for existence, which . . . justifies working at all."[11] Men were returning to the home and participating there as never before—activities such as do-it-yourself projects and sports with their children promised to revitalize family and community life: "A great deal has been done to turn modern home life into a self-rewarding delight."[12] But like the Kellogg's mavericks, she recognized that much remained to be done; "hazards" loomed. It would take a good deal of deliberate, focused effort and will to readjust and adapt the family and community to the coming age of leisure. Old maladaptive habits and work values might persist, complicating and perhaps delaying the transition.

Mead's was an apt prediction of events in Battle Creek. The six-hour holdouts would frequently complain or make jokes about the men's claims to have to work full time. They would repeat the nineteenth-century axiom "work to live, don't live to work" and challenge the men's claims that they could not afford time for normal family duties or community activities, pointing to the optional consumer purchases they made. The mavericks also tended to resist Kellogg's management's efforts to propagandize work. One of the most articulate of the Kellogg's union members I spoke to, Joy Blanchard, spoke for other six-hour workers when she said, "Work was never the most important thing in my life."

Instead, she and her coworkers told stories of experimenting with different kinds of social interactions and relationships—of new opportunities for intimacy and close friendships, for storytelling, games, clubs, choirs, sports, church, shared household projects (quilting, canning, gardening), and informal gatherings. Frequently, they would report that the extra time resulted in conflict: arguments about household duties and daily schedules. However, they most often saw such disagreements as manageable, parts of a normal adjustment. Replying to the "honeydew" cliché, the women defended their efforts to find active things to do with the men, alternatives to sitting around the house or watching TV. The women often saw conflicts and disagreements as normal, healthy parts of living together, offering the chance to negotiate and come to agreement. Several of what were commonly known as "Kellogg's couples" (in which both worked six-hour shifts) talked about having had time and energy to work through disagreements and build the skills necessary for intimacy. When mention was made of the classes offered by the International Ladies' Garment Workers' Union (ILGWU) in marriage and family living, many couples spoke of attempting to persuade their local union to follow the needleworkers' lead. The following exchange between a Kellogg's couple, Art and Donnelly White, is representative of numerous interviews:

ART WHITE: I purposely bid into a [Kellogg's] six-hour department so that Donnelly and I could get up, go to breakfast like we are doing this morning, . . . go to work, work diligently for six hours, then come home and go to supper.

AUTHOR: Now wait a minute. . . . Are you spending more time with your wife here? I thought you and your buddies didn't like those "honeydew days."

ART: Of course, of course. [After the children moved away] there was just Donnelly and I. What you gonna do? Get a divorce?

DONNELLY WHITE: I like Art. I like to be with him a lot. . . .

AUTHOR: Did you think that [six hours] was good for your marriage?

DONNELLY: Yes!

AUTHOR: The [extra] time . . . [you had for] breakfast?

DONNELLY: Oh yes, yes.

ART: She is a very good person to be with.

DONNELLY: Yes [six hours helped our marriage].

ART: You do [think that], Donnelly? It didn't hurt?

DONNELLY: Some people say . . . that too much time around your partner is bad for you, but some people thrive on it.

ART: But we argued sometimes.

DONNELLY: Maybe so, but we always made up. . . . We got good at fighting . . . able to work things out. . . . That was good, better than [another couple,] who never talked and had resentments build up—they were miserable. Couldn't stand each other but had to live together. Never went to breakfast or did things.

ART: I remember them. He [the husband] went to eight [hours] as soon as he could and believed that go to work was all he had to do. . . . He didn't need to put any effort in at home, off work.

DONNELLY: A lot [of the men] were like that—lazy and let-somebody-else-do-it-all when they were off.

AUTHOR: Did some of them think of their jobs as their primary responsibility?

DONNELLY: I guess you could say that. They were proud of working
hard, would brag about it, but some of them were sort of miserable
human beings otherwise.[13]

Some of the mavericks reported that they were spending their extra time
doing things for themselves: shopping, creative projects, hobbies, reading, writing, and spending time alone and in nature. However, interviewers repeatedly
heard stories about the importance of leisure *activities*—of doing things with
friends, working with community groups, and finding interesting and engaging projects. Interviewers repeatedly heard criticisms of empty leisure, devoid
of contacts and interests. Several of the mavericks judged that the passive alternatives offered by consumerism and commercial recreation were simply not
worth the time; as Joy Blanchard observed of those who found nothing better to
do than shop or watch TV, "They [might] just as well go back to work."[14]

Holdouts: Industrial Feminism versus
Prisoners of Men's Dreams

At roughly the same time that my students and I were talking to people who
had worked for Kellogg's and Goodyear, Suzanne Gordon was interviewing
women for *Prisoners of Men's Dreams: Striking Out for a New Feminine Future*.
Gordon interviewed over one hundred women, mostly professionals, and found
them stressed to the breaking point by the competing demands of family and
work, disillusioned by the unfulfilled promises of their jobs, or co-opted by the
"highly competitive, aggressive, and individualist" workplace. What Gordon
described as the "transformative vision" at the heart of the modern feminist
movement had been stymied.[15]

Traditionally, women had "devoted themselves to nurturing, empowering,
and caring for others." In a world

little dedicated to sustaining relationships, encouraging cooperation, or
rewarding altruism rather than greed, women have historically defined,
defended, and sustained a set of insights, values, and activities which, if
never dominant, at least provided a counterweight and an alternative ideal
to the anomie, disconnectedness, fragmentation, and commercialization
of our culture.[16]

As women entered the public world of work, many of them hoped to infuse
cooperation, caring, and mutuality into their new professions, converting
the "hierarchical workplace" into something more convivial and humane.
This "transformative feminism," however, was eclipsed by "equal opportunity

feminism" that embraced the "masculine mystique," valuing "competition above caring, work above love, power above empowerment, and personal wealth above human worth":[17]

> Just as generations of men have succumbed to the lure of [a masculine] American dream, so too have millions of women scrambled after an illusion. . . . Now standing beside [Adam Smith's economic man], we have economic woman—a group of women who have grown so competitive and individualistic that they can think of little but themselves and advancing their careers. [Obsessed by work] too many women believe today that work . . . will be their salvation.[18]

The result of the failure of "transformative feminism" has been "a crisis of caring" as communities and families fail to provide the most fundamental of human needs: people to care for and about each other.[19] While not giving up entirely on reforming modern workplaces, Gordon hoped to revitalize feminism's "transformative vision," primarily by instituting a "National Care Agenda" (government reforms to provide more time for families and communities— parental leave, subsidized day care, health care, national pensions and vacation policies) and by relying on caring professions such as nursing that might be able to address the "crisis of caring."[20] But she also recognized what working women had known for generations, that one of the best hopes for transformative feminism was a general reduction of working hours.

The Kellogg's and Goodyear six-hour holdouts often described a vision similar to Gordon's transformative feminism, claiming that their six-hour day opened additional opportunities to make that vision real. However, they shared few of the initial illusions about work that Gordon found widespread among professional women. For the most part, the Kellogg's mavericks thought of themselves as hard-headed realists, recognizing that jobs in the marketplace, even in the professions, were and would always be about competition (getting ahead, success), power, control, and individual wealth (property or proprietary access to intangible valuables). They had long recognized what Gordon finally concluded in her book: time needed to be freed from the "selfish system" in order to realize women's transformative vision.

The vision Gordon found expressed by professional women toward the end of the twentieth century had been the heart of "Industrial feminism" for over a century. Mildred Moore coined the term and first described industrial feminism in her master's thesis at the University of Chicago in 1915.[21] Beginning with the Lowell women such as Huldah Stone, continuing with immigrants in the needle trades at the turn of the century such as Elizabeth Hasanovitz, and then with workers' education leaders such as Fannia Cohn and then the Kellogg's and Goodyear mavericks (together with labor's allies such as Josephine Goldmark and Dorothy Canfield Fisher), women fought for shorter hours to make room in their lives, and in the lives of the men around them, for cooperation, caring, mutuality, and conviviality. They also shared the modern feminist dream of improving the workplace, not by taking on the Herculean task of reforming the competition, eagerness to possess, and self-seeking that define capitalism, but by using the job as a stepping stone to better things, taming it gradually by shortening the work hours of all and so eventually subordinating work and the marketplace to the more important business of living freely.

Critics of Consumerism and the Harried Leisure Class

One of the explanations historians have offered for the ending of shorter hours has been changes in leisure behavior. The new uses of leisure have been described in various ways: as commodified, alienated, devitalized, and "goods-intensive."[22] Laborites made the same points for generations, viewing commercial recreation as a threat because it offered passive watching rather than active involvement, solitary rather than social experiences; according to the ILGWU's David Dubinsky, what commercial recreation and consumerism lacked was "human fellowship."[23] The Kellogg's and Goodyear mavericks noticed a change in leisure activities as well, remembering a time before mass entertainment when people did more things together: going to local ball games, playing table tennis and other games, visiting, sitting on the front porch, doing community projects, telling stories, going on picnics, tending community gardens, and holding bazaars and reunions. As one of the mavericks put it, "Now people seem to have less time and do things in a hurry." They also noticed that free time involved less socializing and more expense: going shopping; participating in activities that required automobiles, motorcycles, or boats; and visiting restaurants that "encouraged you to leave as soon as you got there."[24]

Rather than continuing to offer the promise of Higher Progress, "mass leisure" was more often seen as a problem during the 1950s and 1960s; boredom was a popular topic in the press and among academics.[25] Unlike the parks and dancehalls at the turn of the century described by Roy Rosenzweig and Kathy Peiss (described in Chapter 4), the new kinds of leisure activities and commercial recreation available after mid-century depended increasingly on spectators and idle consumption—on passive audiences and consumers who contributed little or nothing except their presence and money. Opportunities for conviviality and for challenging existing mores once offered by the saloons Rosenzweig described were increasingly curtailed by the need to maximize profit.[26] Lizabeth Cohen agrees that whereas commercial recreation and consumerism once offered workers opportunities to find community, express ethnic identities, construct working class subculture, and even aspire to a transeconomic equality with other groups, their most recent incarnations have limited civic engagement and perpetuated racial, gender, and class subordinations.[27]

In accord with the economy of scale, businesses found it more profitable to serve more people, faster.[28] Mass-produced entertainment and recreation have tended to reduce the time required to enjoy the goods or services consumed. The result, as the economist Staffan Linder wrote, is the "harried leisure class."

Linder reasoned that the utility, the usefulness and desirability, of any good or service was in part a function of the time spent consuming it. Laborites had long suggested a commonsense version of the theory: people need time to use and enjoy what they purchase, and the more they were able to buy, the more time they would need. Linder, however, documented a change in American leisure behavior from "time intensive" leisure in which less is consumed in more time, to "goods intensive" leisure in which more is consumed in less time, explaining that as work became more productive, leisure's capacity to absorb more goods and services had to expand as well.[29] Linder never adequately explained why consumers of the late twentieth century failed to follow labor's commonsense advice and simply take more leisure to enjoy the products they were able to buy, thus restoring "equilibrium." Rather, quoting Walter Kerr's *Decline of Pleasure*, he described a "growth mania" infecting the industrial nations—an inexplicable willingness to sacrifice "relaxed enjoyment," "the pleasure of cultivating our minds," and even the enjoyment of "the table and bed" to the imperatives of economic growth and consumerism.[30]

The historians' finding that consumerism emerged after World War II as a kind of duty, a necessary part of keeping production going and creating jobs, provides a better explanation of Linder's harried leisure. Lizabeth Cohen notes that consumerism became part of the modern definition of virtue that, along with the job, has come to constitute a substantial part of contemporary morality.[31] Roosevelt's ideology of Full-Time, Full Employment carried with it, as a corollary, the imperative to consume. Along with "harried leisure" and the "growth mania," the results of the consumption imperative were increased divisions between social groups ("marketing segments" divided by class, gender, age, race, and ethnicity), the undermining of working-class commonalities and equality, the weakening of communities, and declining civic engagement.[32] The "consumers' republic" has moved ever closer to a thoroughly commodified public sphere, where little time remains for Dubinsky's human fellowship.

Undoubtedly, many of labor's traditional middle-class supporters followed the need-to-consume-to-create-jobs logic in their turn from shorter hours. Labor leaders, fully embracing Full-Time, Full Employment and what Hannah Arendt called "the modern glorification of work,"[33] subscribed to the consumption imperative as well. However, the men and women who worked for Kellogg's and Goodyear seldom reported that they spent their money because they felt an obligation or that consuming had become a virtue for them. The reasons they gave for spending money were simple: alluring products and services and the absence of a viable alternative.

Previous generations of laborites, such as Huldah Stone, had cautioned their sisters and brothers to spend their wages carefully so that they would have more time to live and escape the capitalist "selfish system"; spending beyond one's means would surely re-enslave a person. Thrift was the avenue to liberation.

However, with the fading of Higher Progress, fewer good reasons remained to be thrifty; fewer enjoyments other than consumerism were available or could even be imagined. Thus, debt mounted,[34] more people began to work longer hours, and a language of necessity thrived that recognized only need building on need and never enough.

Workers who returned to eight-hour days in Akron and Battle Creek talked of their aspirations almost exclusively in terms of the things that money would provide or of finding enough money to pay for what they had begun to speak of as necessities. Rarely did they speak in terms of freedom to do more things with family and friends or to improve their social skills. By contrast, Kellogg's mavericks frequently spoke of freedom's progress in terms of having the chance to spend more time with others doing music and crafts, dancing, playing sports, telling stories, caregiving, and of saving enough to retire on—leaving the plant for good as soon as possible.

Finally, the cacophony of messages urging individuals to buy and keep on buying and to expect the advent of life-centering "good jobs" drowned out those few voices that still extolled the virtues of six hours. As Jacques Ellul observed, one unfortunate result of the ascendancy of the "ideology of work," and one might add, the consumers' republic, has been the inability to imagine an alternative.[35] Jürgen Habermas offered a similar analysis, concluding that "instrumental rationality" has virtually eclipsed other ways to reason and to imagine possibilities. Modern reason has nearly lost its normative, dramaturgical and imaginative, and communicative dimensions, becoming incapable of conceiving realities beyond the sphere of utility and necessity.[36] Other than to note that in shopping centers "consumption and leisure were becoming inseparably intertwined," Lizabeth Cohen and other proponents of a consumerist interpretation of recent American history fail to recognize that alternatives to consumerism (and to the "ideology of work") existed in workers' vision of Higher Progress and in labor's long tradition of higher wages *and* shorter hours.[37] Historians have yet to fully appreciate that the most fundamental of consumer choices, revealing much more about cultural values than ordinary purchases do, was, and remains, the choice between additional leisure or work and wages.

Marginalizing Shorter Hours

Just as had occurred in Battle Creek and Akron, supporters of Full-Time, Full Employment across the nation branded union holdouts as unrealistic or renegade. Progressively shorter work hours, embraced for generations by people spanning the political spectrum, was increasingly defined as radical or communist inspired. Labor's allies, as well, were increasingly seen as radical not because they were socialists or communists but for their defense of shorter hours. Challenges to the new ideologies of "meaningful work" and Full-Time, Full Employment became nearly as threatening as challenges to constitutional democracy.[38]

As early as the 1950s, labor leaders denounced activists too far ahead of the unions. Walter Reuther accused Local 600 at Ford's River Rouge complex of being communist for demanding a thirty-hour week for forty hours' pay (30 for 40), suggesting that theirs was a disguised effort to undermine the nation's efforts to win the Cold War.[39] With the failure of grassroots union efforts and in the absence of national leadership, the continuing efforts of the Communist Party, the League of Revolutionary Black Workers, and the Progressive Labor Party to promote shorter hours did in fact gain prominence. Subsequently, the press offered these developments as further proof of the shorter-hours movement's inherent radicalism.[40]

Leisure's Radicals

Shorter-hours supporters, defending an exposed and vulnerable position, counterattacked. Most, denying any communist or socialist leanings, pointed out that the traditional understanding of American progress was being redefined. Many questioned the morality, rationality, and sustainability of perpetual work creation and permanent economic growth, continuing to suggest vital uses for the opening realm of freedom.

For example, Norman O. Brown, a neo-Freudian populist and professor of classics at Wesleyan, concluded that the "doctrine that play is the essential mode of activity of a free or of a perfected or satisfied humanity has obvious implications. . . . History is transforming the question of reorganizing human society and human nature in the spirit of play from a speculative possibility to a realistic necessity." "Realistic observers" recognized that despite reformers' best efforts to create meaningful jobs, most people were experiencing "increasing alienation from [their] work," a problem made much worse by the likelihood of "mass unemployment" in the future.[41]

However, relief was at hand. Brown quoted Lord Keynes's prediction that nations would "solve the economic problem" before century's end and then face the challenge of leisure. The transition from a work-based to a leisure-based culture would be difficult and require careful preparations—many would resist. Whereas Keynes was pessimistic, "look[ing] with dread at the prospect of the ordinary man's emancipation from work," Brown saw "grounds for optimism" from the "Freudian point of view." Since everyone had experienced the "paradise of play" as children, "underneath the habits of work in every man lies the immortal instinct for play." Hence, the psychological foundations for liberation from work were already prepared—they did not have to be "created from nothing." Brown reasoned, "Nature—or history—is not setting us a goal without endowing us with the equipment to reach it."[42]

In addition to revealing history's destination, the "concept of play," imprinted in the human imagination from childhood, had "analytical applications to history." "Freud becomes relevant when history raises this question:

What does man want over and beyond 'economic welfare' and 'mastery over nature'? . . . Freud suggests that beyond labor there is love."[43]

However, those who were fearful or driven by a need to dominate others (the "rationality of domination") were redefining the promise of leisure as a threat, offering work as the only safe refuge.[44] With Johan Huizinga, Brown concluded that because humans had so long been used to the chains of work and necessity, when technology offered the chance for release they had continued to repress "the play element in culture," beginning a process of "dehumani[zing] culture."[45] Citizens of the modern world had turned their culture to the production of what Herbert Marcuse called the Performance Principle to take the place of Freud's Reality Principle (the objective, rational reasons for culture's repressive forms—primarily work).[46] Modern nations were creating irrational forms of work and new necessities to delay history's inevitable culmination in play. The continuing "surplus"[47] repression required to keep the play impulse at bay had unleashed into history the more unpleasant aspects of the collective psyche, "the death wish":[48] increasing fear, violence, incivility, class antagonisms, irrational political conduct, and insane social behavior.

Brown was more hopeful than Marcuse that the modern world could turn the play impulse to good use, eroticizing and liberating "higher cultural" activities (art, music, literature) previously based on the repression of Eros and making these accessible to all: "resurrecting the body" and freeing industrial civilization from the tyrannies of "continuing domination" and unnecessary ("surplus")[49] repression. "Psychoanalysis offers a . . . way out of the nightmare of endless 'progress' and endless Faustian discontent, a way out of the human neuroses, a way out of history."[50]

Herbert Marcuse agreed that the rational need for repression of Eros and play diminished as technology advanced. He also agreed that tradition, fear, and the desire of the few for "continuing domination" over the many delayed the ending of the nightmare that is history. Diagnosing the psychological dynamic causing humans to continue to work and produce irrationally, Marcuse noted that "productivity tended to contradict the pleasure principle and to become an end in itself."[51]

At times, Marcuse suggested that leisure had become so imbedded in the performance principle that the advent of authentic, meaningful jobs was prerequisite for liberating leisure.[52] It is true that Marcuse was critical of the kinds of devitalized leisure that sustained consumerism and continued domination. Such leisure so submerged the individual in consumerism and in the capitalist system that liberation though leisure alone might have receded as a historical possibility.[53]

However, the *free time* that Marcuse valued was liberated from both alienated work and devitalized leisure. For him, both work and leisure had to be restored beyond capitalism in the emerging realm of freedom. Shorter hours were just as necessary for one as for the other.

No matter how justly and rationally the material production may be organized it can never be a realm of freedom and gratification; but it can release time and energy for the free play of human faculties *outside* the realm of alienated labor. The more complete the alienation of labor, the greater the potential of freedom.[54]

In essence, Marcuse agreed with William Heighton and laborites in the United States who had long argued that the perfection of work, as well as leisure, depended on the reduction of "human labor to its lowest terms":[55]

Since the length of the working day is itself one of the principle repressive factors imposed upon the pleasure principle by the reality principle, the reduction of the working day to a point where the mere quantum of labor time no longer arrests human development is the first prerequisite for freedom. Such reduction by itself would almost certainly mean a considerable decrease in the standard of living. . . . But regression to a lower standard of living, which the collapse of the performance principle would bring about, does not militate against the progress of freedom. The argument that makes liberation conditional upon an ever higher standard of living all too easily serves to justify the perpetuation of repression. The definition of living in terms of [consumer goods] is that of the performance principle itself. Beyond the rule of this principle, the level of living would be measured by other criteria: the universal gratification of the basic human needs, and the freedom from guilt and fear—internalized as well as external, instinctual as well as "rational."[56]

Marcuse identified the essence of working-class radicalism in the exit from capitalism provided by the shorter hours:

Automation threatens to render possible the reversal of the relation between free time and working time: the possibility of working time becoming marginal and free time becoming full time. The result would be a radical transvaluation of values, and a mode of existence incompatible with the traditional culture. Advanced industrial society is in permanent mobilization against this possibility.[57]

The Limits of Growth

Economists and environmental advocates also challenged the new ideology of Full-Time, Full Employment. For well over a century and a half critics of perpetual industrial growth pointed out time and again that a limit will be reached sooner or later. Beginning with John Stuart Mill, economists such as Monsignor John Ryan, Simon Patten, Edward Ross, Walter Weyl, Stewart Chase, and George Soule (and more recently, Martin Joseph Matuštík, Alain Lipietz, Anders Hayden, and Juliet Schor) warned repeatedly of the consequences of economic growth beyond a "mature economy"—beyond the point where basic human needs were effectively and efficiently met for all.[58]

Such critics have viewed eternal economic progress and job creation as irrational projects because they cannot be sustained. John Stuart Mill recognized as early as 1859 that, left unchecked, economic expansion will eventually destroy the natural world and with it all that makes life worth living.[59] Subsequently, economists continued to offer Higher Progress as the remedy, reasoning that progress outside and beyond the marketplace, in nonpecuniary forms, is the rational alternative. If more people resisted the allures of new wealth and were guided by traditional visions of liberation instead of the ideology of Full-Time, Full Employment, they might freely choose additional free time. The "emancipatory potential of consumer choice" might be finally realized when individuals freely choose to live more of their lives outside the job and the marketplace.[60] Making such choices, citizens of the modern world might discover activities, ways of being together with each other, and ways of living with the natural world that would more than compensate for the loss of the illusions of consumerism, careerism, and national power.

That such possibilities were once so evident that Mill thought it "scarcely necessary to remark" about them in 1848 points to a profound historical transformation:

> It is scarcely necessary to remark that a stationary condition of capital and population implies no stationary state of human improvement. There would be as much scope as ever for all kinds of mental culture, and moral and social progress; as much room for improving the Art of Living, and much more likelihood of its being improved, when minds cease to be engrossed with the art of getting on. . . . [I]nstead of serving no purpose but the increase of wealth, industrial improvements would produce their legitimate effect, *that of abridging labor.*[61]

Critics have also recognized that in addition to destroying the environment, open-ended growth beyond "enough" continues to create inequalities of wealth and power that endanger democracies and destabilize nations, resulting in oppression and exploitation, social unrest, and revolutions and wars. Some have suggested that economic growth has already become cancerous, destroying healthy culture and civility and destabilizing the vital functioning of society, thus undermining the economy.[62]

Arguably, the Club of Rome, a group of prominent international scientists, has been the most influential in presenting Mill's case. Their 1972 report *Limits to Growth* (updated and reissued in 2004 as *Limits to Growth: The 30-Year Update*) was a worldwide best seller. After devoting most of the book to supporting Mill's prediction that the destruction of the environment would soon be the result of unbridled economic growth, the report concluded with a paraphrase of Mill's solution: "abridging labour."[63]

The Club of Rome demonstrated, yet again, that the most elementary of economic laws forced the conclusion that the environment and the earth's resources, being finite, would not sustain infinite economic expansion. Limited supply limited demand. Sooner or later (the club predicted 2050), humans would have to deal with the disappearance of work, either as a catastrophe of worldwide unemployment or the boon of leisure. However, the group held out the hope that the nations of the world might still behave rationally. Satisfied with abundance and making sure all had the basic necessities of life, reasonable people might rediscover real progress:

> In particular, those pursuits that many people would list as the most desirable and satisfying . . . education, art, music, religion, basic scientific research, athletics, and social interaction—could flourish. [Such activities] require leisure time. . . . [Thus,] in any equilibrium state [increases in productivity] would result in increased leisure—leisure that could be devoted to any activity that is relatively non-consuming.[64]

Whenever the economy falters, the prospect arises that the latest recession might prove immune to governments' frantic efforts to revive economic growth—the possibility of economic maturity, what Mill called the "stationary state," is now the specter that haunts modern economies. Accompanying this specter is the fear that chronic unemployment will prove the modern project of eternal work creation a failure, and that, as Martin Joseph Matuštík put it, "without a reduced work-week for more people, the global economy can burst with the unemployed who cannot buy what technologies make possible."[65]

Aldo Leopold: In a Plane Perpendicular to Darwin

Since early in the nineteenth century, new recreational, moral, and aesthetic uses and understandings of nature have been forming as alternatives to what Aldo Leopold called the traditional and tragic "Abrahamic concept of land . . . as a commodity belonging to us."[66] After 1970, leaders of America's environmental, conservation, and parks and recreation movements joined economists to reaffirm John Stuart Mill's predictions and represent his vision, building on the growing appreciation of the natural world. Threats to the environment posed by industrial growth coupled with the possibility that increasing leisure offered solutions galvanized the people behind these movements. Examples abound.[67] One of the best, however, is Aldo Leopold.

Leopold's work, including *A Sand County Almanac*, was little appreciated before the 1970s. Environmentalism's dramatic successes and rise to prominence, however, made his book a best seller and Leopold one of the major voices in the environmental movement. His book and Rachel Carson's *Silent Spring* are arguably "the two most important environmental books of the twentieth century."[68]

Admitting that "wild things" had little human value "until mechanization assured us of a good breakfast," Leopold observed that the industrial nations had reached and gone beyond the point of "diminishing returns in progress"— the point where "a still higher 'standard of living' is worth its cost in things natural, wild, and free." The products of industrial progress were less and less worth the increasing toll taken on the natural world. For the sake of simple survival (for, by destroying nature, humans would eventually destroy themselves), humans had to accept limits and deal with the freedom that naturally came after a good breakfast. With laborites, economists, and others in the environmental movement, Leopold proposed an alternative, free relationship with nature as the solution.[69]

Leopold made a case for this alternative based on the new science of ecology, "in a plane perpendicular to Darwin."[70] Having successfully adapted, assuring themselves of basic necessities and of reasonable survival, humans had to adapt again to the reality of freedom to survive. Evolution's challenge to humans now was to find free ways to relate to nature and to each other beyond utility. Accepting this challenge and deliberately entering the realm of freedom, humans would discover there a trans-Darwinian world, designed more by free will and intelligence than by chance and competition.

The challenge required readapting some of the same skill sets humans had used successfully in the struggle for the survival of the fittest: rational thought, imagination, creativity, and resolution. Instead of continuing to use these powers to manipulate nature (which threatened survival), humans had to begin to use them freely to build community, recognize beauty, and feed a growing spiritual hunger for transcendence, wonder, and belonging—innate potentials alienated by the modern world.

Building a "man-land community" in the "plane perpendicular to Darwin," would require exercising and developing what Jürgen Habermas called the "moral rationality"[71] that had allowed human society to exist through the ages: "All ethics so far evolved rest upon a single premise that the individual is a member of a community of interdependent parts. . . . The land ethic simply enlarges the boundaries of the community to include soils, waters, plants, and animals, or collectively: the land."[72]

The insights about nature revealed by Darwin's *Origin of Species*, "that men are only fellow-voyagers with other creatures in the odyssey of evolution . . . should have given us, by this time, a sense of kinship with fellow-creates; a wish to live and let live; a sense of wonder over the magnitude and duration of the biotic enterprise."[73]

The enlarging "man-land community" would be valuable in and for itself.[74] Nevertheless, it would provide humans with beauty, recreation, and a much needed escape from self-absorption into a sense of wonder, of belonging ("harmony with"), and of responsibility for a reality and purpose greater than themselves: "It is inconceivable to me that an ethical relation to land can exist without love, respect, and admiration for land."[75]

The product of rational choice rather than chance, the "man-land community" would have to be deliberately willed into being. Gradually forming on the basis of reason, vision, belief, and commitment, it would have to be taught and learned. Individuals and nations would have to progress (consciously evolve) toward a goal conceived in imagination and held in memory. Reason alone would not suffice. Other forms of human understanding, sensitivity, and discernment needed to be nurtured: the appreciation of beauty, a sense of wonder, and the ability to reason morally, understand intuitively, enjoy, and love.[76]

With many others in the environmental movement, Leopold saw that technology offered an escape from unsustainable economic growth in the form of shorter work hours. Moreover, the leisure that was made possible by industrial progress offered all people access to the trans-Darwinian plane.[77] He feared and objected to commercialized leisure and recreation to be sure, believing that driving around the countryside and other casual, effortless contacts with nature constituted just another kind of exploitation—what the historian Paul Sutter called a "dysfunctional leisure-based relationship with nature."[78] However, his objections to Herbert Hoover's conservation efforts were about the use of leisure, not its importance—like many in the environmental movement, he took for granted that leisure would increase.[79] What was needed was careful planning to encourage and promote "wild-leisure": those experiences of the outdoors that blended the aesthetic with the rational and empirical, in which nature itself taught humans how to be free.[80]

Professionals, schools, and government could assist nature in this process, providing outdoor recreation opportunities and public facilities and encouraging citizens to enter the natural world. However, once outside, individuals found nature employing an ingenious teaching strategy of its own, in harmony with their inborn senses of beauty and wonder. Instructing in the arts of freedom and teaching by means of a "conservation aesthetic," nature led toward the "land ethic,"[81] toward what literary scholar Sherman Paul called "the leisure-time practice of the husbandry of wild things."[82]

Outdoor Recreation: The Essence of Ecology

Contributing to the still-ongoing discourse about Higher Progress, Leopold explained that outdoor recreation was a five-stage developmental process that formed an "ethical sequence."[83] Outdoor recreation began with a natural attraction to "the land" and a naive desire for trophies. These were common starting points, responsible for the influx of automobiles and hunters into the wilds. However, once outside, motorists and hunters eventually discovered a richer pleasure in "the feeling of isolation in nature" that led to a new perspective, a "change of scene" (familiar to the women at Lowell) that provided instructive ways to view both the city and the land. Then followed the even richer intellectual pleasures of ecology: the understanding and "perception of the natural processes . . . evolution, [and] ecology." These four preparatory stages culminated in "the husbandry of the wild".[84] assumption of moral responsibility for the "man-land community," enjoyment of the rich pleasures of caring for and belonging to the natural world, and cultivation of "love, respect, and admiration" of the natural world.[85]

Other prominent conservationists and preservationists rang various changes on Leopold's main points. Historian James Glover notes that, from his youth, Bob Marshall, cofounder of the Wilderness Society with Benton MacKaye and Leopold, was concerned with "the growth of leisure and . . . with recreation as a social issue."[86] In his chapter for the "Copland Report" (one of the most important documents in the history of American forestry), Marshal detailed the ways that "the forest for recreation" could be made a reality and offered as an alternative, nondestructive way of using the nation's natural resources to enrich the growing leisure of its people. He estimated that "for the not distant future . . . [the workweek would be] as low as 24 hours and in the majority of cases at least as low as 30 hours." Moreover, he agreed with many in the forest service who recognized that public lands could not be reserved for the wealthy. He insisted that since "all classes of people" would have more leisure, the nation's natural resources had to be made available for all.[87]

Percy MacKaye's brother Benton agreed:

> Whatever else the future holds for us . . . [we can be certain of] less work and more leisure. . . . If we are tending toward leisure, then half the task of statesmanship is to stimulate our culture. To preserve the source thereof (within our dwelling-place and land) is the other half.[88]

Widely recognized as the driving force behind the creation of the Appalachian Trail, Benton MacKaye helped preserve in the natural world what his brother tried to create in the city with the "Civic Theatre": free public spaces for democratic recreation.[89]

After 1980, Full-Time, Full Employment virtually eclipsed Higher Progress. Yet even after the eclipse, pockets of resistance remained; laments for Higher Progress could still be heard. The parks and recreation movement and what remains of leisure studies (under siege for the last twenty years) in America's colleges continue to harbor a vitally important few who still understand and teach the importance of the Western leisure tradition and its relevance to the modern world; brave souls such as Douglas Sessoms, Thomas Goodale, Ken Mobily, John Hemingway, and Geoffrey Godbey have devoted their careers to preserving that tradition. The vision of Higher Progress still inspires parks and recreation professionals who manage and advocate for public spaces and provide leisure services in cities around the nation.

The Eclipse of Higher Progress and the Emergence of Overwork

One of the primary purposes of this book has been to support the hypothesis that the loss of the original American dream is one of the main reasons that interest in shorter hours ended and that working hours began to increase over the last thirty years. However, as working hours grew in the absence of Higher Progress and in the presence of the ideology of Full-Time, Full Employment, the issue of shorter working hours reappeared in the late 1980s and the 1990s in a new form: as a solution to a range of problems created by what scholars and journalists began to describe as overwork. No longer understood as the road to Higher Progress, the reduction of work time was redefined as a remedy for a nation too busy for its own good.

Beginning in the late 1980s, less than two decades after the problem of too much leisure had been a popular media topic, concerns about overwork spread among businesspeople and politicians as well as academics and journalists. Juliet Schor's *The Overworked American* was followed by numerous popular and scholarly publications identifying the problem and suggesting solutions—most often some form of small-scale, limited recovery of lost leisure. Conferences and symposiums about the "time famine" were held around the nation.[1] For the last two decades journalists and freelance writers have followed the story, publishing hundreds of accounts of overworked individuals, stressed families, and anemic communities languishing for want of time.[2]

Some have formed associations to deal with overwork. Led by John de Graaf (producer of the 1994 PBS documentary *Running Out of Time*), the organization Take Back Your Time launched a nationwide campaign. Patterned after Earth Day, Take Back Your Time seeks to do for overworked Americans what environmentalists accomplished: to begin a national discussion that will influence public opinion and initiate changes in public policy. The movement describes itself as "a major U.S./Canadian initiative to challenge the epidemic of overwork, over-scheduling and time famine that now threatens our health, our families and relationships, our communities and our environment."[3]

Noting that Americans work an average of nine weeks a year (350 hours) more than Western Europeans, the group chose October 24 as Take Back Your Time Day to spread awareness of how much longer Americans work each year: if we lived in any of the Western European nations, we would have the rest of the year off. The organization features its policy agenda on its web page:

- Guaranteeing paid leave for all parents for the birth or adoption of a child. . . .
- Guaranteeing at least one week of paid sick leave for all workers. . . .
- Guaranteeing at least three weeks of paid annual vacation leave for all workers. . . .
- Placing a limit on the amount of compulsory overtime work that an employer can impose. . . .
- Making Election Day a holiday. . . .
- Making it easier for Americans to choose part-time work.[4]

Joe Robinson, author of *Work to Live*, has been campaigning for legislation that would provide Americans with at least three weeks of paid vacation a year.[5] Since the publication of *Your Money or Your Life* in 1992, Vicki Robin and the New Road Map Foundation have been showing others how to achieve financial independence by "breaking free from auto-pilot consumerism" and choosing more life and less money and work.[6] Finding common cause, the voluntary simplicity movement has adopted the overwork issue. The magazine *Simple Living* and voluntary simplicity study circles maintain that thrift is still a virtue and that living a simple life pays off in a wealth of time, more than compensating for the useless gewgaws and burdensome trophies sought for in the ceaseless drive for more that consumes modern life.[7]

For obvious reasons, the travel, tourism, and restaurant industries have become interested in the issue. In June 2000, Shell Oil reported in a nationwide survey titled "What Happened to the Weekend—and the Rest of Leisure Time?" that nearly half the working population have little or no break over the weekend because they are too busy doing necessary chores—things they had no time for during the week. Nearly two-thirds reported that they have little or no discretionary time Saturday and Sunday.[8]

More recently, Hilton Hotels launched a Leisure Time Advocacy campaign, appointing a board of scholars and activists. On its website, Hilton outlined the campaign's purpose:

Our present-day, "hard-working" culture has created a leisure time deficit. Increased workloads, workweeks that extend into weekends, long commutes, and crunched family schedules have left little time for leisure activities including vacations. Society is desperate for more leisure time to relax and rejuvenate. More than 65 percent of Americans say they are stressed and under pressure, with nearly seven of 10 Americans saying they need more fun in their life, are in need of a long vacation, or, just simply need a break. As a result of the pressures of juggling all of life's balls and having little if any leisure time, Americans suffer negative effects, including failing health, psychological stress and strained personal relationships. The time-starved everywhere need a new "leisure ethic" to balance this strong "work ethic." That is why the Hilton Family of Hotels has formed the Leisure Time Advocacy™ (LTA). Through LTA, the Hilton Family hopes to encourage, persuade and excite people to embrace more leisure activities, enjoy some hard-earned time off and reflect on all that life has to offer.[9]

Following suit, Taco Bell launched a still-active advertising campaign based on the premise that so many people regularly work past dinnertime that they need a place to eat late at night, a "FourthMeal." Working with Take Back Your Time, Panera Bread continues to point out, "We're all feeling the pressure of our 24/7 lives, a pace that has very real consequences for our families and relationships, our health and our communities." Calling for Americans to take the time to "reclaim dinnertime," Panera cites research gathered by the Families and Work Institute specifying the "very real consequences" of and providing an excellent summary of the current critique of overwork:

> We are eating on the run. . . . We are not taking the time to exercise. We are not taking time to socialize with friends and family. . . . The obesity rate for both adults and children is at critical levels; we are seeing rising rates of other stress-related diseases . . . [and] high blood pressure. . . . Studies on building stronger families found that parents rank time with children higher than every other factor, including income. . . . Families are in flux, rarely coming together. . . . We are taking fewer vacations.[10]

Panera also traced the historical source of these problems to longer hours and to technology that is working in the opposite direction of labor-saving devices, increasing time pressure:

> Americans are working longer hours than we did 20 years ago. One in three American employees is chronically overworked. Fifty-four percent of American employees have felt overwhelmed at some time in the past month by how much work they had to complete. . . . Technology [now] keeps us connected to work at all hours of the day/night/weekend. Our fast-paced technology culture has contributed to the expectation that we should all move fast and produce at a machine's pace. . . . [Technology now] reduces our face-to-face connections.[11]

Because of the public concern about the nation's time famine, politicians began to analyze the problem and promise relief. During the last years of Bill Clinton's administration, his Council of Economic Advisors issued its report "Families and the Labor Market, 1969–1999: Analyzing the 'Time Crunch.'" The council concluded that American parents in 1999 had twenty-two fewer hours each week to spend at home compared with 1969, prompting most parents to regret the loss of opportunities to be with their children.[12] During President Clinton's second term, he and other Democrats attempted to address the national concerns about overwork by trying to make business more family friendly, proposing child-care legislation and regulations that would have required companies to give their employees better control of their work schedules, allowing them to take time to care for a sick child or go to an occasional family event.[13] Republicans, suspicious of government regulation, pushed instead for "comp time," proposing amendments to the Fair Labor Standards Act that would have allowed employers to compensate workers for working overtime with additional time rather than additional money—for instance, an employee putting in ten hours' overtime could take off fifteen hours sometime in the future.[14] However, Democrats blocked the bill in Congress.

During the 1992 presidential campaign, Eugene McCarthy pledged to confront the issue by amending the Fair Labor Standards Act. Bill Clinton repeated that "we are working more now for less" during his campaigns in the 1990s. During her bid for the Democratic presidential nomination in 2008, Hillary Clinton recalled a letter[15] she and forty-two other senators had sent to President George W. Bush's secretary of labor, Elaine L. Chao, in 2003 that outlined her and the other senators' position on jobs and working hours legislation:

> Our citizens are working longer hours than ever before—longer than in any other industrial nation. At least one in five employees now has a work week that exceeds 50 hours. Protecting the 40-hour work week is vital to balancing work responsibilities and family needs. It is certainly not family friendly to require employees to work more hours for less pay.[16]

Various stopgap measures have appeared. Amy Saltzman detected a national trend that she called "downshifting," in which young professionals were leaving the fast track to find jobs that were simpler and not as time consuming.[17] Flexible schedules and telecommuting (working at home by computer over the Internet) have become increasingly popular. Recently, the *New York Time* reported that several companies are offering a new kind of retention bonus: a chance to take a bit more time off work.[18]

Beginning in the 1990s and continuing into the twenty-first century, Canada and several European nations, as well as private companies in these nations, attempted to create more jobs by reducing work hours, introducing legislation similar to the 1933 Black-Connery bill (see Chapter 6). When unemployment reached double digits in the early 1990s, the French began a debate about reducing their workweek that culminated in legislation mandating a thirty-five-hour week. Shorter-hours advocates in Europe, pointing out that economic growth rates would have to remain substantially above record-high historical rates for several years to bring unemployment down below double digits, questioned whether Full-Time, Full Employment through economic growth and governmental work-creation efforts was still a viable, defensible governmental policy.

The French thirty-five-hour week was only moderately successful and was scrapped in 2005 even though it had become widely popular—the French regularly bragged about being less stressed, happier, and more productive than Americans and other Europeans. Arguably, private companies have provided more successful and practical models for work sharing. In the mid-1990s Volkswagen cut working hours to just under thirty per week, leading the way for several other German firms (including BMW and the nation's coal industry) to deal with chronic unemployment in their industries. Bell Canada made comparable efforts to reduce unemployment, as did the Paris-based Thompson Electronic Tubes Company and Italy's Fiat.[19]

In the late 1990s, Ron Healey, an influential business consultant, initiated a "30/40 plan" together with several companies around the Indianapolis area.[20] Offering workers the same pay for working thirty hours a week as they had previously received for working forty, Healey was able to attract much needed skilled workers to plastic manufacturers and bakeries unable to pay higher wages. Healey's successes were hailed as indications of things to come in 1997 by *Good Morning America*, in feature articles in the *New York Times*, and on the cover of *US News and World Report*.[21]

However, additional government regulation of working hours is no longer part of the political debate in the United States. During the economic crisis that began in 2008, and with unemployment rates approaching 10 percent in 2009, politicians seldom, if at all, mentioned the traditional shorter-hours unemployment remedy. With few exceptions, the press has ignored the issue. For the most part there is a disconnect between the problem of overwork and the problem of unemployment. Intolerably high unemployment remains as immune to economic growth and government efforts to create jobs today as it did in earlier times, a fact stressed by union leaders and economists during the 1963 and 1979 congressional hearings (see Chapter 6). But that immunity has not resulted in a return to the traditional shorter-hours solution. Americans cling to the hope that Full-Time, Full Employment will eventually return.

The political will to regulate working hours simply does not exist today in the United States. Indeed, during George W. Bush's administration political trends ran in the opposite direction, toward deregulation of existing work limits, even those historic achievements of the Fair Labor Standards Act. Organized labor has devoted most of its efforts related to the hours of labor to protecting existing legislation against political threats.

Few companies have followed Kellogg's or Volkswagen's leads and stepped up to assume responsibility for their industries' and communities' unemployment problems by offering opportunities for employees to work shorter hours. Healey's 30/40 initiative has not spread beyond the Indianapolis area, even though it thrives in companies such as Metro Plastics in Noblesville, Indiana, continuing to represent a working business model for the rest of the nation. Company official Ken Hahn reported in December 2010, "We are very proud of the fact we have kept 30/40 implemented for many years now. It has been a tremendous benefit to us as well our employees."[22]

Conclusion

I have attempted to complete the journeyman's task of the historian in this book, describing and explaining the end of shorter hours and the rise of Full-Time, Full Employment. But I am not content with the role of an objective observer. Even though I was trained by some fine historians at Chapel Hill and have spent most of my career writing history, I am a professor of leisure studies, following the educational tradition represented by Robert Maynard Hutchins and Dorothy Canfield Fisher. For over thirty-seven years I have taught and written about the Western leisure heritage and the alternatives it offers the modern technological world. I have also undertaken in my classes and in this book to re-present the traditional vision of Higher Progress that was the inspiration for the century-long shorter-work-hours process in the United States. Thus I remain an advocate for James Truslow Adams's American dream—a dream that might once again become the inspiration for political and economic reform and cultural regeneration. As an advocate, I also hope to reveal the implicit assumptions, and advocacy, of economists and historians who today tend to assume that perpetual economic growth and the expansion of government to produce new jobs are normative—representing the essential values of our culture for which there are no reasonable, moral, or historical alternatives.[23]

Because of the advent of the ideology of Full-Time, Full Employment and the resulting overwork, today's shorter-work-hours advocates may seem quixotic, trying to oppose irresistible social forces and trends. E. P. Thompson's observation that "in mature Capitalist society all time must be consumed, marketed, put to use; it is offensive for the labor force merely to 'pass the time'" appears to some to be the inexorable outcome of capitalism.[24] The situation seems bleak—one may well wonder whether any realistic hope remains for the resurrection of the shorter-hours process.

Indeed, re-presenting shorter hours merely as remedy for overwork is not enough to cause significant changes. It is doubtful that recent efforts to combat overwork will delay capitalism's colonization of more and more of human life. Those struggling to find remedies for overwork have not been bold enough, their horizons constricted by short-term goals. Historically, the vision of Higher Progress was necessary for the start and continuation of shorter hours.

Lacking the ability to imagine an inspiring alternative to eternal economic growth and everlasting work creation, reformers have little hope for substantial change today.[25]

The traditional American dream needs to be re-presented as a compelling and inspiring alternative to the current dream of eternal consumption, wealth, and work that now threatens human communities and the natural world. The original American dream carries with it an imminently realistic means for its realization: the "progressive shortening of the hours of labor." With the recovery of the dream, the renaissance of shorter hours might follow as more and more of us voluntarily choose the "larger liberty," freely exercising the most fundamental of all consumer choices for new leisure rather than new wealth and work.[26]

Individuals might find in Higher Progress good reasons to work less and then, acting in the free market, sell less of their time to their jobs, thereby expanding the realm of freedom. There they might realize the true "emancipatory potential of consumer choice," just as Americans did for over a century and a half.[27]

What is needed now is a reassessment of what work, wealth, and power are for. We need to ask again if there is something better than living to work. We need to relearn that America once stood for better things than eternally increasing wealth, everlasting consumerism, and unending extensions of its might and power. We need an inspiring alternative to the environmentalists' austerity proposal, that all should live parsimonious lives. We need a practical, inspiring alternative to tax cuts for the wealthy, uncertain and expensive government stimulus packages and bailouts, perpetual military mobilization, and mounting government debt. We need a stirring alternative to evermore wealth, larger government, and the desperate project of work without end.

We need to recover the original American dream of Higher Progress as a wealth of time to live. We need to hear again the words of Jonathan Edwards: "Labour to get thoroughly convinced that there is something else needs caring for more." We need to listen again to Walt Whitman, passionately calling us to the "Open Road," urging us to live out our humanity to its fullest—to search out and experience "the thing for itself" and to realize "only the soul is of itself . . . all else has reference to what ensues." We need to hear again the voices of industrial feminists such as Fannia Cohn urging us to cultivate "deep community" in a shared "spirit of intimacy," making progress in both aspects of our lives, "Bread and Roses."

We are prevented from realizing the original American dream by no inexorable political or economic reality. Shorter working hours remains the portal to the "realm of freedom," offering an eminently more practical and sustainable future than the pursuit of eternal economic growth and everlasting job creation. What is lacking is only belief and commitment. What is needed is the vigorous re-presenting of those voices that remind us of the still-unrealized possibilities of the original American dream. We need committed salesmen and saleswomen, such as Robert Hutchins and the Kellogg's six-hour women, to hawk the attractions of Higher Progress—competing with those who spend fortunes on advertising to persuade us to consume ever more goods and services or to chase this or that job-creating political will-o'-the-wisp.

With the revival of the original American dream the will to change might reemerge, either by government regulation of work hours or, much better still, at the level of individual firms such as Kellogg's and Metro Plastics and through individual choices in the marketplace. Higher Progress will be possible once again when more of us choose freely to liberate more of our lives from the economy, making the most basic of consumer choices to forgo new spending and luxuries, as well as modern illusions about the everlasting need for more wealth and work. Free people choosing more freedom is the best hope for the future.

NOTES

Additions to these notes may be found at http://ir.uiowa.edu/leisure_pubs/1. Asterisks mark the notes that have additions online.

PREFACE

1. John Maynard Keynes, *Essays in Persuasion* (New York: Norton, 1963), 367.

2. J. D. Owen, "Workweeks and Leisure: An Analysis of Trends, 1948–75," *Monthly Labor Review* 99, no. 8 (1976): 3–8.

3. References supporting this claim may be found in Benjamin Hunnicutt, *Work without End: Abandoning Shorter Hours for the Right to Work* (Philadelphia: Temple University Press, 1988), 316–317nn3–5.*

4. Juliet Schor, *The Overworked American: The Unexpected Decline of Leisure* (New York: Basic Books, 1991).

5. Juliet Schor, "The (Even More) Overworked American," in *Take Back Your Time: Fighting Overwork and Poverty in America*, ed. John de Graaf (San Francisco: Berrett-Koehler, 2003).

6. Schor, "The (Even More) Overworked American," 6–11.

7. Arlie Hochschild and Anne Machung, *The Second Shift* (New York: Penguin, 2003).

8. Andrew Curry, "Why We Work," *U.S. News and World Report*, February 16, 2003, 50.

9. Schor, "The (Even More) Overworked American," 6–11; Joe Robinson, *Work to Live: The Guide to Getting a Life* (New York: Berkley, 2003), 3.

10. Susan E. Fleck, "International Comparisons of Hours Worked: An Assessment of the Statistics," *Monthly Labor Review* 132, no. 5 (2009): 3.*

11. See, for example, Richard Posner, *Aging and Old Age* (Chicago: University of Chicago Press, 1995), 39, 83, 350; and Henry J. Aaron and Gary T. Burtless, *Retirement and Economic Behavior* (Washington, DC: Brookings Institution, 1984), 117.*

12. Eduardo Porter, "Retirement Becomes a Rest Stop," *New York Times*, February 9, 2005.

13. Patrick Purcell, "Older Workers: Employment and Retirement Trends," *Congressional Research Service*, September 16, 2009, available at http://assets.opencrs.com/rpts/RL30629_20090916.pdf.

14. Murray Gendell, "Older Workers: Increasing Their Labor Force Participation and Hours of Work," *Monthly Labor Review* 131, no. 1 (2008): 41.

15. Ibid. See also Purcell, "Older Workers."

16. Gerald Friedman, review of *Work without End*, by Benjamin Kline Hunnicutt, *Annals of the American Academy of Political and Social Science* 505 (September 1989): 190–192. Hunnicutt, *Work without End*; Benjamin Hunnicutt, *Kellogg's Six-Hour Day* (Philadelphia: Temple University Press, 1996).

17. Walt Whitman, *Democratic Vistas*, in *Prose Works 1892*, vol. 2, *Collect and Other Prose*, ed. Floyd Stovall (New York: New York University Press, 1964), 410. I have adopted Whitman's term "higher progress" and use it frequently in this book; capitalization (Higher Progress) indicates that the term is used to refer in a general way to extraeconomic, nonpecuniary progress.

18. James Truslow Adams, *The Epic of America* (1931; repr., New York: Blue Ribbon Books, 1941), 405, 406, 412, 415 (italics in original). For a discussion of Adams as the originator of the term "American dream," see James Cullen, *The American Dream: A Short History of an Idea That Shaped a Nation* (New York: Oxford University Press, 2003), 7, 191.

19. "Prevalence of the Five-Day Week in American Industry," *Monthly Labor Review* 23 (December 1926): 1167. See also C. M. Wright, "Epoch-Making Decisions in the Great American Federation Labor Convention at Detroit," *American Labor World*, 1926, 22–24; American Federation of Labor, *Proceedings of the 46th Annual Convention* (Washington, DC: AFL, 1926), see especially "Report of the Committee on the Shorter Workday," 195–207.

INTRODUCTION

1. F. L. Broderick, *Right Reverend New Dealer: John A. Ryan* (New York: Macmillan, 1963).

2. John Ryan, *The Church and Labor* (New York: Macmillan, 1920), xiv, 83, 170, 260.

3. John Maynard Keynes, *Essays in Persuasion* (New York: Norton, 1963), 367.

4. Walt Whitman, *Democratic Vistas*, in *Prose Works 1892*, ed. Floyd Stovall (New York: New York University Press, 1964), 410.

5. J. A. Ryan, *Declining Liberty and Other Papers* (New York: Macmillan, 1927), 323.

6. A. H. Silver, "Leisure and the Church," *Playground* 20 (January 1927): 539.

7. Gordon Wood, "Jefferson in His Time," *Wilson Quarterly* 17, no. 2 (1993): 38.

8. Ibid.*

9. Gordon Wood, *Revolutionary Characters: What Made the Founders Different* (New York: Penguin Press, 2006), 105.

10. Ibid. See also Gordon Wood, *The Creation of the American Republic, 1776–1787* (Chapel Hill: University of North Carolina Press, 1969–1998), xiii.

11. Max Weber, *The Protestant Ethic and the Spirit of Capitalism*, trans. Talcott Parsons (1930, 1958; repr., New York: Dover Publications, 2003).

12. Samuel Hopkins, *Works of Samuel Hopkins, D.D., with a Memoir of His Life and Character*, 3 vols. (Boston: Doctrinal Tract and Book Society, 1852), 2:286–287.

13. John Adams to Abigail Adams, May 12, 1780, Adams Family Papers, Massachusetts Historical Society, available at http://www.masshist.org/digitaladams/aea/cfm/doc .cfm?id=L17800512jasecond.

14. Henry Adams, *History of the United States of America during the Administrations of Thomas Jefferson* (1890; repr., New York: Library of America, 1986), 125.

15. Benjamin Franklin, *Works of the Late Dr. Benjamin Franklin: Consisting of His Life, Written by Himself*, 2 vols. (New York: Samuel Campbell, 1794), 2:74.

16. Gordon S. Wood, *Revolutionary Characters*, 104.

17. Ibid.

18. John Rogers Commons, Ulrich B. Phillips, Eugene A. Gilmore, Helen L. Sumner, and John B. Andrews, eds. *A Documentary History of American Industrial Society*, 5 vols. (Cleveland: A. H. Clark, 1910), 5:80.

19. William Heighton, "An Address to the Members of Trade Societies and to the Working Classes Generally," reprinted in Philip Foner, *William Heighton: Pioneer Labor Leader of Jacksonian Philadelphia* (New York: International, 1991), 69.

20. Benjamin Hunnicutt, *Work without End: Abandoning Shorter Hours for the Right to Work* (Philadelphia: Temple University Press, 1988), 81.

21. AFL-CIO, *The Shorter Work Week: Papers Delivered at the Conference on Shorter Hours of Work Sponsored by the American Federation of Labor and the Congress of Industrial Organizations* (Washington, DC: Public Affairs Press, 1956), 3.

22. H. Richard Niebuhr, *The Kingdom of God in America* (Middletown, CT: Wesleyan University Press, 1988).

23. Commons et al., *Documentary History*, 5:80.

24. *Workingman's Advocate*, August 28, 1830, 2. See Chapter 2.

25. Commons et al., *Documentary History*, 5:80.

26. "Larger liberty" was a common laborite term in the nineteenth century, most often used in reference to free time.

27. Jacques Rancière, *La Nuit des Prolétaires* (Paris: Fayard, 1981). Trans. John Drury as *The Nights of Labor: The Workers' Dream in Nineteenth-Century France* (Philadelphia: Temple University Press, 1989). See Chapter 2.

28. Andrew Menard, "The Enlarged Freedom of Frederick Law Olmsted," *New England Quarterly* 83, no. 3 (2010): 508–538. See also John Mitchell, "Frederick Law Olmsted's Passion for Parks," *National Geographic* 207 (March 2005): 32–51.

29. Sherman Gwinn, "Days of Drudgery Will Soon Be Over: An Interview with Walter S. Gifford," *American Magazine* 56 (November 1928): 25.

30. *Monthly Labor Review* 23 (December 1926): 1167. See also C. M. Wright, "Epoch-Making Decisions in the Great American Federation Labor Convention at Detroit," *American Labor World*, May 1926, 22–24.

31. See "Leisure's Radicals" in Chapter 9.

32. Aldo Leopold, *A Sand County Almanac: With Essays on Conservation from Round River* (1949; repr., New York: Random House, 1990), viii.

33. Sigurd F. Olson, "Leisure Time: Man's Key to Self Realization—The Out-of-Doors," *Minnesota Journal of Education*, April 1958; Olson, *Open Horizons* (1969; repr., Minneapolis: University of Minnesota Press, 1998), 139, 183.

34. H. Marcuse, *Eros and Civilization: A Philosophical Inquiry into Freud* (New York: Beacon, 1962), viii.

35. David R. Roediger and Philip Sheldon Foner, *Our Own Time: A History of American Labor and the Working Day* (New York: Greenwood Press, 1989).

36. Just as I use "Higher Progress," capitalized, to represent the first, forgotten American dream, I use "Full-Time, Full Employment," capitalized, to represent the new dream of eternal economic growth and work without end that has eclipsed the first.

CHAPTER 1

1. J.G.A. Pocock, "Virtue and Commerce in the Eighteenth Century," *Journal of Interdisciplinary History* 3 (Summer 1972): 118.

2. Wood concluded, "Classical virtue had flowed from the citizen's participation in politics; government had been the source of his civic consciousness and public spiritedness. [By contrast, during the early Republic,] modern virtue flowed from the citizen's participation

in society, not in government, which the liberal-minded increasingly saw as the source of the evils of the world. It was society—the affairs of private social life—that bred sympathy and the new domesticated virtue. Mingling in drawing rooms, clubs, and coffee-houses—partaking of the innumerable interchanges of the daily comings and goings of modern life—created affection and fellow-feeling, which were all the adhesives really necessary to hold an enlightened people together. . . . All human beings had 'implanted in our breasts' this 'love of others,' this 'moral instinct'; these 'social dispositions' were what made democracy possible." Gordon Wood, *The Creation of the American Republic, 1776–1787* (Chapel Hill: University of North Carolina Press, 1969–1998), x–xiii. See also Gordon Wood, "Jefferson in His Time," *Wilson Quarterly* 17 (Spring 1993): 38–53.*

   3. H. Richard Niebuhr, *The Kingdom of God in America* (Middletown, CT: Wesleyan University Press, 1988), 169.

   4. Ibid., xxi; John Wilson, ed., "Editor's Introduction," in *The Works of Jonathan Edwards*, vol. 9, *A History of the Work of Redemption*, by Jonathan Edwards (New Haven, CT: Yale University Press, 1989), 95. For additional Niebuhr references to the "American dream," see Niebuhr, *The Kingdom of God in America*, 5, 46–48.

   5. Niebuhr, *The Kingdom of God in America*, 14. Niebuhr suggested that the kingdom of God in America might be thought of as a "guiding idea which unfolds itself" through time.

   6. Before the first Great Awakening in America, premillennialism was the accepted view of the coming kingdom. Premillennialism taught that Christ would return unexpectedly, interrupting and ending history. Thus, premillennialism tended to be pessimistic and fatalistic: humans had little or no role to play in history, and progress was an illusion. By contrast, postmillennialists such as Edwards believed that they might be able to prepare for Christ's return, helping to establish the kingdom of God on earth before the end of time. Hence postmillennialists were more optimistic about the future and engaged in trying to improve earthly life. See James H. Moorhead, *World without End: Mainstream Protestant Visions of Last Things, 1880–1925* (Bloomington: Indiana University Press, 1999), 5–6.

   7. Edwards, Samuel Hopkins, and others during the colonial and Revolutionary periods used "ease" more often than "leisure" to describe time freed by machines that might be used for other, "higher" purposes.

   8. Jonathan Edwards, "Miscellanies," in *The Philosophy of Jonathan Edwards from His Private Notebooks*, ed. Harvey G. Townsend (Eugene: University of Oregon Press, 1955), 207–208, no. 262.

   9. Jonathan Edwards, "Cares of This Life Hinder the Word of God" (Matthew 13:22), in *Sermons, Series II: 1728–1729* of *Works of Jonathan Edwards Online*, ed. Harry S. Stout and Kenneth P. Minkema, available at http://edwards.yale.edu.*

   10. Niebuhr, *The Kingdom of God in America*, 112–113.

   11. Jonathan Edwards, *A Narrative of Many Surprising Conversions in Northampton and Vicinity. Written in 1736. Together with Some Thoughts on the Revival in New England* (Worcester, MA: Moses W. Grout, 1832), 487, 432.

   12. Edwards, *A Narrative of Many Surprising Conversions*, 12, 22. See also George M. Marsden, *Jonathan Edwards: A Life* (New Haven, CT: Yale University Press, 1993), 159–160.*

   13. Jonathan Edwards, "Christian Liberty," in *Sermons and Discourses, 1720–1723*, of *Works of Jonathan Edwards Online*, ed. Wilson H. Kimnach, available at http://edwards.yale.edu/archive.

   14. Peter Jauhiainen, "An Enlightenment Calvinist: Samuel Hopkins and the Pursuit of Benevolence" (Ph.D. diss., University of Iowa, 1997), 364 (italics added).

   15. Samuel Hopkins, *The Works of Samuel Hopkins: With a Memoir of His Life and Character*, 3 vols. (Boston: Doctrinal Tract and Book Society, 1852), 2:286–287. See also Samuel Hopkins, *The System of Doctrines Contained in Divine Revelation*, 2nd ed., 2 vols. (Boston: Lincoln and Edmands, 1811), 2:286–287.

16. Joseph A. Conforti, "Samuel Hopkins and the New Divinity: Theology, Ethics, and Social Reform in Eighteenth-Century New England," *William and Mary Quarterly* 34, no. 4 (1977): 582. For the Zen Buddhist comparison, see Oliver Wendell Elsbree, "Samuel Hopkins and His Doctrine of Benevolence," *New England Quarterly* 8, no. 4 (1935), 539.

17. Hopkins, *Works of Samuel Hopkins*, 2:272.

18. James H. Moorhead identified Edwards as "the putative father of American postmillennialism." Moorhead, *World without End*, 5–6. Perry Miller called Edwards the "greatest artist of the apocalypse." Ruth Bloch, *Visionary Republic: Millennial Themes in American Thought, 1756–1800* (New York: Cambridge University Press, 1985), 16. Robert R. Mathisen, *Critical Issues in American Religious History: A Reader* (Waco, TX: Baylor University Press, 2001), 174.

19. Edwards, "Sermon on Christian Liberty."

20. Minister of the Federal Street Church in Boston, Massachusetts, from 1803 to 1842, Channing was by most accounts the leading Unitarian minister and theologian during the first decades of the nineteenth century. David Robinson concluded, "New Englanders generally recognized him as the key spokesman for the liberal or Unitarian theology." Robinson, "The Legacy of Channing: Culture as a Religious Category in New England Thought," *Harvard Theological Review* 74, no. 2 (1981): 221–239.

21. Robinson, "The Legacy of Channing," 221. Channing was never a fire-breathing abolitionist and shared the racist views common in his day. However, he did actively oppose slavery, writing and speaking against this "peculiar institution" in his later life.

22. Robinson, "The Legacy of Channing," 228.*

23. The movement to reduce working hours had spread nationwide by the time of the Civil War, providing some of the first evidence of working-class self-consciousness in the United States. See Chapter 4. For the prevalence of the rhetoric of "self-improvement," "self-cultivation," and "self-education" among workers and their supporters during the Jacksonian era, see David R. Roediger and Philip Sheldon Foner, *Our Own Time: A History of American Labor and the Working Day* (New York: Greenwood Press, 1989), 14, 17, 21, 39, 41, 54, 151, 153. Roediger and Foner noted that "sisterhood of ten-hour workers" had produced a rhetoric of "militant self-improvement" in the early 1840s (59).

24. William Ellery Channing, *The Works of William E. Channing* (Boston: American Unitarian Association, 1891), 58.

25. Ibid., 34, 46 (italics added).

26. Ibid., 103.

27. William Henry Channing, *The Life of William Ellery Channing*, 6th ed. (Boston: American Unitarian Association, 1899), 152, 153 (italics added). Compare Chapter 2.

28. Ibid., 65, 109, 596.

29. Ibid., 34.

30. W. E. Channing, *The Works of William E. Channing*, 39.

31. For "higher life," see ibid., 106, 229, 241, 248, 359, 360, 361, 362, 265, 418, 437, 573, 598, 618.

32. Ibid., 121.

33. For Channing's essay on slavery, see "Slavery," in ibid., 688–743.

34. Ibid., 710.

35. Ibid.*

36. Ibid.

37. "On the Elevation of the Laboring Classes," in ibid., 39–40.

38. Ibid.

39. Ibid. (italics added). A common interpretation of Channing's "occupations" has been that he must be referring to new kinds of rewarding work—what Nicholas Knowles Bromell called a "miraculous transformation" of labor. See Bromell, *By the Sweat of the Brow:*

Literature and Labor in Antebellum America (Chicago: University of Chicago Press, 1993), 26. But Channing made it clear that the "occupations" he had in mind were extraeconomic, done in one's free time, involving "another state of being."

40. W. E. Channing, *The Works of William E. Channing*, 46.

41. Ibid., 112.

42. Ibid., 112. See also John Williams, "William Ellery Channing's Philosophy of Physical Education and Recreation," *Quest* 4, no. 1 (1965): 49–52.

43. W. E. Channing, *The Works of William E. Channing*, 111–112.

44. Ibid., 19–20.*

45. See Chapters 3 and 10.

46. W. E. Channing, *The Works of William E. Channing*, 35.

47. Ibid.

48. Ibid., 894.

49. Ibid., 35.

50. Ibid., 54.

51. Ibid.

52. Ibid., 361.

53. Ibid., 56–57.

54. Ibid., 57.

55. Ibid., 52–54; see also 242, 360.*

56. Ibid., 360.

57. Ibid., 53.

58. Hunnicutt, *Work without End*, 90–92.

59. W. E. Channing, *The Works of William E. Channing*, 103.

CHAPTER 2

1. Hegel, Kant, and other nineteenth-century philosophers often used the term "realm of freedom," but Marx and Engels grounded the term, and some of the concepts associated with it, in the historical process of shorter working hours. It is worth pointing out that workers in the United States had worked out a similar connection long before during their struggle for ten hours.

2. Maurice Godelier, "Aide-Memoire for a Survey of Work and Its Representations," *Current Anthropology* 21 (December 1980): 831–835.*

3. See Karl Marx, *A Contribution to the Critique of Political Economy*, trans. N. I. Stone (Chicago: Charles H. Kerr, 1911).*

4. E. P. Thompson, "Time, Work-Discipline and Industrial Capitalism," *Past and Present* 38 (December 1967): 56–97.

5. Thompson, "Time, Work-Discipline and Industrial Capitalism," 85.*

6. David Roediger and Philip Foner, *Our Own Time: A History of American Labor and the Working Day* (New York: Verso, 1989), 2.

7. David J. Saposs, "Colonial and Federal Beginnings," in *History of Labour in the United States*, by John R. Commons, David J. Saposs, Helen L. Sumner, E. B. Mittelman, H. E. Hoagland, John B. Andrews, and Selig Perlman (New York: Macmillan, 1921), 1:25–164.

8. Ibid., 1:103–106. See also Roediger and Foner, *Our Own Time*, 8–9.

9. Sean Wilentz, *Chants Democratic* (1984; 20th anniversary ed., New York: Oxford University Press, 2004), 105.

10. Alan Trachtenberg, *Incorporation of America: Culture and Society in the Gilded Age* (New York: Hill and Wang, 1982), 73. See also Roediger and Foner, *Our Own Time*, 49.

11. Thompson, "Time, Work-Discipline and Industrial Capitalism," 95.

12. Roediger and Foner, *Our Own Time*, 17.

13. Roy Rosenzweig, *Eight Hours for What We Will: Workers and Leisure in an Industrial City, 1870–1920* (New York: Cambridge University Press, 1983), 222–228.

14. Ibid., 7.

15. S. J. Ross, "Workers on the Edge: Work, Leisure, and Politics in Industrializing Cincinnati: 1830–1890" (Ph.D. diss., Princeton University, 1980), iii–v, 317–404; see also J. T. Cumbler, *Working-Class Community in Industrial America: Work, Leisure, and Struggle in Two Industrial Cities, 1880–1930* (Westport, CT: Greenwood Press, 1979), 7–12, 28–38, 114–128; Rosenzweig, *Eight Hours for What We Will*.

16. Roediger and Foner, *Our Own Time*, ix, 10.

17. Ibid., 19.

18. Ibid., 21.

19. Jacques Rancière, *La Nuit des Prolétaires* (Paris: Fayard, 1981). Trans. John Drury as *The Nights of Labor: The Workers' Dream in Nineteenth-Century France* (Philadelphia: Temple University Press, 1989).

20. "Something as broad as freedom" is Roediger and Foner's resonant term. Roediger and Foner, *Our Own Time*, 99.

21. Jacques Rancière, "Preface to the Hindi translation of *The Nights of Labor*," in *Sarvahara Raatein: Unneesaveen sadi ke Frans mein Mazdoor Swapn*, trans. Abhay Kumar Dube (Delhi, India: Vani Prakashan, 2008), available at http://hydrarchy.blogspot.com/2009/01/ranciere-2-new-preface-to-hindi.html.

22. Compare Orlando Patterson, *Freedom in the Making of Western Culture* (New York: Basic Books, 1992).*

23. Rancière, "Preface to the Hindi translation of *The Nights of Labor*."

24. Ibid. (italics added). Rancière's workers held on to an original understanding of *their* "work" as meaningful effort performed outside and "independent of the market economy" during what we now would call their "leisure." See Jacques Rancière, "Preface."

25. Rancière, *The Nights of Labor*, vii. See also Chris Turner, "Introduction to Rancière," *New Formations*, no. 3 (Winter 1987): 56.*

26. Rancière, *The Nights of Labor*, vii.

27. Ibid.

28. Ibid.

29. Ibid.

30. Ibid., 125.

31. In the *Voice of Industry* on December 26, 1845, Young reported on one of Burritt's lectures that he called a "truly worthy effort." However, Young was critical of Burritt's glorifying labor as "indispensable to [human] happiness" and hoped that he would "be induced to turn his attention more directly to the evils of the present system of labor and their degrading tendency."*

32. *Voice of Industry*, May 7, 1847.

33. Jama Lazerow, *Religion and the Working Class in Antebellum America* (Washington, DC: Smithsonian Institution Press, 1995), 194–195.

34. In her first letter to the *Voice of Industry*, writing in the third person, Huldah Stone announced that she had been appointed correspondent to the paper by the "Ladies Labor Reform Association" (later FLRA); see *Voice of Industry*, July 31, 1845.

35. *Voice of Industry*, September 9, 1845.

36. *Voice of Industry*, October 2, 1845.

37. *Voice of Industry*, May 1, 1846.

38. Roediger and Foner, *Our Own Time*, 21.

39. Ibid., 13.

40. Jürgen Habermas described the "lifeworld" as forming "communities of discourse," finding examples in fledgling worker communities building in the modern era.

Jürgen Habermas, *The Theory of Communicative Action: Lifeworld and System: A Critique of Functionalist Reason*, trans T. McCarthy (Boston: Beacon Press, 1987). See also John L. Hemingway, "Emancipating Leisure: The Recovery of Freedom in Leisure," *Journal of Leisure Research* 28, no. 1 (1996): 27.*

41. *Voice of Industry*, May 7, 1847 (italics added).

42. Thomas Jefferson, "Declaration of Causes and Necessity of Taking Up Arms," July 6, 1775.*

43. *Voice of Industry*, December 19, 1845.

44. Ibid.

45. *Workingman's Advocate*, September 12, 1835, 7, 5.

46. *Workingman's Advocate*, May 16, 1835, 6, 40.

47. *The Mechanic*, July 27, 1835.

48. Quoted in David R. Roediger, *The Wages of Whiteness: Race and the Making of the American Working Class* (New York: Verso, 1999), 51.

49. *Voice of Industry*, April 3, 1846. Seth Luther spoke in support of the convention's resolutions in an address following the formal adoption of the resolution.

50. *Voice of Industry*, April 3, 1846.

51. *The Mechanic*, May 25, 1844.

52. *The Mechanic*, July 13, 1844.

53. *Voice of Industry*, November 7, 1845.

54. Ibid.

55. *Voice of Industry*, April 4, 1846.

56. Letter to John Adams, Monticello, September 12, 1821, in Jefferson, *Light and Liberty: Reflections on the Pursuit of Happiness*, ed. Eric Petersen (New York: Modern Library, 2004), 67.

57. *Voice of Industry*, October 10, 1845, and May 21, 1847.

58. *Voice of Industry*, December 26, 1845.

59. *Voice of Industry*, April 23, 1847. See also Lazerow's account of this exchange in Lazerow, *Religion and the Working Class in Antebellum America*, 1–3, 13, 14.

60. *Voice of Industry*, April 23, 1847, 175–178.

61. Commons et al., *History of Labour in the United States*, 1:192, 305.

62. Reprinted in the *Voice of Industry*, October 2, 1845. The *Star of Bethlehem* was a Universalist paper, sympathetic to labor, published for a time in Lowell and edited by A. A. Miner.

63. Commons et al., *History of Labour in the United States*, 1:385.

64. *Workingman's Advocate*, April 20, 1833, 4, 36 (italics added).

65. *The Mechanic*, May 11, 1844.

66. *The Mechanic*, May 18, 1844.

67. *Voice of Industry*, August 21, 1845.

68. Daniel T. Rodgers, *The Work Ethic in Industrial America, 1850–1920* (Chicago: University of Chicago Press, 1978), 90. See also James Gilbert, *Work without Salvation: America's Intellectuals and Industrial Alienation, 1880–1910* (Baltimore: Johns Hopkins University Press, 1877), v, 153, 181.*

69. *Voice of Industry*, April 23, 1847.

70. Commons et al., *History of Labour in the United States*, 1:69.*

71. Proclaiming, "I am a mechanic and proud of the title," Hewitt wrote that "avarice cannot long be allowed to run riot in its present oppressive course." The factory system was "working its own destruction." *The Mechanic*, May 11, 1844.

72. Benjamin Franklin, *Works of the Late Dr. Benjamin Franklin: Consisting of His Life, Written by Himself*, 2 vols. (New York: Samuel Campbell, 1794), 2:74.

73. Reprinted in *Workingman's Advocate*, August 28, 1830, 2.

74. Ibid.

75. *The Mechanic*, May 11, 1844.

76. Ibid.; see also *The Mechanic*, May 18, 1844.

77. The *Boston Transcript* published a paraphrased version of the *Sentinel* article. See also *Workingman's Advocate*, March 19, 1831, 2, 31.

78. *Workingman's Advocate*, September 19, 1835.

79. *Voice of Industry*, August 8, 1845.

80. The phrase "selfish system" might have originated with Benjamin Phelon's columns in *The Mechanic* (in January and February 1845), after which the phrase was used extensively in the labor press.

81. *Workingman's Advocate*, October 20, 1832, 4, 10 (italics added).

82. Jacques Rancière, "Preface."

83. *Voice of Industry*, September 18, 1845.

84. *Workingman's Advocate*, August 28, 1830, 2.

85. *Voice of Industry*, July 31, 1845.

86. *The Mechanic*, May 11, 1844.

87. *Voice of Industry*, April 3, 1846.

88. *Voice of Industry*, April 4, 1847.

89. *Voice of Industry*, April 3, 1846.

90. Ibid., July 27, 1844 (italics in original).

91. Ibid., August 24, 1844. Lazerow, *Religion and the Working Class in Antebellum America*, 136.*

92. *Voice of Industry*, July 31, 1845.

93. Ibid.

94. Reprinted in *Voice of Industry*, April 3, 1946.

95. For discussion of the need for an infrastructure of public, free places to serve workers' leisure, see *The Mechanic*, August 31, 1844, and January 18, 1845.

96. Lazerow, *Religion and the Working Class in Antebellum America*, 32, 193. Lazerow makes a distinction between "what a later generation of labor reformers would call 'leisure time'" (198) and how workers wrote and spoke about their new free time during the ten-hour movement.

CHAPTER 3

1. Walt Whitman, *Democratic Vistas*, in *Prose Works 1892*, ed. Floyd Stovall (New York: New York University Press, 1964), 369–370.

2. Louis Untermeyer, ed., *The Poetry and Prose of Walt Whitman* (New York: Simon and Schuster, 1949), 805. Here Untermeyer described *Democratic Vistas* as "a mixture of savage bitterness and desperate hope."

3. Whitman, *Democratic Vistas*, 370.

4. Untermeyer, *The Poetry and Prose of Walt Whitman*, 805.

5. Ed Folsom outlined and used such a representation strategy in the Fifteenth Annual Presidential Lecture, "What Do We Represent? Walt Whitman, Representative Democracy, and Democratic Representation," February 15, 1998, at the University of Iowa.*

6. For Whitman's understanding of progress as the advance of freedom, see, for example, the opening lines of *Democratic Vistas*, 361–362.*

7. Whitman, *Democratic Vistas*, 410 (italics added). Mark Van Doren's quotation of this passage may be found in Untermeyer, *The Poetry and Prose of Walt Whitman*, 1195.

8. Perennially, historians and politicians interpret American history as the gradual unfolding of the liberal assumptions implicit in the Declaration of Independence. They often assert that the promises that all "men" are born with "unalienable" rights to "life, liberty, and

the pursuit of happiness" were gradually claimed, and are in the process of being claimed, in contexts never imagined by the Founders and by groups initially excluded—those without property, African Americans, women, gays and lesbians, and so on. Martin Luther King, in his "I Have a Dream" speech in 1963, and Barack Obama, in his keynote address to the Democratic National Convention in 2004, followed this interpretation.*

9. David D. Anderson, "Walt Whitman: Nineteenth-Century Man," *Walt Whitman Birthplace Bulletin* 3 (April 1960): 3–5.

10. *Brooklyn Daily Eagle*, November 24, 1947 (italics added). See also June 23, 1846; July 28, 1846; October 8, 1846; April 20, 1847; May 3, 1847.

11. Whitman, *Democratic Vistas*, 410.*

12. Whitman, *Democratic Vistas*, 363, 731.

13. Robert T. Rhode, "Culture Followed the Plow, However Slowly," *Kentucky Philological Review* 15 (2001): 49–56.

14. Whitman, *Democratic Vistas*, 353, 484.

15. Leadie M. Clark, *Walt Whitman's Concept of the American Common Man* (New York: Philosophical Library, 1955), 32.

16. Whitman, *Democratic Vistas*, 538–539 (italics added).

17. Alan Trachtenberg, *The Incorporation of America: Culture and Society in the Gilded Age* (New York: Hill and Wang, 1982), 32, 73. See also Granville Hicks, *The Great Tradition: An Interpretation of American Literature since the Civil War*, rev. ed. (New York: Biblo and Tannen, 1967), 24; and M. Wynn Thomas, "Whitman and the Dreams of Labor" in *Walt Whitman: The Centennial Essays*, ed. Ed Folsom and Guido Villa (Iowa City: University of Iowa Press, 1994). Thomas observed that "the old republican dream of labor getting its just rewards and of *everyone* enjoying modest comforts" was "a dream which Trachtenberg specifically associates with Whitman" (144; italics in original).

18. Kenneth Cmiel, "Whitman the Democrat," in *A Historical Guide to Walt Whitman*, ed. David S. Reynolds (Oxford: Oxford University Press, 2000), 227. See also Jerome Loving, "The Political Roots of *Leaves of Grass*" in Reynolds, *A Historical Guide to Walt Whitman*, 97–119.

19. Nathaniel Hawthorne wrote "The Celestial Railroad" in 1843. An allegory based on Bunyan's *Pilgrim's Progress*, the short story was partly founded on the widespread hope that economic progress was preparing the way for something like Whitman's Higher Progress. In "The Celestial Railroad," Vanity Fair represented the concern that the excesses of wealth and the satisfaction with mere economic achievements would delay pursuit of the nation's real destination and higher destiny.

20. Whitman, "Song of the Open Road," in *Leaves of Grass: The Comprehensive Reader's Edition*, ed. Harold W. Blodgett and Sculley Bradley (New York: New York University Press, 1965), 155.

21. Ibid. See also George Kateb, "Walt Whitman and the Culture of Democracy," *Political Theory* 18, no. 4 (1990): 545–571; and Whitman, *Leaves of Grass: The Comprehensive Reader's Edition*, 157.*

22. W. B. Fulghum, "Whitman's Debt to Joseph Gostwick" *American Literature* 12 (January 1941): 491–496.*

23. Ibid.

24. Whitman, *Leaves of Grass*, in Untermeyer, *The Poetry and Prose of Walt Whitman*, 110, 115. See also Whitman, *Democratic Vistas*, 394.*

25. Whitman, "Song of Myself," in Untermeyer, *The Poetry and Prose of Walt Whitman*, 95.

26. Ibid., 115.

27. See also Whitman, "Drum Taps," in Untermeyer, *The Poetry and Prose of Walt Whitman*, 288.*

28. Whitman, "Song of Myself," in Untermeyer, *The Poetry and Prose of Walt Whitman*, 114, 117.

29. Whitman uses a variety of words to describe free times beyond ordinary jobs and chores. In addition to "loafe," he writes of "leisure," "ease" or being "at ease," "intervals," "rambles," and "recreation." Whitman seemed to have been struggling to find the right word for the new, refined freedom.

30. Whitman, "Song of Myself," in Untermeyer, *The Poetry and Prose of Walt Whitman*, 95.*

31. Ibid.

32. See Walt Whitman, *Notebooks and Unpublished Prose Manuscript*, ed. E. Grier. 4 vols. (New York: New York University Press, 2007), 4:1469.

33. Eugen Fink, "The Oasis of Happiness: Toward an Ontology of Play," Ute Saine and Thomas Saine's translation of selections from Fink's *Oase des Glücks: Gedanken zu einer Ontologie des Spiels*, in "Game, Play, Literature," special issue, *Yale French Studies* 41 (1968): 19–30.*

34. Walt Whitman, *Walt Whitman's Workshop: A Collection of Unpublished Manuscripts*, ed. Clifton Joseph Furness (Cambridge, MA: Harvard University Press, 1964), 132, see also 185. Other Whitman references to play include *Democratic Vistas*, 806, 836; and "Song of Myself" and "Song at Sunset," in Untermeyer, *The Poetry and Prose of Walt Whitman* 95, 440.

35. Whitman also used the metaphor of "free play" or the "play of" to explain some of his central concepts such as "personalism." Whitman, *Democratic Vistas*, 396.*

36. Parts of *Democratic Vistas* were originally published as the essay "Personalism."

37. Kateb, "Whitman and the Culture of Democracy," 551.

38. Ibid.*

39. Whitman, *Democratic Vistas*, 414.*

40. Ibid.

41. Recently, scholars have noted the similarity between Whitman's "adhesiveness" and some of Jürgen Habermas's constructs, such as "intersubjectivity." See Charles Molesworth, "Whitman's Political Vision," *Raritan* 12 (Summer 1992): 98–112.

42. See, for example, one of the first to use the trope, Lewis Mumford, *The Golden Day: A Study in American Experience and Culture* (New York: Norton, 1926).

43. For "discussional," see Jürgen Habermas and T. McCarthy, *The Theory of Communicative Action: Reason and the Rationalization of Society* (New York: Beacon Press, 1985).*

44. "Gray detail" is the phrase Foucault used to describe aspects of his "genealogy" project, which he defined as the "union of erudite knowledge and local memories . . . a reactivation of local knowledges . . . in opposition to scientific hierarchisation of knowledges." Quoted in Benjamin Hunnicutt, "Habermas's *Musse* and Foucault's *Genealogy*: Ways out of the Postmodern Black Hole," *Leisure Sciences* 28 (December 2006): 437–441.*

45. Compare Habermas, *The Theory of Communicative Action*. See also Molesworth, "Whitman's Political Vision."

46. Whitman, *Democratic Vistas*, 396.

47. Whitman's preface to the 1855 edition of *Leaves of Grass*, in Untermeyer, *The Poetry and Prose of Walt Whitman*, 513.

48. Ibid., 514.

49. Robert Olsen, "Whitman's *Leaves of Grass*: Poetry and the Founding of a 'New World' Culture," *University of Toronto Quarterly* 64 (Spring 1995): 305–323.

50. Whitman's preface to the 1855 edition of *Leaves of Grass*, 504.

51. Kerry A. Larson, *Whitman's Drama of Consensus* (Chicago: University of Chicago Press, 1988), xx–xxi, 11–12; see also Mark Maslan, *Whitman Possessed: Poetry, Sexuality, and Popular Authority* (Baltimore: Johns Hopkins University Press, 2001), 5, 92–116.

52. Hunnicutt, "Habermas's *Musse* and Foucault's *Genealogy*: Ways out of the Postmodern Black Hole," 440.*

53. Olsen, "Whitman's Leaves of Grass," 305–323.

54. Ed Folsom and Kenneth M. Price, *Re-Scripting Walt Whitman: An Introduction to His Life and Work* (Maiden, MA: Blackwell, 2005), 33.*

55. Olsen, "Whitman's Leaves of Grass."*

56. Whitman's preface to the 1855 edition of *Leaves of Grass*; see also Whitman, "By Blue Ontario's Shore," in Untermeyer, *The Poetry and Prose of Walt Whitman*, 496, 238.

57. Betsy Erkkila, *Whitman the Political Poet* (New York: Oxford University Press, 1989), 252. Sean Wilentz, *Chants Democratic: New York City and the Rise of the American Working Class* (New York: Oxford University Press, 1984), 256–263. See also Thomas F. Haddox, "Whitman's End of History," *Walt Whitman Quarterly Review* 22 (Summer 2004): 1–22.

58. Arthur Wrobel, "*Democratic Vistas* (1871)," in *Walt Whitman: An Encyclopedia*, ed. J. R. LeMaster and Donald D. Kummings (New York: Garland, 1998), 178.

59. See Chapter 2.

60. See Chapter 2.

61. For other examples of the *Eagle*'s reporting and editorializing about shorter hours, see March 27, 1826, October 26, 1846, April 23, 1947, and November 30, 1849. A letter published in the *Eagle* on September 9, 1846, and signed "A Democrat" included the rhetoric that accompanied the ten-hour fight. The letter quoted a Van Buren supporter: "The administration of Mr. Van Buren introduced the ten hour system upon the public works of the Government, and many a laborer has blessed him, morning and evening, for this contributing to the comfort of himself and family. *This reform so necessary to the moral, physical and religious culture of the people*, should be introduced into every manufactory in the land—but I know of no power in the Constitution that can compel its adoption. You must enforce it by the omnipotent influences of public opinion" (italics added). See also Thomas Brasher, "Organized Labor versus Whitman's 'Immutable Truth,'" *Walt Whitman Review* 6 (December 1960): 63–66.

62. A story of his about a boy held as a "wage slave" was serialized in the *Brooklyn Eagle* beginning January 29, 1847.

63. Whitman, *Democratic Vistas*, 409–410.

64. Whitman, "No Labor-Saving Machine," in Untermeyer, *The Poetry and Prose of Walt Whitman*, 131.

65. Whitman, "The Return of Heroes," in Untermeyer, *The Poetry and Prose of Walt Whitman*, 358.

66. Haddox, "Whitman's End of History." See also Horace Traubel, *With Walt Whitman in Camden* (Carbondale: Southern Illinois University Press, 1964), 5:393, 427.*

67. Whitman, *Democratic Vistas*, 402 (italics added). Whitman's "pleasant western settlement" continues one of his long expositions that begins just before he introduces "the wife of a mechanic." Trying to imagine a place in society for "feminine excellence" that "knew that there are intervals," he proceeds to outline his western utopia where time was available for "the rest of life, the main thing."*

68. Whitman, *Democratic Vistas*, 401.

69. Whitman's preface to the 1855 edition of *Leaves of Grass*, 441.

70. Whitman to Emerson, August 1856, in Untermeyer, *The Poetry and Prose of Walt Whitman*, 522.

71. Whitman, "Song of the Open Road," 159 (italics added).

72. Ralph Waldo Emerson, *Society and Solitude* (Boston: Fields and Osgood, 1870), 149.

73. Whitman's preface to the 1855 edition of *Leaves of Grass*, 440–441.

74. David Karsner, *Horace Traubel, His Life and Work* (New York: E. Arens, 1919), 57–58.

75. Horace Traubel, *The Conservator* 24, no. 6: 2. See also William English Walling, *Whitman and Traubel* (New York: A. C. Boni, 1916), 120.

76. Mark Van Doren, quoted in Untermeyer, *Poetry and Prose of Walt Whitman*, 1228.

77. See Rhode, "Culture Followed the Plow, However Slowly." Rhode makes the case that Whitman, together with Abraham Lincoln and Henry Ward Beecher, saw labor-saving machines such as the steam plow "increasing personal freedom and, thereby, encouraging artistic accomplishment" (50).

78. Anderson, "Walt Whitman: Nineteenth-Century Man."

79. Daniel Rodgers, *The Work Ethic in Industrial America, 1850–1920* (University of Chicago Press, 1979), 1.

80. Henry Seidel Canby, *Classic Americans: A Study of Eminent American Writers from Irving to Whitman, with an Introductory Survey of the Colonial Background of Our National Literature* (New York: Harcourt, 1932), 198–205.

81. Henry David Thoreau, *Walden: Or Life in the Woods* (E. P. Dutton, New York: 1908), 61.

82. Ibid., 95–96. See also Thoreau's 1937 commencement address at Harvard on the "commercial spirit," one of the finest expressions of the forgotten American dream. F. B. Sandborn, ed., *The Writings of Henry David Thoreau*, vol. 6 (Boston: Houghton Mifflin, 1906), 9.

83. Charles Dudley Warner, "What Is Your Culture to Me?" *Scribner's Monthly* 4, no. 4 (1872): 476.

84. Ibid., 472, 473, 474.

85. Ibid., 474–475.

86. Ibid., 477.

87. Glyndon G. Van Deusen, *Horace Greeley, Nineteenth-Century Crusader* (Philadelphia: University of Pennsylvania Press, 1953), 28, 45.

88. Ibid., 68–69.

89. Horace Greeley, *Hints toward Reforms, Lectures, Addresses and Other Writings* (New York: Fowlers and Wells, 1855), 33–34. For Greeley's "profession of . . . faith in a better future" for labor, see *Voice of Industry*, May 21, 1847, 2.

90. Jeter Isely, *Horace Greeley and the Republican Party, 1853–1861* (New York: Octagon Books, 1965), 212.

91. Greeley, *Hints toward Reform*, 33–34.

92. Leon Case and Horace Greeley, *The Great Industries of the United States* (Chicago: Burr and Hyde, 1872), 146.

93. Edward Everett, *Importance of Practical Education and Useful Knowledge: Being a Selection from His Orations and Other Discourses* (New York: Harper and Brothers, 1847), 291–292.

94. David Roediger and Philip Foner, *Our Own Time: A History of American Labor and the Working Day* (New York: Verso, 1989), 85, see also 95.

95. *New York Times*, May 24, 1870, 2.

96. Rhode, "Culture Followed the Plow, However Slowly," 51–52.

97. Henry Ward Beecher, "Mowing Machines and Steam Plows," *Farmer's Magazine* 8 (1855), 1. See also Henry Ward Beecher, *Eyes and Ears* (Boston: Ticknor and Fields, 1862), 70.

98. Rodgers, *The Work Ethic in Industrial America*, 97–98.

99. Henry Ward Beecher, "Moral Theory of Civil Liberty" (sermon preached July 4, 1869), *The Plymouth Pulpit: Sermons Preached in Plymouth Church* (Brooklyn, NY: J. B. Ford, 1871), 301–302.

100. Rhode, "Culture Followed the Plow, However Slowly." See also Abraham Lincoln, "Address to the Wisconsin State Agricultural Society, Milwaukee, Wisconsin, Sept. 30, 1859," reprinted in Andrew Delbanco, ed., *The Portable Abraham Lincoln* (New York: Penguin, 2009), 181. It is fitting to end this catalog of nineteenth-century supporters of Higher Progress with Lincoln. However, others, including Charles Sumner, Karl Heinzen, William F. Channing, Gerrit Smith, Josiah Abbott, and William Lloyd Garrison, supported eight-hour days in terms of the progress of freedom and civilization. See Roediger and Foner, *Our Own Time*, 85. Often overlooked, Chauncey Smith, a prominent patent attorney during the late nineteenth century, made an eloquent case for Higher Progress though shorter hours. See Chauncey Smith, "The Influence of Inventions upon Civilization: A Paper Read before the Chiefs and Commissioners of the Several Bureaus of Labor Statistics in the United States," in *Annual Report of the Bureau of Michigan Labor and Industrial Statistics*, by Michigan Bureau of Labor and Industrial Statistics (Lansing, MI: Bureau of Labor Statistics, 1886), 25–36.

CHAPTER 4

1. William Heighton, "An Address to the Members of Trade Societies and to the Working Classes Generally," reprinted in Philip Foner, *William Heighton: Pioneer Labor Leader of Jacksonian Philadelphia* (New York: International, 1991), 69.

2. Karl Marx, *Capital: A Critique of Political Economy*, trans. Samuel Moore and Edward Aveling (New York: Modern Library, 1906), 329.

3. Daniel Rodgers, *The Work Ethic in Industrial America, 1850–1920* (Chicago: University of Chicago Press, 1979), 155.

4. Massachusetts Bureau of Statistics of Labor (MBSL), *Twentieth Annual Report* (Boston: Wright and Potter, 1889), 447. See also Rodgers, *The Work Ethic*, 157.

5. Gerald N. Grob, *Workers and Utopia: A Study of Ideological Conflict in the American Labor Movement, 1865–1900* (Evanston, IL: Northwestern University Press, 1961), 149.

6. Samuel Gompers, "Testimony before the Committee on Labor of the U.S. House of Representatives," in *The Samuel Gompers Papers*, vol. 5, *An Expanding Movement at the Turn of the Century, 1898–1902*, ed. Stuart Bruce Kaufman and Peter J. Albert (Urbana: University of Illinois Press, 1986), 482.

7. Bill Haywood, quoted in Rodgers, *The Work Ethic*, 156.

8. George Gunton, *Wealth and Progress: A Critical Examination of the Wages Question* (New York: D. Appleton, 1897), 247.

9. Rodgers, *The Work Ethic*, 156.

10. Rodgers noted that workers' interest in shortening their work hours at the time did not spring from "all the complex intellectual rationale behind the eight-hour campaign" but from an "essential . . . obvious appeal: the promise of the relief from toil." Rodgers, *The Work Ethic*, 160.

11. David Montgomery, "Gutman's Nineteenth-Century America," *Labor History* 19 (Summer 1978): 419.

12. Benjamin Hunnicutt, *Work without End: Abandoning Shorter Hours for the Right to Work* (Philadelphia: Temple University Press, 1988), 12–14.

13. Certainly, the historical relationship between shorter hours and higher wages was more complex. During the last part of the nineteenth century, labor leaders such as Ira Steward argued that, in theory, working less resulted in higher wages and that workers did not have to choose between the two. However, in practice most employees had bosses who, reluctant to grant either, made the either-or choice clear. For a discussion of how the "consumer choice," work and wages or leisure, became an explicit part of the labor movement, see "Abundance, an Exact Science" in Chapter 6.

14. MBSL, *Twelfth Annual Report*, 449.

15. Ibid.

16. Ibid. The MBSL report showed that most workers who had specific ideas about what to do were spending (or planned to spend) their new leisure with their families and friends. See also Kathy Peiss, *Cheap Amusements: Working Women and Leisure in Turn-of-the-Century New York* (Philadelphia: Temple University Press, 1986), 15.

17. Stuart Ewen and Elizabeth Ewen, *Channels of Desire: Mass Images and the Shaping of American Consciousness* (Minneapolis: University of Minnesota Press, 1992), 36.

18. Mikhail Bakhtin, *Rabelais and His World* (Cambridge, MA: MIT Press, 1968), introduction, 83, 92 (italics in original). See Susan G. Davis, *Parades and Power: Street Theatre in Nineteenth-Century Philadelphia* (Philadelphia: Temple University Press, 1986), 38–39.*

19. E. P. Thompson, "Time, Work-Discipline and Industrial Capitalism," *Past and Present* 38 (December 1967): 56–97. See also Ivan Illich, *Tools for Conviviality* (New York: Harper and Row, 1973).*

20. Max Weber, *The Protestant Ethic and the Spirit of Capitalism*, trans. Talcott Parsons (1930; repr., Mineola, NY: Dover, 2003), 53, 89.*

21. "Crisis of work" is James Gilbert's term. See J. B. Gilbert, *Work without Salvation: America's Intellectuals and Industrial Alienation, 1880–1910* (Baltimore: Johns Hopkins University Press, 1977), vii–xv, 31–66, 181.

22. See Roy Rosenzweig, *Eight Hours for What We Will: Workers and Leisure in an Industrial City, 1870–1920* (New York: Cambridge University Press, 1983), 54.

23. Peiss, *Cheap Amusements*, 57.

24. Bakhtin, *Rabelais and His World*, 83, 92 (italics added).

25. Lizabeth Cohen, *Making a New Deal: Industrial Workers in Chicago, 1919–1938* (New York: Cambridge University Press, 1990), 100; Vicki L. Ruiz, *From out of the Shadows: Mexican Women in Twentieth-Century America* (New York: Oxford University Press, 1998), especially the chapter "Confronting 'America,'" 33–50; George Sanchez, *Becoming Mexican American: Ethnicity and Acculturation in Chicano Los Angeles, 1900–1943* (New York: Oxford University Press, 1993), 171–203.

26. Rosenzweig, *Eight Hours for What We Will*, 58.*

27. Rosenzweig, *Eight Hours for What We Will*, 58 (italics in original).

28. Peiss, *Cheap Amusements*, 185–186.

29. Ibid., 4, 40.

30. Randy McBee, *Dance Hall Days: Intimacy and Leisure among Working-Class Immigrants in the United States* (New York: New York University Press, 2000).

31. Nan Enstad, *Ladies of Labor, Girls of Adventure: Working Women, Popular Culture, and Labor Politics at the Turn of the Twentieth Century* (New York: Columbia University Press, 1999), 16–17 (italics added).

32. Angela McRobbie, *Feminism and Youth Culture: From "Jackie" to "Just Seventeen"* (1991; repr., New York: Macmillan, 1995), 14.

33. Richard Butsch, *For Fun and Profit: The Transformation of Leisure into Consumption* (Philadelphia: Temple University Press, 1990), 13. See also Stephen Hardy, *How Boston Played: Sport, Recreation, and Community, 1865–1915* (Knoxville: University of Tennessee Press, 2003); Dominic Cavallo, *Muscles and Morals: Organized Playgrounds and Urban Reform, 1880–1920* (University of Pennsylvania Press, 1981); and Cary Goodman, *Choosing Sides: Playground and Street Life on the Lower East Side* (New York: Schocken Books, 1979).*

34. Chad Montrie, "'I Think Less of the Factory than of My Native Dell': Labor, Nature, and the Lowell 'Mill Girls,'" *Environmental History* 9, no. 2 (2004): 275–295.

35. Montrie, "'I Think Less of the Factory than of My Native Dell,'" 277.

36. Dianne D. Glave and Mark Stoll, *To Love the Wind and the Rain: African Americans and Environmental History* (Pittsburgh, PA: University of Pittsburgh Press, 2006), 63–65;

see also Dianne Glave, *Rooted in the Earth: Reclaiming the African American Environmental Heritage* (Chicago: Lawrence Hill Books, 2010), 64, 100, 122, 123.

37. Roy Rosenzweig and Elizabeth Blackmar, *The Park and the People: A History of Central Park* (Ithaca, NY: Cornell University Press, 1992), 18.

38. Ibid., 526.

39. Ibid., 235.

40. J. Joseph Huthmacher, "Urban Liberalism and the Age of Reform," *Mississippi Valley Historical Review* 49, no. 2 (1962): 238.

41. Rosenzweig and Blackmar, *The Park and the People*, 338.

42. Ibid., 423–424.

43. Ibid., 526.

44. Ibid., 530.

45. Elizabeth Hasanovitz, *One of Them: Chapters from a Passionate Autobiography* (Boston: Houghton Mifflin, 1918), 96.*

46. Ibid., 198.

47. Ibid., 199.

48. Rosenzweig and Blackmar, *The Park and the People*, 526, 530.

49. Hasanovitz, *One of Them*, 91.

50. Ibid., 18.

51. Ibid., 1–2.

52. Ibid., 162 (italics in original).

53. Ibid., 315.

54. Ibid., 25, 159.

55. Ibid., 93, 308, 24–25.

56. Rosenzweig, *Eight Hours for What We Will*, 58.

57. Diane Balser, *Sisterhood and Solidarity: Feminism and Labor in Modern Times* (Cambridge, MA: South End Press, 1987), 41–42. Eric Arnesen, ed., *Encyclopedia of U.S. Labor and Working-Class History* (New York: Routledge, 2007), 1:395, 1512.

58. David Roediger and Philip Foner, *Our Own Time: A History of American Labor and the Working Day* (New York: Verso, 1989), 178.

59. Ibid., 178.

60. Ibid.

61. Mary Marcy, *Shop Talks on Economics* (Chicago: Charles H. Kerr, 1911), 54, 56.

62. Susan Stone Wong, "From Soul to Strawberries: The International Ladies' Garment Workers' Union and Workers' Education, 1914–1950," in *Sisterhood and Solidarity: Workers' Education for Women, 1914–1984*, ed. Joyce Kornbluh and Mary Frederickson (Philadelphia: Temple University Press, 1984), 42.

63. Kenneth C. Wolensky, Nicole H. Wolensky, and Robert P. Wolensky, *Fighting for the Union Label: The Women's Garment Industry and the ILGWU in Pennsylvania* (University Park: Pennsylvania State University Press, 2002), 89.

64. See Barbara Smith and G. Steinem, *The Reader's Companion to U.S. Women's History* (New York: Houghton Mifflin Harcourt, 1999), 380; and Annelise Orleck, *Common Sense and a Little Fire: Women and Working-Class Politics in the United States, 1900–1965* (Chapel Hill: University of North Carolina Press, 1995), 308.

65. See, for example, Stuart Bruce Kaufman, *Samuel Gompers and the Origins of the American Federation of Labor, 1848–1896* (Westport, CT: Greenwood Press, 1973), xi.

66. Wong, "From Soul to Strawberries," 43.

67. Rand School of Social Science, Dept. of Labor Research, *The American Labor Year Book* (New York: Rand School of Social Science, 1924), 221.

68. Orleck, *Common Sense and a Little Fire*, 164, 181.

69. Cohn managed to sustain workers' education during the economic downturn of the early 1920s, years that saw ILGWU membership decline by more than 16 percent. Ibid., 182.

70. Ibid., 164, 184, 173. Sometimes called "discursive democracy," the term "deliberative democracy" was first used in the 1980s by Joseph M. Bessette. See Joseph M. Bessette, *The Mild Voice of Reason: Deliberative Democracy and American National Government* (Chicago: University of Chicago Press, 1997). The concept has been developed by Jürgen Habermas, Joshua Cohen, and Amy Gutman, among others. The constituent principles of deliberative democracy that Joshua Cohen outlined nearly match what Fannia Cohn thought workers' education should be. See Joshua Cohen, "Deliberative Democracy and Democratic Legitimacy," in *The Good Polity*, ed. A. Hamlin and P. Pettit (Oxford: Blackwell, 1989), 18–30.

71. Fannia Cohn, "Experiments of the Philadelphia Waistmakers' Union: Local No. 15," *Ladies' Garment Worker* 9 (January 18, 1918): 27.

72. Orleck, *Common Sense and a Little Fire*, 182.*

73. Fannia Cohn, "Woman's Eternal Struggle: What Workers' Education Will Do for Woman," pamphlet reprinted from the January 1932 issue of *Pioneer Woman*.

74. While losing many of her socialist and communist friends, she found numerous new middle-class supporters. They included historians Mary and Charles Beard and labor journalist Arthur Gleason, who helped her found the Workers' Education Bureau (WEB) in the early 1920s.

75. Workers' Education Bureau, *Workers' Education in the United States, Report of the Proceedings of the Second National Conference on Workers' Education Held at the New School for Social Research New York City on April 22nd and 23rd, 1922* (New York: Workers' Education Bureau, 1922), 54.

76. Workers' Education Bureau, *Workers' Education*, 66.

77. Quoted in Orleck, *Common Sense and a Little Fire*, 176.

78. Annelise Orleck, "Fannia Cohn," in Arnesen, *Encyclopedia of U.S. Labor and Working-Class History*, 1:272.

79. Orleck, *Common Sense and a Little Fire*, 16.

80. Fannia Cohn, *Labor Unions and the Community* (New York: Workers' Education Bureau of America, 1946), 6 (italics in original).

81. Cohn, "Woman's Eternal Struggle."*

82. Orleck, *Common Sense and a Little Fire*, 16. For a discussion of "deep community," see Janice G. Raymond, *A Passion for Friends* (North Melbourne, Victoria, Australia: Spinifex Press, 2001), 86, 110, 160. See also Marilyn Friedman's review of Raymond's book, "Individuality without Individualism," *Hypatia* 3, no. 2 (1988), 131–137.

83. Workers' Education Bureau, *Workers' Education*, 54.

84. Orleck, *Common Sense and a Little Fire*, 187.

85. Cohn, "Woman's Eternal Struggle." For Cohn's feminist views, see Wong, "From Soul to Strawberries," 49.

86. Cohn, "Woman's Eternal Struggle."

87. Fannia Cohn, *Learning, Playing, Action: A Program of Progressive Workers' Education* (New York: ILGWU, 1946), 3.

88. Workers' Education Bureau, *Workers' Education*, 60.

89. Cohn, *Learning, Playing, Action*, 11.

90. Ibid., 3.

91. Ivan Illich's term is appropriate here because Cohn seems to have anticipated parts of his critique of modern culture. Ivan Illich, *Tools for Conviviality* (New York: Harper and Row, 1973). 11.

92. Cohn, *Learning, Playing, Action*, 5A.*

93. Mildred Moore, "A History of the Women's Trade Union League of Chicago" (master's thesis, University of Chicago, 1915), 29.

94. Ibid., 28–30.

95. Josephine Goldmark, *Fatigue and Efficiency: A Study in Industry* (New York: Russell Sage Foundation, 1912), 286–287.*

96. See Stanley Shapiro, "The Passage of Power: Labor and the New Social Order," *Proceedings of the American Philosophical Society* 120, no. 6 (1976): 464–474. See also *New Republic* 14 (February 16, 1918): 2. As late as July 1919, Gleason still maintained that labor's future lay with guild socialism.*

97. Arthur Gleason, *What the Workers Want: A Study of British Labor* (New York: Harcourt, Brace and Howe, 1920), 4. On the basis of years of reporting in England, he concluded, "Step by step the new order is being established. It is being done without armed insurrection, or bloodshed. It is gentle revolution of the good-humored British brand" (4).

98. Gleason, *What the Workers Want*, 182 (italics in original).

99. Arthur Gleason, *The Book of Arthur Gleason: My People* (New York: W. Morrow, 1929), 203.

100. Arthur Gleason, *Workers' Education: American Experiments* (New York: Bureau of Industrial Research, 1921), 51; for Gleason's complicated views on progress, see *What the Workers Want*, 17, 97, 131.

101. Gleason, *Workers' Education*, 10.

102. Ibid., 68.

103. Ibid.

104. Letter from Gompers to John Kirchner, February 28, 1889, in *The Samuel Gompers Papers: The Early Years of the American Federation of Labor, 1887–1890*, ed. Stuart Bruce Kaufman (Champagne: University of Illinois Press, 1987), 2:187.

105. Gleason, *Workers' Education*, 11.

106. Ibid., 13.

107. Ibid., 14.

108. Ibid., 29.

109. Ibid., 11.

110. Ibid., 35.

111. Ibid., 55 (italics added).

112. Ibid., 56.

113. Orleck, *Common Sense and a Little Fire*, 184. See also Grant Overton, *When Winter Comes to Main Street* (New York: Doran, 1922), i–iii.

114. Gompers failed to find "anything in common between the democracy of America and the cruel, ruthless tyranny of Moscow." *New York Times*, April 15, 1923, 2.

115. *New York Times*, March 6, 1923, 23; *New York Times*, April 20, 1925, 12.

116. *New York Times*, April 20, 1925, 12.

117. *New York Times*, July 10, 1925, 16.

118. Ibid.

119. Alfred Dwight Sheffield, *Joining in Public Discussion* (New York: Workers' Bookshelf, George Doran, 1922), 170.

120. Ibid., vi–vii (italics added).

121. Ibid., viii.

122. Ibid., see section 1, "Qualifying Oneself to Contribute," 21.

123. Ibid.

124. Ira Steward, *The Eight Hour Movement: A Reduction of Hours Is an Increase of Wages* (Boston: Boston Labor Reform Association, 1865), 4 (italics added).

125. Ibid., 13.

126. Ibid., 15.

127. Gunton, *Wealth and Progress*, 356.

128. Steward, *The Eight Hour Movement*, 18.

129. Ibid., 14 (italics in original).

130. Ibid., 12 (italics in original).

131. Gunton, *Wealth and Progress*, 235, 318, see also 95–96, 241, 341, 344, 352.*

132. Ira Steward, *The Eight Hour Movement*, 41.

CHAPTER 5

1. Wright quoted Whitman's "Song of the Universal." Whereas Whitman used words such as "ideal" and "American idea" to describe his vision, the last few verses of his poem, which Wright omitted, leave no doubt that "plan of Thee" is what Whitman thought of as the original American dream:

Is it a dream?
Nay but the lack of it the dream,
And failing it life's lore and wealth a dream,
And all the world a dream.

2. Daniel T. Rodgers, *The Work Ethic in Industrial America, 1850–1920* (Chicago: University of Chicago press, 1979), 28. See also James Gilbert, *Work without Salvation: America's Intellectuals and Industrial Alienation, 1880–1910* (Baltimore: Johns Hopkins University Press, 1977), vii–xv, 31–66, 181. Gilbert wrote of the "social crisis . . . that typified the late part of the [nineteenth] century up to the First World War . . . the intensified feeling that work, the sacred myth of mobility and individualism, was undergoing a rapid and crucial degeneration," which "by the turn of the century . . . had become . . . unavoidable" (vii).

3. Rodgers, *Work Ethic*, 90, 197.

4. Ibid., 93.

5. Ibid., 123.

6. Rodgers did caution his readers that his focus was on middle-class writers in the northeastern part of the United States. See ibid., introduction.

7. Sean Wilentz, *Chants Democratic: New York City and the Rise of the American Working* Class, *1788–1850* (New York: Oxford University Press, 1984), 113.

8. E. P. Thompson, "Time, Work-Discipline and Industrial Capitalism," *Past and Present* 38 (December 1967): 56–97.*

9. Frank Lloyd Wright, "The Art and Craft of the Machine," in *Frank Lloyd Wright: Essential Texts*, ed. Robert C. Twombly (New York: Norton, 2009), 43. The essay was first published as Frank Lloyd Wright, "The Art and Craft of the Machine," *Brush and Pencil* 8, no. 2 (1901): 77–90. Wright modified this original essay, publishing the changed texts in various places. References here are to Twombly's version.

10. Some Wright scholars believe that this paper is "his first great manifesto." Others, such as Bruce Brooks Pfeiffer, see it as more of a "summation of ideas and concepts that he had been presenting to the public for years." Frank Lloyd Wright, *Frank Lloyd Wright Collected Writings*, 5 vols., ed. Bruce Brooks Pfeiffer (New York: Rizzoli, 1992–1995), 1:58. Because he was responding to William Morris's challenge, however, he made the essay something more than a mere summation.

11. John Sergeant, *Frank Lloyd Wright's Usonian Houses: The Case for Organic Architecture* (New York: Whitney Library of Design, 1976), 127; Richard "Jix" Lloyd-Jones, great-nephew of Jenkin Lloyd Jones, interview by author, Iowa City, IA, October 10, 2010.

12. Wright, "The Art and Craft of the Machine."*

13. Like Whitman, Wright often contrasted his vision of a democratic culture with the European feudal past, characterized by exclusiveness.

14. Wright, "The Art and Craft of the Machine," 44.

15. Ibid., 44, 45.

16. Ibid., 50.

17. Ibid., 51.

18. Ibid., 50.

19. Ibid.

20. Ibid.

21. Frank Lloyd Wright, *The Living City* (New York: Horizon Press, 1958), 85–86. See also H. I. Brock, "A Pioneer in Architecture That Is Called Modern," *New York Times,* June 29, 1930.

22. Wright, "The Art and Craft of the Machine," 54.

23. Wright, *Frank Lloyd Wright Collected Writings,* 5:262.*

24. Wright, "The Art and Craft of the Machine," 63 (italics added).

25. Wright frequently used the term "American Ideal." See, for example, *Frank Lloyd Wright: Essential Texts,* 109, 241.

26. Frank Lloyd Wright, *The Disappearing City* (New York: W. F. Payson, 1932); Frank Lloyd Wright, *When Democracy Builds* (Chicago: University of Chicago Press, 1945). *The Living City* was an extensive rewrite and update of *When Democracy Builds,* which was published in 1945. *When Democracy Builds* was itself a revision of his 1932 book, *The Disappearing City.*

27. Wright, *Frank Lloyd Wright Collected Writings,* 2:19. Wright's students created a physical model of Broadacre City in 1934.

28. B. B. Pfeiffer, *The Essential Frank Lloyd Wright: Critical Writings on Architecture* (Princeton, NJ: Princeton University Press, 2008), 212.

29. Ibid. See also Wright, *Frank Lloyd Wright Collected Writings,* 2:74.*

30. Neil Levine, "Introduction," in *Modern Architecture: Being the Kahn Lectures for 1930,* by Frank Lloyd Wright (1931; repr., Princeton, NJ: Princeton University Press, 2008), 112. See also Paul E. Corcoran, "Utopian Masterminds," review of *Urban Utopias in the Twentieth Century, Ebenezer Howard, Frank Lloyd Wright, and Le Corbusier,* by Robert Fishman, *Review of Politics* 41, no. 3 (1979): 458–460.

31. Wright, *Frank Lloyd Wright Collected Writings,* 2:96–97.*

32. Wright, *Frank Lloyd Wright Collected Writings,* 5:191. Wright said, "Taking a human being for my scale, I brought the whole house down in height to fit a normal person. . . . Clarity of design and perfect significance both are first essentials of the spontaneously born simplicity of the lilies of the field who neither toil nor spin." *Frank Lloyd Wright Collected Writings,* 2:54.

33. See, for example, Wright, *Frank Lloyd Wright Collected Writings,* 2:68. See also Wright, *Frank Lloyd Wright Collected Writings,* 2:65.*

34. Wright, *When Democracy Builds,* 52.

35. Ibid., 62.

36. Wright, like Whitman, might have been influenced by the German Romantic philosophers. See Robert Fishman, *Urban Utopias in the Twentieth Century: Ebenezer Howard, Frank Lloyd Wright, Le Corbusier* (New York: Basic Books, 1977), 128.*

37. Wright, *When Democracy Builds,* 64.

38. Wright, *The Living City,* 149.

39. Wright, *An Autobiography* (1943; repr., Petaluma, CA: Pomegranate, 1977), 326 (italics in original). See also Wright, *Frank Lloyd Wright Collected Writings,* 2:74.*

40. Wright, *Frank Lloyd Wright Collected Writings,* 2:45. For additional references to the instinct to shelter, see Wright, *An American Architecture,* ed. E. Kaufmann (New York: Horizon Press, 1955), 61; and Wright, *Frank Lloyd Wright Collected Writings,* 5:220.

41. Wright, *Frank Lloyd Wright Collected Writings,* 5:125.

42. Wright, *Frank Lloyd Wright Collected Writings*, 5:125, 239.

43. Wright, *Modern Architecture: Being the Kahn Lectures for 1930* (Princeton NJ: Princeton University Press, 2008), 111.

44. Baker Brownell and Frank Lloyd Wright, *Architecture and Modern Life* (New York: Harper, 1938), 122.

45. Ibid., 304–305. See also Wright, *Frank Lloyd Wright Collected Writings*, 2:77.*

46. Wright, *Frank Lloyd Wright Collected Writings*, 2:76, 348.

47. Wright, *The Living City*, 152.

48. Robert C. Twombly, "Undoing the City: Frank Lloyd Wright's Planned Communities," *American Quarterly* 24, no. 4 (1972): 546–547.*

49. See Frank Lloyd Wright, Terence Riley, Peter Reed, and Anthony Alofsin, *Frank Lloyd Wright, Architect* (New York: Museum of Modern Art, 1994), 77. See also William R. Drennan, *Death in a Prairie House: Frank Lloyd Wright and the Taliesin Murders* (Madison, WI: Terrance Books, 2007), 156.

50. Corcoran, "Utopian Masterminds," 459. See also Donald Leslie Johnson, "Frank Lloyd Wright in Moscow," *Journal of the Society of Architectural Historians* 46, no. 1 (1987): 65–79.*

51. Twombly, *Frank Lloyd Wright, His Life and Architecture*, 412–413. See also Sergeant, *Frank Lloyd Wright's Usonian Houses*, 127.

52. Brownell, *Architecture and Modern Life*, 87.

53. Ibid., 242–243.

54. Ibid., 87. See also Donald Leslie Johnson, "Frank Lloyd Wright in Moscow: June 1937," *Journal of the Society of Architectural Historians*, 46, no. 1 (1987): 65–79.

55. Wright, *Frank Lloyd Wright Collected Writings*, 2:77.

56. Twombly, *Frank Lloyd Wright*, 412–413.

57. Wright, *Frank Lloyd Wright Collected Writings*, 2:13–14 (italics in original).

58. Patrick Meehan, ed., *The Master Architect: Conversations with Frank Lloyd Wright* (New York: Wiley, 1958), 122.

59. "ART 1938: Usonian Architect: Frank Lloyd Wright's Taliesin," *Time*, October 5, 1983, 23.*

60. Historians and art critics have remarked on the consistency of Wright's key ideas represented by Broadacre City. See Wright, *Frank Lloyd Wright Collected Writings*, 4:45.

61. Wright, *The Living City*, 219.

62. Ibid., 116.

63. The first part of the quote, ending with "Real Leisure," is from "The Future of the City," *Saturday Review*, May 14, 1955, quoted in Wright, *Frank Lloyd Wright Collected Writings*, 5:135. The final quote is from Wright, *The Living City*, 221, see also 328.

64. J. L. Hemingway, "Emancipating Leisure: The Recovery of Freedom in Leisure," *Journal of Leisure Research* 28, no. 1 (1996): 30; see also Michael Martin, *Verstehen: The Uses of Understanding in Social Science* (New Brunswick, NJ: Transaction, 2000), 221; and Habermas, *The Theory of Communicative Action*, 120.*

65. Percy MacKaye, *The Civic Theatre in Relation to the Redemption of Leisure* (New York: Mitchell, Kennerley, 1912).

66. Percy MacKaye, *Epoch: The Life of Steele MacKaye, Genius of the Theater, in Relation to His Times and Contemporaries* (New York: Boni and Liveright, 1927), xvi; Percival Chubb, *Festivals and Plays in Schools and Elsewhere* (New York: Harper and Brothers, 1912), introduction and 5, 15–16, 122–124. See also Thomas Dickinson, *The Case of American Drama* (Boston: Houghton Mifflin, 1915), 193.*

67. MacKaye, *The Civic Theatre*, 18.

68. Ibid., 19.*

69. MacKaye, *The Civic Theatre*, 18, 20.

70. MacKaye was careful to distinguish his ideas about leisure from Torstein Veblen's. Veblen, *The Theory of the Leisure Class* (New York: Macmillan, 1912). He explained, "[By] 'popular leisure' I mean the leisure of workers, not the leisure of the leisure class." MacKaye, *The Civic Theatre*, 24.

71. MacKaye, *The Civic Theatre*, 15, 97.

72. Letter from MacKaye to Carl Glick, September 4, 1938, Carl Glick Papers, Box 1, MacKaye folder, University of Iowa Library, special collections; letter from Glick to MacKaye, January 23, 1938, Carl Glick Papers, Box 1, MacKaye folder, University of Iowa Library, special collections.*

73. MacKaye, *The Civic Theatre*, 17. For MacKaye's interest in Central Park, see MacKaye, *Caliban by the Yellow Sands* (New York: Doubleday, Page, 1916), xx.

74. MacKaye, *The Civic Theatre*, 30.

75. Ibid., 69.

76. Ibid., 157.

77. Ibid.

78. Ibid., 186.

79. Ibid., 187, 197.

80. Ibid., 188, 65. See also Michael Peter Mehler, "Percy MacKaye: Spatial Formations of a National Character" (Ph.D. diss., University of Pittsburgh, 2010), 19, 39, 41, 51, 190.

81. Walter Lippmann, review of *The Civic Theatre*, by Percy MacKaye, *New York Times*, January 12, 1912. See also W. Lippmann, "Free Time and Extra Money," *Woman's Home Companion* 57 (April 1930): 31; and Benjamin Kline Hunnicutt, *Work without End: Abandoning Shorter Hours for the Right to Work* (Philadelphia: Temple University Press, 1988), 260–265.*

82. Carl Glick and A. McCleery, *Curtains Going Up* (New York: Pitman, 1939), iii.

83. A more complete account of the parks and recreation movement's response to the prospect of an age of leisure may be found in Hunnicutt, *Work without End*, chap. 4.

84. See Kenneth Macgowan, *Footlights across America* (New York: Harcourt, Brace, 1929).

85. Of special interest are Mabie's and Glick's papers, held by the University of Iowa Library, special collections.*

86. His daughter Maryo Gard Ewell's introduction to his *Grassroots Theatre: A Search for Regional Arts in America* (Madison: University of Wisconsin Press, 1999) is indispensable. See also Robert Edward Gard Papers, 1910–1980, Steenbock Library, University of Wisconsin, Madison.

87. Paul Green, *Dramatic Heritage* (New York: S. French, 1953), 4.

88. "Kahn Sees Suburbs Best Art Centers," *New York Times*, July 6, 1930.*

CHAPTER 6

1. *Monthly Labor Review* 23 (December 1926): 1167; Hannah Arendt, *The Human Condition* (Chicago: University of Chicago Press, 1958), 85.

2. Jay Sorenson, *The Life and Death of Trade Unionism in the USSR, 1917–1928* (New Brunswick, NJ: Aldine Transaction, 2010), 138. Neither Karl Marx nor Engels believed work could ever become play-like and intrinsically rewarding.

3. William Green, "Leisure for Labor: A New Force Alters Our Social Structure," *Magazine of Business* 56 (August 1929): 136–137.

4. Ibid.*

5. *Monthly Labor Review* 23 (December 1926): 1167. See also C. M. Wright, "Epoch-Making Decisions in the Great American Federation Labor Convention at Detroit," *American Labor World*, 1926, 22–24; and U.S. Department of Labor, Bureau of Labor

Statistics, *Handbook of Labor Statistics 1924–1926* (Washington, DC: U.S. Government Printing Office, 1927), 818.

6. William Green, "The Five-Day Week," *American Federationist* 33 (October 1926): 567–574.*

7. Jean Trepp McKelvey, *AFL Attitudes toward Production, 1900–1932* (Westport, CN: Greenwood Press, 1974), 5. See also C. Gordon, *New Deals: Business, Labor, and Politics in America, 1920–1935* (Cambridge: Cambridge University Press, 1994), 90.

8. J. C. Lane, "The Five-Day Week Is Now a Vivid Industrial Issue," *New York Times*, October 17, 1926, section 9, p. 6.

9. Ibid.; Harry A. Millis, "The Union in Industry: Some Observations on the Theory of Collective Bargaining," *American Economic Review* 25, no. 1 (1935), 1–13.

10. Millis, "The Union in Industry," 1–13.

11. Paul H. Douglas, *The Theory of Wages* (New York: Macmillan, 1934), 310–314.

12. *Hours of Work: Hearings before the Select Subcommittee on Labor of the Committee on Education and Labor, House of Representatives, Eighty-eighth Congress, First Session, on H.R. 355, H.R. 3102, and H.R. 3320, Bills to Reduce the Maximum Workweek under the Fair Labor Standards Act of 1938, as Amended, and to Increase the Overtime Penalty Rate*, part 2 (1964), pp. 221, 290.

13. Ibid., 290. Eli Ginzberg, an economist at Columbia, agreed with Douglas. Ibid., 230.

14. AFL-CIO, *The Shorter Work Week: Papers Delivered at the Conference on Shorter Hours of Work* (Washington, DC: Public Affairs Press, 1956), 45–46.

15. Ira Steward, *The Eight Hour Movement: A Reduction of Hours Is an Increase of Wages* (Boston: Boston Labor Reform Association, 1865), 4.

16. George Gunton, *Wealth and Progress: A Critical Examination of the Wages Question and Its Economic Relation to Social Reform* (New York: D. Appleton, 1890), 197.

17. *Recent Economic Changes in the United States: Report of the Committee on Recent Economic Changes, of the President's Conference on Unemployment, Herbert Hoover, Chairman, Including the Reports of a Special Staff of the National Bureau of Economic Research* (New York: McGraw-Hill, 1929), xvi.

18. Ibid., xv.

19. Ibid., xvii.

20. Benjamin Kline Hunnicutt, *Work without End: Abandoning Shorter Hours for the Right to Work* (Philadelphia: Temple University Press, 1988), chap. 5.

21. H. Ford and S. Crowther, "The Fear of Overproduction," *Saturday Evening Post* 203 (July 12, 1930): 3.

22. Hunnicutt, *Work without End*, 47.

23. H. Ford, "Why I Favor Five-Days' Work with Six-Days' Pay," interview, *World's Work* 52 (October 1926): 613. See also H. Ford, *My Philosophy of Industry and Moving Forward* (New York: Coward-McCann, 1929), 88.

24. T. N. Carver, "Shorter Working Time and Unemployment," *American Economic Review* 20 (March 1932): 8; see also T. N. Carver, *The Economic Revolution in the United States* (Boston: Allen, 1925), 59–65, 162.

25. Hunnicutt, *Work without End*, 83.

26. Constance Southworth, "Can There Be General Overproduction? No!" *Journal of Political Economy* 32 (December 1924): 722–723.

27. Henry Dennison, "Would the Five-Day Week Decrease Unemployment?" *Magazine of Business* 54 (November 1928): 50.

28. Henry Ford and S. Crowther, "Unemployment or Leisure," *Saturday Evening Post* 203 (August 1930): 19; H. L. Slobodin, "Unemployment or Leisure—Which?" *American Federationist* 37 (October 1930): 1205–1208; Green, "Leisure for Labor," 136–137; W. Green, "Shorter Hours," *American Federationist* 38 (January 1931): 22.

29. Stuart Chase, *The Economy of Abundance* (New York: Macmillan, 1934), 16–22; Arthur Pound, "Out of Unemployment into Leisure" *Atlantic Review* 146 (December 1930): 784–792; William Green, "Thirty Hour Week," *American Federationist* 40 (November 1933): 1174.*

30. Hunnicutt, *Work without End*, chap. 5.

31. Benjamin Hunnicutt, *Kellogg's Six-Hour Day* (Philadelphia: Temple University Press, 1996), chap. 1; see also Harvey Swados, "Less Work—Less Leisure," *Nation* 186 (February 2, 1958): 153–158.

32. "Big Gain in Work-Sharing," *New York Times*, January 15, 1933, N2.

33. "Job Sharing: Five Million Helped by Work-Spreading, Teagle Committee Estimates," *Business Week* 14 (February 1, 1933): 1–2.

34. Hunnicutt, *Work without End*, 114, 231–232.

35. *New York Times*, May 16, 1932; May 21, 1932; May 26, 1932; June 30, 1932; July 30, 1932; September 22, 1932; October 5, 1932.*

36. "Labor's Ultimatum to Industry: Thirty-Hour Week," *Literary Digest* 114 (December 10, 1932): 3–4; "Labor Will Fight," *Business Week* 14–15 (December 14, 1932): 32; "The Labor Army Takes the Field: A Shorter Work Week to Make Jobs," *Literary Digest* 115 (April 15, 1933): 6.

37. Ellis Hawley, ed., *Herbert Hoover as Secretary of Commerce: Studies in New Era Thought and Practice* (Iowa City: University of Iowa Press, 1981), 44, 111.

38. *Business Week*, February 15, 1933, 3.

39. See Ellis Hawley, *Herbert Hoover and the Crisis of American Capitalism* (Cambridge, MA: Schenkman, 1973), 13, 28, 117.*

40. Hunnicutt, *Work without End*, 151–153.

41. Ibid.

42. Hugh Johnson, *The Blue Eagle from Earth to Egg* (Garden City, NY: Doubleday, 1935), 205.

43. The Wagner bill proved to be the single most important labor legislation ever enacted in the United States, granting labor the basic rights to recruit and organize.

44. Hunnicutt, *Work without End*, 220–224.

45. Just as I use "Higher Progress," capitalized, to represent the first, forgotten American dream, I use "Full-Time, Full Employment," capitalized, to represent the new dream of eternal economic growth and work without end that has eclipsed the first.

46. Ibid., 159.

47. Ibid., 191.

48. Arthur M. Schlesinger Jr., *The Age of Roosevelt*, vol. 3, *The Politics of Upheaval* (Boston: Houghton Mifflin, 1960), 690–692.

49. Rexford Tugwell, *Roosevelt's Revolution* (New York: Macmillan, 1977), 239.

50. Robert M. Hutchins, *The University of Utopia* (Chicago: University of Chicago Press, 1965), ix.

51. Ibid.

52. Hunnicutt, *Work without End*, 180.

53. David Roediger and Philip Foner, *Our Own Time: A History of American Labor and the Working Day* (New York: Verso, 1989), 258.

54. Milo Keynes, *Essays on John Maynard Keynes* (Cambridge: Cambridge University Press, 1980), 135–140; see also W. Nordhaus and J. Tobin, "Is Growth Obsolete?" in *The Measurement of Economic and Social Performance*, ed. M. Moss (New York: Columbia University Press, 1975). Nordhaus and Tobin developed a new "measure of economic welfare" by adding the value of leisure to the traditional GNP measurements, concluding that leisure represents over half of total consumer income.

55. Hunnicutt, *Work without End*, 207.

56. Ibid., chap. 8.

CHAPTER 7

1. For Wright's continuing interest in increased leisure, see Wright, *When Democracy Builds* (Chicago: University of Chicago Press, 1945), 44.*

2. Ibid., 56.

3. Ibid., 46.

4. Ibid., 88.

5. See, for example, Peter Blake, *Frank Lloyd Wright, Architecture and Space* (New York: Penguin, 1964), 338. See also Brendan Gill, *Many Masks: A Life of Frank Lloyd Wright* (New York: Putnam, 1987), 415.*

6. Wright, *When Democracy Builds*, 56.

7. Wright, *The Living City*, 73. The coming of the new ideology of Full-Time, Full Employment is described in Chapter 6.

8. Wright, *The Living City*, 75, see also 73, 94, 135, 164.

9. Ibid., 41. See also Wright, *When Democracy Builds*, 48.

10. Wright, *The Living City*, 34.

11. Ibid., 78, 158.

12. Ibid., 128.

13. Ibid., 217.*

14. For Hutchins's use of the term "American dream," see John Oakes, "A Nonconformist Conscience," *New York Times*, October 14, 1956, BR17. See also Robert Hutchins, "A Letter to the Reader," in *Gateway to the Great Books*, vol. 1, *Introduction, Synoptical Guide*, ed. Robert M. Hutchins and Mortimer Adler (Chicago: Encyclopedia Britannica, 1963), 12. *Time* quoted Hutchins as saying, "The essence of the American dream is and always has been freedom." See "Liberties Termed Anti-Red Weapon," *Time*, November 1, 1956, 9.

15. Robert M. Hutchins, "Introduction to the Second Edition," in *The University of Utopia* (Chicago: University of Chicago Press, 1965), vii.

16. Hutchins, *The University of Utopia*, vii.

17. Ibid., viii.

18. Ibid., vii.*

19. Ibid., viii.

20. Ibid., ix.

21. Ibid.

22. Ibid.

23. Robert Hutchins, *The Great Conversation: The Substance of a Liberal Education*, in *Great Books of the Western World*, ed. Robert M. Hutchins and Mortimer Adler, 54 vols. (Chicago: Encyclopedia Britannica, 1952), 1:7.

24. Hutchins, *The Great Conversation*, 23.

25. Hutchins, *The University of Utopia*, 8.

26. Ibid.

27. Ibid., 68.*

28. Ibid., 51; Robert M. Hutchins, *Education for Freedom* (Baton Rouge: Louisiana State University, 1943), 39.

29. Hutchins, *The Great Conversation*, 3.

30. Ibid., 14.

31. Hutchins, *The University of Utopia*, 14.

32. Robert M. Hutchins, "The University and Character," *The Commonweal*, April 22, 1938, 710–711.*

33. Hutchins, *The University of Utopia*, 68. Hutchins highlighted such virtues by describing their opposites: the lack of openness in "the man who believes he knows everything" and the lack of attentiveness, responsibility, and mutuality in the "man who does not want to talk to anybody" (68).

34. Tyrants and priests could force or fool people to accept this or that value or belief for a time. But democracies and free people depend on persuasion rather than force, conscious agreement rather than coercion or subterfuge. Hutchins, *The University of Utopia*, 71–72.

35. Hutchins, "The University and Character," 710.

36. Hutchins, *The University of Utopia*, 56–62.

37. James Richard Connor, "The Social and Educational Philosophy of Robert Maynard Hutchins" (master's thesis, University of Wisconsin, Madison, 1954), 26. See also Frank K. Kelly, *Court of Reason: Robert Hutchins and the Fund for the Republic* (New York: Free Press, 1981), 38.

38. Robert M. Hutchins, "Something New in Education," *Rotarian*, February 1933, 7, 8.

39. Benjamin Hunnicutt, *Work without End: Abandoning Shorter Hours for the Right to Work* (Philadelphia: Temple University Press, 1988), 118.*

40. Committee on Economic Security, "Report to the President" (Washington, DC: Government Printing Office, 1935), 47, 48.*

41. Tugwell is widely recognized as one of the leading theorists responsible for the construction of a "socially managed economy." See *American Studies* 25 (January 1, 1984): 96. See also Clyde Weaver, "Review: Tugwell on Morningside Heights," *Town Planning Review* 55, no. 2 (1984): 228–236.

42. Hunnicutt, *Work without End*, 258.

43. Ibid., 254.

44. Rexford Tugwell, "The Theory of Occupational Obsolescence," *Political Science Quarterly* 46 (1931): 194.

45. Rexford Tugwell, "The Third Economy," *Vital Speeches* 1 (April 22, 1935): 451.

46. Rexford G. Tugwell and L. H. Keyserling, eds., *Redirecting Education*, 2 vols. (New York: Columbia University Press, 1934), 1:93.

47. Ibid., 1:193.

48. Ibid., 1:109.

49. Ibid. See also Rexford Tugwell, "Government in a Changing World," *Review of Reviews* 88 (August 1933): 33–34.*

50. Lawrence Cremin, *American Education: the Metropolitan Experience, 1876–1980* (New York: Harper and Row, 1988).

51. Marvin Lazerson, "Lawrence Cremin and the American Dilemma," review of *American Education: The Metropolitan Experience, 1876–1980*, by Lawrence Cremin, *American Journal of Education* 99 (November 1990): 95–104.

52. Cremin, *American Education*.

53. Hutchins, *Education for Freedom*, 34, 79.

54. Ibid., 17.

55. Hutchins, *Education for Freedom*, 89.

56. See, for example, Philip Kinsley, "Hutchins Views Education as a Pathway to Life," *Chicago Tribune*, October 1, 1939, 23.

57. Hutchins, *The University of Utopia*, 8.

58. Hutchins, *Education for Freedom*, 25.

59. Hutchins, *The Great Conversation*, 29.*

60. Ibid., 8.

61. Robert M. Hutchins, "Education for Freedom," *Harpers' Magazine* 183 (October 1941): 513.

62. Hutchins, *Education for Freedom*, 35.

63. Hutchins, *University of Utopia*, ix.

64. Ibid., ix.

65. Ibid., 26.

66. Hutchins, *Education for Freedom*, 46–47.

67. Ibid., 45, 83. See also Hutchins, *The Great Conversation*, 19.

68. Hutchins, *Education for Freedom*, 44–45.

69. Ibid.

70. Robert M. Hutchins, "The Next Fifty Years," *Science*, n.s., 94 (October 10, 1944): 333–335.

71. Ibid.

72. Robert M. Hutchins, "The Public Library: Its Place in Education," *Library Quarterly* 20, no. 3 (1950): 186.

73. Ibid., 181.

74. Ibid., 182.

75. Ibid.

76. Mortimer Adler, *Great Ideas: A Synopticon of the Great Books of the Western World*, in *Great Books of the Western World*, ed. Robert M. Hutchins and Mortimer Adler, 54 vols. (Chicago: Encyclopedia Britannica, 1952).

77. Hutchins, "The Public Library," 182.

78. Ibid., 183

79. Ibid., 180.

80. Ibid., 180.*

81. Hutchins, *Education for Freedom*, 17.

82. "Education: Chicago's Adjustment," *Time*, January 4, 1932; "Education: Report Card," *Time*, December 29, 1952.

83. "Education: Worst Kind of Troublemaker," *Time*, November 21, 1949.

84. Robert M. Hutchins, *The Higher Learning in America* (New Haven, CT: Yale University Press, 1936), 5.*

85. Hutchins, *The University of Utopia*, 5–6.

86. Ibid., 6.

87. Hutchins, *Education for Freedom*, 46–47.

88. Hutchins, *The Great Conversation*, 1.*

89. Mary Ann Dzuback, *Robert M. Hutchins: Portrait of an Educator* (Chicago: University of Chicago Press, 1991), 234–235; Milton Mayer, *Robert Maynard Hutchins: A Memoir* (Berkeley: University of California Press, 1993), 295, 408.

90. "Radio: Viewers," *Time*, February 19, 1951; for "wisecracks," see "Education: "Worst Kind of Troublemaker"; for "Hutchinsisms," see "Education: Bigger—but Better," *Time*, July 26, 1948.

91. Robert Hutchins, "A Letter to the Reader," 12 (italics in original).

92. Dzuback, *Robert M. Hutchins*, 234, 274.

93. Hutchins, "The Public Library," 183.

94. Ibid.*

95. Ibid., 184.

96. "Education: Trouble in Chicago," *Time*, May 1, 1944. See also Mayer, *Robert Maynard Hutchins*, 340.*

97. "Education: Culture C.O.D.," *Time*, June 16, 1947.

98. "Books: Latter Day Beard," *Time*, October 18, 1943.*

99. "Education: No Time for Infants," *Time*, September 30, 1946.

100. "Education: Culture C.O.D."

101. "Services: Cashing In on Culture," *Time*, April 20, 1962.

102. J. Donald Adams, "Speaking of Books," *New York Times*, September 6, 1959.

103. Alex Beam, *A Great Idea at the Time: The Rise, Fall, and Curious Afterlife of the Great Books* (New York: Public Affairs Books, 2008), 4.*

104. "Services: Cashing In on Culture."

105. Ibid.

106. "Education: Culture C.O.D."*

107. "Services: Cashing In on Culture."

108. "Education: New Job for a Salesman," *Time*, January 1, 1951.

109. Robert M. Hutchins and Mortimer Adler, eds., *The Great Ideas Today: Work, Wealth, and Leisure* (Chicago: Encyclopedia Britannica, 1965), 2, 3.

110. Yale Brozen, "Automation and Jobs," in *The Great Ideas Today: Work, Wealth, and Leisure*, 25.

111. Ibid., 26.

112. Theobald was a well-known economist and futurist during the 1950s–1980s.

113. Adolf A. Berle, "Jobs for the Displaced: A Public Responsibility," in *The Great Ideas Today: Work, Wealth, and Leisure*, 29.

114. J. M. Keynes, *General Theory of Employment* (New York: Harcourt, Brace, 1936). That the economy could stabilize at any level of unemployment was one of the influential claims Keynes made in this, perhaps his most influential, book.

115. Berle, "Jobs for the Displaced," 29, 38.*

116. Ibid., 38.

117. Ibid., 33 (italics added).

118. Ibid., 34.

119. Ibid., 34–38.

120. Robert Hutchins and Mortimer Adler, "Wealth and Happiness," in *The Great Ideas Today: Work, Wealth, and Leisure*, 90.*

121. Ibid.

122. Ibid., 92.

123. Ibid., 103.

124. Louis O. Kelso and Mortimer Adler, *The New Capitalists* (New York: Random House, 1961), 87–88.

125. Ibid., 88 (italics in original).

126. Hutchins and Adler, *The Great Ideas Today*, 441.*

CHAPTER 8

1. A. H. Raskin, "AFL Reaffirms 30-Hour Week Plan," *New York Times*, November 30, 1940, 1.

2. David R. Roediger and Philip Sheldon Foner, *Our Own Time: A History of American Labor and the Working Day* (New York: Greenwood Press, 1989), 261–262.

3. "Green Says 30-Hour Week Must Come as 'Only Practical Way' to Spread Work," *New York Times*, October 26, 1944, 10.

4. William A. McGaughey, *A Shorter Workweek in the 1980s* (Minneapolis, MN: Thistlerose, 1981), 44.

5. See G. J. Santoni, "The Employment Act of 1946: Some History Notes," *Federal Reserve Bank of St. Louis Review*, November 1986.*

6. Dwight Eisenhower, *Crusade in Europe* (Baltimore: Johns Hopkins University Press, 1997), 319.*

7. Santoni, "The Employment Act of 1946."

8. Samuel Gompers, "Testimony before the Committee on Labor of the U.S. House of Representatives," in *The Samuel Gompers Papers*, vol. 5, *An Expanding Movement at the Turn of the Century: 1898–1902*, ed. Stuart Bruce Kaufman and Peter J. Albert (Urbana: University of Illinois Press, 1986), 482.

9. American Federation of Labor and Congress of Industrial Organizations, *Proceedings of the Third Constitutional Convention of the AFL-CIO*, vol. 1 (San Francisco: AFL-CIO, 1959), 638. See also *American Federationist* 68, no. 7 (1961): 6.

10. George Shultz and John Coleman, *Labor Problems: Cases and Readings*, 2nd ed. (New York: McGraw-Hill, 1959), 67.

11. For a fuller description of the study, see this book's website (http://ir.uiowa.edu/leisure_pubs/1) and Benjamin Hunnicutt, *Kellogg's Six-Hour Day* (Philadelphia: Temple University Press, 1996), 76.

12. Letter of "mill girl," *Voice of Industry*, April 23, 1847.

13. David Dubinsky, "Union Education for Leisure," *Education* 71 (October 1950): 114.

14. Ibid.

15. Ibid., 115.

16. Ibid., 117.

17. David Dubinsky, "Union Education for Leisure," 113–117.*

18. David M. Lewis-Colman, *Race against Liberalism: Black Workers and the UAW in Detroit* (Champaign: University of Illinois Press, 2008), 19.

19. "Father of the Twenty-Five-Hour Week," *Fortune* 65 (March 1962): 189–190.*

20. Edward Cohen-Rosenthal, "Enriching Workers' Lives," *Change* 2, no. 5 (1979): 64–66.

21. Roediger and Foner, *Our Own Time*, 257.

22. Ibid. See also J. D. Owen, "Workweeks and Leisure: An Analysis of Trends, 1948–75," *Monthly Labor Review* 99, no. 8 (1976): 3–8.

23. Roediger and Foner, *Our Own Time*, 266.

24. Ronald Edsforth, "Why Automation Didn't Shorten the Work Week: The Politics of Work Time in the Automobile Industry," in *Autowork*, ed. Robert Asher, Ronald Edsforth, and Stephen Merlino (Albany: State University of New York Press, 1995), 160.

25. A. H. Raskin, "If We Had a Twenty-Hour Week," *New York Times*, February 4, 1962, 191.

26. Roediger and Foner, *Our Own Time*, 262.

27. Edsforth, "Why Automation Didn't Shorten the Work Week," 170.

28. "Profits Face New Labor Attack," *Nation's Business*, February 1958, 70.

29. *IUD Bulletin*, September 1956, 1.

30. Roediger and Foner, *Our Own Time*, 266.

31. Edsforth, "Why Automation Didn't Shorten the Work Week," 168.

32. Roediger and Foner, *Our Own Time*, 262.

33. Ibid., 267. Even after the tide had turned in 1963, nearly half of AFL-CIO union members continued to support a thirty-five-hour week.

34. Raskin, "If We Had a Twenty-Hour Week," 191.

35. Ibid. See also "How Long a Week?" *New York Times*, March 4, 1963, 14.

36. Felix Belair, "Economist Warns On Shorter Week," *New York Times*, March 21, 1961, 16.

37. Richard E. Mooney, "Heller Opposes a Work-Week Cut," *New York Times*, May 27, 1962, 54.

38. Tom Wicker, "Kennedy Predicts Cut in Work Week," *New York Times*, September 29, 1963, 1.

39. "Meany Presses Support for Shorter Work Week," *New York Times*, October 21, 1963, 6.

40. Wicker, "Kennedy Predicts Cut in Work Week," 1.

41. John F. Kennedy, News Conference 62, October 9, 1963, available at http://www.jfklibrary.org/Research/Ready-Reference/Press-Conferences/News-Conference-62.aspx.

42. Nelson Lichtenstein, *The Most Dangerous Man in Detroit: Walter Reuther and the Fate of American Labor* (New York: Basic Books, 1995), 365.

43. "Text of President Kennedy's Message to Congress on Tax Reduction and Revisions," *New York Times*, January 25, 1963, 6.

44. AFL-CIO, *The Shorter Work Week: Papers Delivered at the Conference on Shorter Hours of Work* (Washington, DC: Public Affairs Press, 1956), 3.

45. Ibid., 5–6.

46. Ibid., 16.

47. Ibid., 32.

48. Ibid. The quotations are Frank Honigsbaum's, director of research, International Brotherhood of Paper Makers, who paraphrased Brooks's extemporaneous remarks.

49. Albert Epstein, economist for the International Association of Machinists, made similar remarks. AFL-CIO, *The Shorter Work Week*, 24.

50. Ibid., 60.*

51. Ibid., 20.

52. Ibid., 34.

53. Ibid., 28.

54. Ibid., 29.

55. Ibid., 35.

56. *Hours of Work: Hearings before the Select Subcommittee on Labor of the Committee on Education and Labor, House of Representatives, Eighty-eighth Congress, First Session, on H.R. 355, H.R. 3102, and H.R. 3320, Bills to Reduce the Maximum Workweek under the Fair Labor Standards Act of 1938, as Amended, and to Increase the Overtime Penalty Rate*, parts 1 and 2 (1963–1964).

57. Ibid., part 1, p. 1.

58. Ibid., part 1, p. 122.

59. Ibid., part 2, pp. 445, 457.

60. Ibid., part 2, p. 477.

61. Ibid., part 1, p. 221.

62. Ibid., part 1, p. 224.

63. Ibid., part 1, p. 105.

64. Ibid., part 2, p. 683.

65. Ibid., part 2, p. 476.

66. Ibid., part 1, pp. 221–222.

67. Ibid., part 2, p. 424.

68. Ibid., part 2, p. 445.

69. Ibid.

70. Ibid., part 2, p. 446.

71. Ibid., part 2, p. 489.

72. Ibid.

73. Ibid., part 2, p. 496.

74. Ibid., part 2, p. 512.

75. Ibid., part 2, p. 651.

76. *To Revise the Overtime Compensation Requirements of the Fair Labor Standards Act of 1938: Hearings before the Subcommittee on Labor of the Committee on Education and Labor, House of Representatives, Ninety-sixth Congress, First Session, on H.R. 1784* (1979).

77. Ibid., 268.

78. "Union Labor: Less Militant, More Affluent," *Time*, September 17, 1965.

79. Steve Fraser, "The 'Labor Question,'" in *The Rise and Fall of the New Deal Order, 1930–1980*, ed. Steve Fraser and Gary Gerstle (Princeton, NJ: Princeton University Press, 1989), 55–58; Richard Butsch, *For Fun and Profit: The Transformation of Leisure into Consumption* (Philadelphia: Temple University Press, 1990), 3–17; Nelson Lichtenstein, "The View from Jackson Place," *Labor History* 37 (Spring 1996): 167–168. See also Lichtenstein, *The Most Dangerous Man in Detroit*; for an analysis and critique of "goulash capitalism," see Michael

Rogin, "How the Working Class Saved Capitalism: The New Labor History and *The Devil and Miss Jones*," *Journal of American History* 89, no. 1 (2002): 87–114.

80. Hannah Arendt, *The Human Condition* (Chicago: University of Chicago Press, 1958), 85, see also 4.*

81. David Riesman, with Nathan Glazer and Reuel Denney, *The Lonely Crowd: A Study of the Changing American Character* (New Haven, CT: Yale University Press, 1950). See also Robert Hutchins, *The University of Utopia*, 2nd ed. (1952; repr., Chicago: University of Chicago Press, 1965), 8. Hutchins considered support of shorter hours part of the essence of America's "liberal tradition." See Chapter 7.

82. "Memorial Minute: David Riesman, Author of 'The Lonely Crowd,'" *Harvard University Gazette*, November 13, 2003.*

83. Riesman, *The Lonely Crowd*, 326.

84. Ibid., 343.

85. Ibid., 373.

86. David Riesman, "Some Observations on Changes in Leisure Attitudes," *Antioch Review* 12, no. 4 (1952): 417–436.

87. David Riesman, "Preface to the 1961 Edition," in Riesman, *The Lonely Crowd* (1961; repr., New Haven, CT: Yale University Press, 2001), lxvii.

88. David Riesman, "The Dream of Abundance Reconsidered," *Public Opinion Quarterly* 45, no. 3 (1981): 300.

89. William Heighton, "An Address to the Members of Trade Societies and to the Working Classes Generally," reprinted in Philip Foner, *William Heighton: Pioneer Labor Leader of Jacksonian Philadelphia* (New York: International, 1991), 69.*

90. Hannah Arendt, *The Portable Hannah Arendt*, ed. Peter Baehr (New York: Penguin, 2003), 169.*

91. R. Lee, "Leisure—Blessing or Bane?" *Presbyterian Life* 15 (August 1, 1962): 5–6.

92. Quoted in Robert Kubey and Mihaly Csikszentmihalyi, *Television and the Quality of Life: How Viewing Shapes Everyday Experience* (Hillsdale, NJ: Lawrence Erlbaum Associates, 1990): 20–21.

93. B. F. Skinner, *Walden Two* (1948; repr., New York: Hackett, 2005), 76.

94. B. F. Skinner, *Beyond Freedom and Dignity* (1971; repr., New York: Hackett, 2002), 178.

95. The invisible hand of the market has, of course, replaced God as the source of direction and authority.

96. Deirdre N. McCloskey, *The Bourgeois Virtues: Ethics for an Age of Commerce* (Chicago: University of Chicago Press, 2006).*

97. See, for example, *Donald Trump's Golf War*, a British documentary directed by Scott Brown and produced by Patricia Macleod, originally aired in the United Kingdom on BBC Two on March 1, 2011.

CHAPTER 9

1. AFL-CIO, *The Shorter Work Week: Papers Delivered at the Conference on Shorter Hours of Work* (Washington, DC: Public Affairs Press, 1956), 37.*

2. Benjamin Hunnicutt, *Kellogg's Six-Hour Day* (Philadelphia: Temple University Press, 1996), 239. In a statement typical of the men's response to the prospect of leisure, one commented: "[Six hours was] too much wasted time, less money, not as productive."

3. David R. Roediger and Philip Sheldon Foner, *Our Own Time: A History of American Labor and the Working Day* (New York: Greenwood Press, 1989), 276.

4. Hunnicutt, *Kellogg's Six-Hour Day*, 122–125.

5. Ibid., 170.

6. See, for example, "Essay: Union Labor: Less Militant, More Affluent," *Time*, September 17, 1967.*

7. James McQuiston, interview by author, August 11, 1989, Battle Creek, MI.

8. AFL-CIO, *The Shorter Work Week*, 39. See also Hunnicutt, *Kellogg's Six-Hour Day*, 12, 145.

9. See Hunnicutt, *Kellogg's Six-Hour Day*, 83.

10. *To Revise the Overtime Compensation Requirements of the Fair Labor Standards Act of 1938: Hearings before the Subcommittee on Labor of the Committee on Education and Labor, House of Representatives, Ninety-sixth Congress, First Session, on H.R. 1784* (1979), 268.

11. Margaret Mead, "The Pattern of Leisure in Contemporary American Culture," *Annals of the American Academy of Political and Social Science* 313 (September 1957): 14. Mead continued, "Hours of work which permit a man to spend more time at home, length of vacation, amount of strain and over-work, all are valued as to how they will affect family life. As once it was wrong to play so hard that it might affect one's work, now it is wrong to work so hard that it may affect family life" (15). The September 1957 issue of the *Annals of the American Academy of Political and Social Science* was devoted to "Recreation in the Age of Automation."

12. Ibid., 15.

13. Art and Donnelly White, retired Kellogg's workers, interview by author, August 12, 1989, Battle Creek, MI.

14. Joy Blanchard, interview by author, August 10, 1989, and July 24, 1993, Battle Creek, MI.

15. Susanne Gordon, *Prisoners of Men's Dreams: Striking Out for a New Feminine Future* (New York: Little, Brown, 1991), 5. See also Carol Wekesser, *Feminism: Opposing Viewpoints* (New York: Greenhaven Press, 1995), 206.

16. Gordon, *Prisoners of Men's Dreams*, 5.

17. Ibid., 6.

18. Ibid., 9.

19. Ibid., 12.

20. Ibid., introduction, 6, 12, 14.

21. Mildred Moore, "A History of the Women's Trade Union League of Chicago" (master's thesis, University of Chicago, 1915), 28–30.

22. Staffan Linder, *The Harried Leisure Class* (New York: Columbia University Press, 1970), 31.

23. David Dubinsky, "Union Education for Leisure," *Education* 71 (October 1950): 113–117.

24. Anonymous, retired female Kellogg's worker, interview by author, July 24, 1993, Battle Creek, MI; Cecelia Bissell, retired Kellogg's worker, interview by Rebecca Woodward, November 21, 1991, Battle Creek, MI.

25. See Eric Larrabee and Rolf Meyersohn, *Mass Leisure* (New York: Free Press, 1958).*

26. Lizabeth Cohen, *Making a New Deal: Industrial Workers in Chicago, 1919–1939* (New York: Cambridge University Press, 2008), xxvi.

27. Lizabeth Cohen, *A Consumers' Republic: The Politics of Mass Consumption in Postwar America* (New York: Knopf, 2003). See also Gary Cross, *An All-Consuming Century: Why Commercialism Won in Modern America* (New York: Columbia University Press, 2000); and David Steigerwald, "All Hail the Republic of Choice: Consumer History as Contemporary Thought," *Journal of American History* 93, no. 2 (2006): 385–403.

28. Richard Butsch, *For Fun and Profit: The Transformation of Leisure into Consumption* (Philadelphia: Temple University Press, 1990), 3–19.

29. Linder, *The Harried Leisure Class*, 95.

30. Ibid. See also Walter Kerr, *The Decline of Pleasure* (New York: Time, 1966).*

31. Cohen, *A Consumers' Republic*, 8–9, 295. Cohen writes, "In the postwar Consumers' Republic, a new ideal emerged—*the purchaser as citizen*. . . . Now the consumer satisfying personal material wants actually served the national interest, since economic recovery . . . depended on a dynamic mass consumption economy" (8–9; italics in original).

32. Robert Putnam, *Bowling Alone: The Collapse and Revival of American Community* (New York: Simon and Schuster, 2000).

33. Hannah Arendt, *The Human Condition* (Chicago: University of Chicago Press, 1958), 85.

34. Juliet Schor, *The Overspent American: Why We Want What We Don't Need* (New York: Harper Perennial, 1999).

35. Jacques Ellul, "L'idéologie du Travail," *Foi et Vie* 79, no. 4 (1980): 80.

36. J. L. Hemingway, "Emancipating Leisure: The Recovery of Freedom in Leisure," *Journal of Leisure Research* 28, no. 1 (1996): 27–43.

37. Cohen, *A Consumers' Republic*.

38. Andre Gorz, bidding farewell to the working classes, identified shorter hours as the lasting essence of working-class identity and a fundamental threat to capitalism. See Andre Gorz, *Critique of Economic Reason* (New York: Verso, 2011).

39. Nelson Lichtenstein, *The Most Dangerous Man in Detroit: Walter Reuther and the Fate of American Labor* (New York: Basic Books, 1995), 290.

40. David R. Roediger and Philip Sheldon Foner, *Our Own Time: A History of American Labor and the Working Day* (New York: Greenwood Press, 1989), 272.

41. Norman O. Brown, *Life against Death: The Psychoanalytical Meaning of History* (1959; repr., Middletown, CT: Wesleyan University Press, 1985), 36–37.

42. Brown, *Life against Death*, 36.

43. Ibid., 17.

44. "Rationality of domination" is Herbert Marcuse's term; see Marcuse, *Eros and Civilization* (1959; repr., New York: Routledge, 1987), 36.

45. Brown, *Life against Death*, 37.

46. Ibid., ix.

47. Marcuse, *Eros and Civilization* (1959; repr., New York: Routledge, 1987), 38.

48. Ibid., 129.*

49. Ibid., 140.

50. Brown, *Life against Death*, 19.

51. Marcuse, *Eros and Civilization* (1959; repr., New York: Routledge, 1987), 141.

52. Ibid., 142.

53. Robert M. Hutchins and Mortimer Adler, eds., *The Great Ideas Today: Work, Wealth, and Leisure* (Chicago: Encyclopedia Britannica, 1965), 103.*

54. Herbert Marcuse, *Eros and Civilization* (New York: Vintage Books, 1961), 156 (italics added).

55. William Heighton, "An Address to the Members of Trade Societies and to the Working Classes Generally," reprinted in Philip Foner, *William Heighton: Pioneer Labor Leader of Jacksonian Philadelphia* (New York: International, 1991), 69.

56. Marcuse, *Eros and Civilization* (New York: Vintage Books, 1961), 152–153.

57. Herbert Marcuse, *Eros and Civilization* (New York: Vintage Books, 1961), xii.

58. Juliet Schor, *Plenitude: The New Economics of True Wealth* (New York: Penguin Press, 2010); Martin Joseph Matuštík, *Specters of Liberation: Great Refusals in the New World Order* (Albany: State University of New York, 1998); Anders Hayden, *Sharing the Work, Sparing the Planet: Work Time, Consumption and Ecology* (London: Zed Books, 1999).

59. J. S. Mill, *Principles of Political Economy*, 7th ed. (1848; repr., London: Longmans Green, 1871), 454.

60. Cohen, *Making a New Deal*, xxvi.

61. Mill, *Principles of Political Economy*, 454–455 (italics added).

62. Robert D. Putnam, *Bowling Alone*.

63. Donella H. Meadows, Dennis H. Meadows, Jorgen Randers, and William W. Behrens III, *The Limits to Growth: A Report for the Club of Rome's Project on the Predicament of Mankind* (New York: Universe Books, 1972); Donella Meadows, Jorgen Randers, and Dennis Meadows, *The Limits to Growth: The 30-Year Update* (White River Junction, VT: Chelsea Green, 2004).

64. Meadows et al., *The Limits to Growth*, 175–176.

65. Matuštík, *Specters of Liberation*, 220.

66. Aldo Leopold, *A Sand County Almanac: With Essays on Conservation from Round River* (1949; repr., New York: Random House, 1990), viii.

67. For a detailed account of the parks and recreation movement's preparation for the coming age of leisure, see Benjamin Kline Hunnicutt, *Work without End: Abandoning Shorter Hours for the Right to Work* (Philadelphia: Temple University Press, 1988), 109–116.

68. Sean Duffy, "*Silent Spring* and *A Sand County Almanac*: The Two Most Significant Environmental Books of the 20th Century," *Nature Study* 44 (February 1991): 6–8.

69. Leopold, *A Sand County Almanac*, xvii, 163.

70. Aldo Leopold, *Round River* (New York: Oxford University Press, 1953), 159.

71. Ibid. Jürgen Habermas, Richard Rorty, and Leszek Kolakowski, *Debating the State of Philosophy*, ed. Józef Niznik and John T. Sanders (New York: Praeger, 1996), 46.

72. Leopold, *A Sand County Almanac*, 239.

73. Ibid., 117.

74. Ibid., 17.

75. Ibid., 261.

76. Ibid., 17. Laura Westra writes, "Aldo Leopold's influence on environmental ethics cannot be overstated." Laura Westra, "From Aldo Leopold to the Wildlands Project," *Environmental Ethics* 23 (Fall 2001): 261.

77. Aldo Leopold, "Wilderness as a Form of Land Use," *Journal of Land and Public Utility Economics* 1, no. 4 (1925): 398–404; Aldo Leopold, "Wildlife in American Culture," *Journal of Wildlife Management* 7, no. 1 (1943); Aldo Leopold, "A Man's Leisure Time," in *A Sand County Almanac*, 181; Aldo Leopold, "The Last Stand of the Wilderness," *American Forests and Forest Life*, October 1925; Aldo Leopold, Susan Flader, and J. Baird Callicott, *The River of the Mother of God and Other Essays* (Madison: University of Wisconsin Press, 1991), 141, 142, 196.*

78. Paul Sutter, quoted in Turner James Morton, "From Woodcraft to 'Leave No Trace': Wilderness, Consumerism, and Environmentalism in Twentieth-Century America," *Environmental History* 7, no. 3 (2002): 467.

79. Carl E. Krog, "'Organizing the Production of Leisure': Herbert Hoover and the Conservation Movement in the 1920's," *Wisconsin Magazine of History* 67, no. 3 (1984): 199–218.

80. My colleague and friend Sherman Paul observed, "The conservation movement . . . had begun as a hobby and—this is Leopold's strategy—must again become one, farther down the line than vigilant protest, now in the leisure-time practice of the husbandry of wild things." Sherman Paul, "The Husbandry of the Wild," *Iowa Review* 17, no. 2 (1987): 16. See also Sherman Paul, *For Love of the World: Essays on Nature Writers* (Iowa City: University of Iowa Press, 1992), 51–61. For Leopold on "wild-leisure," see Charles J. List, "The Virtues of Wild Leisure," *Environmental Ethics* 27 (Winter 2005): 355–373.*

81. Leopold, *A Sand County Almanac*, 280.

82. Paul, "The Husbandry of the Wild." Just before his death in 1995, Sherman Paul wrote, "The reduction of hours of work . . . involves . . . a reconsideration of the kind of

education we provide and the use of (personal, communal, civic) leisure. All this, to my mind, falls under the idea of restoration, an idea that preoccupies me . . . and everything needs restoring, rethinking, renewing, remaking, as it seems the ancient Hebrews knew, for their word *Tikkun* means to mend or heal, and *tikkun olam* means the healing and repair of the world and, with the idea of justice, is the primary obligation of everyone." Letter to and in the possession of the author, dated August 1993.*

83. See Leopold, "The Ethical Sequence," in *A Sand County Almanac*, 238.

84. Paul, "The Husbandry of the Wild."

85. Leopold, *A Sand County Almanac*, 261.

86. James M. Glover, "Romance, Recreation, and Wilderness: Influences on the Life and Work of Bob Marshall," *Environmental History Review* 14, no. 4 (1990): 175–176.

87. Bob Marshall, "The Forest for Recreation," in Senate Doc. 12, 73rd Congress (1933), 466.

88. Benton MacKaye, *From Geography to Geotechnics* (Ann Arbor: University of Michigan Press, 1968), 139–141. See also Benton MacKaye, *The New Exploration: A Philosophy of Regional Planning* (Urbana: University of Illinois Press, 1990), 115–118, 143.

89. Percy MacKaye, *The Civic Theatre in Relation to the Redemption of Leisure* (New York: Mitchell, Kennerley, 1912).*

CHAPTER 10

1. A conference titled "Our Time Famine" was held at the University of Iowa in 1996; another was held in 2010 titled "Balanced Lives." For years, the organization Take Back Your Time has organized annual observances (conferences, symposia, speakers, and press releases) around the nation each October 24. For more information, see the organization's website at http://www.timeday.org.

2. See, for example, Arlie Hochschild, *The Time Bind: When Work Becomes Home and Home Becomes Work* (New York: Henry Holt, 2001); Arlie Hochschild and A. Machung, *The Second Shift* (New York: Penguin Books, 2003); Al Gini, *The Importance of Being Lazy: In Praise of Play, Leisure, and Vacations* (New York: Taylor and Francis, 2006); Al Gini, *My Job, My Self: Work and the Creation of the Modern Individual* (New York: Routledge, 2001); Witold Rybczynski, *Waiting for the Weekend* (New York: Penguin Books,1992); Karl Hinrichs, William Roche, and Carmen Sirianni, *Working Time in Transition: The Political Economy of Working Hours in the Industrial Nations* (Philadelphia: Temple University Press, 1991); Joe Dominguez and Vicki Robin, *Your Money or Your Life: Transforming Your Relationship with Money and Achieving Financial Independence* (New York: Penguin Books, 1999); Barbara Brandt, *Whole Life Economics: Revaluing Daily Life* (Gabriola Island, BC: New Society, 1995); Madeleine Bunting, *Willing Slaves: How the Overwork Culture Is Ruling Our Lives* (New York: Harper Perennial, 2005); Ellen Galinsky, *Overwork in America: When the Way We Work Becomes Too Much* (New York: Families and Work Institute, 2005); and Tim Robinson, *Work, Leisure and the Environment: The Vicious Circle of Overwork and Over Consumption* (Northampton, MA: Edward Elgar, 2006).

3. See http://www.timeday.org.*

4. See "Time to Care Public Policy Agenda" at http://www.timeday.org/time_to_care .asp.

5. Joe Robinson, *Work to Live: The Guide to Getting a Life* (New York: Perigee, 2003).

6. See "About the New Road Map Foundation" at http://www.financialintegrity.org/ index.php?title=About_the_New_Road_Map_Foundation. See also Dominguez and Robin, *Your Money or Your Life*, chap. 9.

7. Duane Elgin, *Voluntary Simplicity: Toward a Way of Life That Is Outwardly Simple, Inwardly Rich* (New York: William Morrow, 1993).*

8. Gregory T. Orr, *Evaluation of Alternate Work Schedules at Eastman Chemical Company* (Knoxville: University of Tennessee and Eastman Division of Eastman Chemical Company, 2000), 1, available at http://www.uiowa.edu/~lsahunni/173/shell.pdf.

9. Hilton recently took down its website. See also Hilton Family of Hotels, Leisure Time Advocacy Group, "White Paper: The Importance of Reclaiming and Preserving American Leisure Time," August 20, 2003, 5–10.*

10. See http://www.reclaimdinnertime.com/pace.php.*

11. Ibid.

12. Council of Economic Advisers, "Families and the Labor Market, 1969–1999: Analyzing the 'Time Crunch'" (Washington, DC: Council of Economic Advisers, Executive Office of the President, 1999), available at http://clinton4.nara.gov/media/pdf/famfinal.pdf.*

13. Alison Mitchell, "Banking on Family Issues, Clinton Seeks Parents' Votes," *New York Times*, June 25, 1996, A19.*

14. Sana Siwolop, "Overtime vs. Time Off: A Debate over a Choice," *New York Times*, August 18, 1996, F10.*

15. Steven Greenhouse, "Democrats Protest Changes to Overtime Rules," *New York Times*, July 1, 2003, AL9.

16. See "Positions and Views of Hillary Clinton on Jobs," Vote NY, 2003, available at http://vote-ny.org/PoliticianIssue.aspx?Id=NYClintonHillaryRodham&Issue=BUSJobs.*

17. Amy Saltzman, *Downshifting: Reinventing Success on a Slower Track* (New York: HarperCollins, 1991).

18. Steven Greenhouse, "The Retention Bonus? Time," *New York Times*, January 8, 2011.

19. Susan E Fleck, "International Comparisons of Hours Worked: An Assessment of the Statistics," *Monthly Labor Review*, May 2009, 3.*

20. See "Reinventing the Workday," *Livelihood*, available at http://www.pbs.org/livelyhood/workday/reinventing/guru.html.

21. Susan Wells, "Honey, They've Shrunk the Workweek," *New York Times*, June 15, 1997, 9; *U.S. News and World Report*, November 1997. See also "Plan Offers Fewer Hours at Same Pay," *Indianapolis Business Journal*, June 19, 1997, 3.*

22. E-mail communication with author, December 8, 2010.

23. Dominique Méda, "New Perspectives on Work as Value," *International Labour Review* 135, no. 6 (1966): 633–643. Compare Alan Wolfe, "State of the Debate: The Moral Meanings of Work," *American Prospect*, no. 34 (September 1, 1997): 8–12.

24. E. P. Thompson, "Time, Work-Discipline and Industrial Capitalism," *Past and Present* 38 (December 1967): 90–91.*

25. Jacques Ellul writes that the "Ideology of Work" leads to the "obvious consequence" that "most people are unable to comprehend what life would be like for a person who does not work." Jacques Ellul [P. Mendes, pseud.], "L'idéologie du Travail," *Foi et Vie* 79, no. 4 (1980): 25–33 (author's translation).

26. Thus, this book may contribute to the recent historical investigations of consumerism. The ways that people use consumer products in culturally significant ways are certainly important historical topics. However, consumerism understood as the consumption of leisure, and as alternative to the range of other kinds of consumption and thus as the alternative to the capitalist "selfish system," has been neglected. Certainly, America's changing consumer preferences vis-à-vis leisure or work are as revealing as consumption patterns in kitchen appliances or automobiles.

27. Lizabeth Cohen, *Making a New Deal: Industrial Workers in Chicago, 1919–1939* (Cambridge: Cambridge University Press, 2008), xxvi.*

INDEX

Benjamin Kline Hunnicutt is a Historian and Professor at the University of Iowa. He is also the author of *Kellogg's Six-Hour Day* and *Work without End: Abandoning Shorter Hours for the Right to Work* (both Temple).